Anthropological Explorations in Queer Theory

MARK GRAHAM
Stockholm University, Sweden

LONDON AND NEW YORK

First published 2014 by Ashgate Publishing

Published 2016 by Routledge
2 Park Square, Milton Park, Abingdon, Oxfordshire OX14 4RN
711 Third Avenue, New York, NY 10017, USA

First issued in paperback 2016

Routledge is an imprint of the Taylor & Francis Group, an informa business

Copyright © 2014 Mark Graham

Mark Graham has asserted his right under the Copyright, Designs and Patents Act, 1988, to be identified as the author of this work.

All rights reserved. No part of this book may be reprinted or reproduced or utilised in any form or by any electronic, mechanical, or other means, now known or hereafter invented, including photocopying and recording, or in any information storage or retrieval system, without permission in writing from the publishers.

Notice:
Product or corporate names may be trademarks or registered trademarks, and are used only for identification and explanation without intent to infringe.

British Library Cataloguing in Publication Data
A catalogue record for this book is available from the British Library

The Library of Congress has cataloged the printed edition as follows:
Graham, Mark, 1960–
  Anthropological explorations in queer theory / by Mark Graham.
    pages cm. – (Queer interventions)
Includes bibliographical references and index.
  ISBN 978-1-4094-5066-5 (hardback)
  1. Queer theory. I. Title.

HQ76.25.G7294 2014
306.7601–dc23

2014004285

ISBN 13: 978-1-138-70218-9 (pbk)
ISBN 13: 978-1-4094-5066-5 (hbk)

Contents

List of Figures *vii*
Preface *ix*

Introduction 1

1 Things 19

2 Sexonomics 37

3 Smells 55

4 Species 71

5 Intersections 91

6 Failures 107

7 Explications 127

References *147*
Index *165*

For Stefan

List of Figures

P.1	The Flush Bar, courtesy of Stockholm Vatten.	ix
5.1	Map of Gravelly Hill Interchange in Birmingham. *Source*: OpenStreetMap from Wikimedia, reproduced on a Creative Commons Licence.	95
5.2	Aerial view of Gravelly Hill Interchange, Birmingham a.k.a. Spaghetti Junction, September 2008. *Source*: Wikimedia, reproduced on a Creative Commons Licence.	96
5.3	Motorway, railway and waterway at Gravelly Hill Interchange, Birmingham, © Optimist on the run, 2009 / CC-BY-SA-3.0 & GFDL-1.2. *Source*: Wikimedia, reproduced on a Creative Commons Licence.	97

Preface

P.1 The Flush Bar, courtesy of Stockholm Vatten.

Consider the picture above. It depicts a queue outside the entrance to the 'Flush Bar' (*Spol Bar*) guarded by a doorman – a turd – whose job is to vet the hopefuls eagerly awaiting to be flushed down the toilet. The doorman appears to be male. His sign reads: 'We don't let in any television soap stars here'. The celebrity hopefuls include a used and irritated tampon, whose bubble reads 'Can't even a red-headed babe slip in?', together with a condom with a scary Halloween face, a used cotton bud complete with sunglasses and gendered as female (note the full red lips and long blond 'hair'), and an angry cigarette butt who threatens to 'stub himself out' (*fimpa*) on the doorman if refused entry. At the back of the queue stands another couple, two turds waiting their turn. 'She' is shorter than 'he' is, has longer eyelashes, fuller lips and, like the used tampon, breasts. This heterosexual couple evidently expects to be allowed in without any problems. Their sign reads: 'Hi, Surely we can go in first, we're on the S.H.I.T list'.

This scenario is taken from Swedish informational material intended to encourage people to be selective about what they flush down the lavatory. The sign on the floor next to the turd couple reads:

32 tonnes of rubbish are flushed down the toilets of Stockholm every week.

The commonest are cotton buds, tampons, paper towels, condoms, cigarette butts, cotton wool balls and sanitary towels.

Some of the rubbish gets caught in the pipes and causes blockages, the rest that reaches the sewage plant is taken care of in an environmentally friendly way.

There are only three things that should go down the toilet – pee, poop and toilet paper!

The campaign was directed primarily at children and teenagers who are expected to be familiar with the sight of a queue of people seeking entry into a trendy club. But what is so striking is the gendering and sexualising of the objects. In the case of a tampon, the gendering is perhaps predictably female. The condom is presumably male although the Halloween face is generic. The cigarette butt is also male, although there is nothing inherently male about cigarettes. Cotton buds are often used to remove women's make-up but this is not their only function by any means. Perhaps most striking is the heterosexual turd couple at the back of the queue, even faecal matter has to be forced into a heteronormative framework.[1]

Heteronormative demands are not limited to educational material for school children. In October 2009, Uganda attracted considerable international media attention when parliamentarian David Bahati attempted to introduce his Anti-Homosexuality Bill whose clauses included life imprisonment and the death penalty for homosexual acts and a three-year prison term for anyone who does not report someone they know to be homosexual. Christian and Muslim clerics supported and still support the legislation which was inspired in part by evangelical Christian activists from the USA. Bahati justified the measure as protection of children from 'recruitment' by homosexuals. One of the casualties of the extreme homophobia in Uganda was gay rights activist David Kato, who was beaten to death in his own home in January 2011. The Ugandan parliament passed the Anti-Homosexuality Act on 20 December 2013 and it received the presidential signature on 24 February 2014. The proposed death penalty clause was replaced by life imprisonment. In Russia, conditions for the lgbt population

---

1 The campaign was used at Hammarby Sjöstad, Stockholm, Sweden's largest sustainable urban development (www.Hammarbysjostad.se).

PREFACE

worsen. Punitive legislation includes a new law that makes 'propaganda of non-traditional sexual relations' in the presence of minors illegal. Gay rights organisations are denounced as 'foreign agents' that must be registered or face crushing fines and their work labelled foreign infiltration. Critics denounce the legislation as a manoeuvre designed to deflect attention from domestic worries. Meanwhile in France and in England and Wales legislation has recently been passed (in May and July 2013 respectively) legalising gay marriage, albeit in the face of strong religious opposition, especially in France.

The above are but a few examples of how sexuality increasingly figures in a host of current political and social debates. Sexuality is the arrival lounge for internal and external forces, transnational gay and lesbian politics, confrontations between tradition and modernity, post-colonial fundamentalisms, questions of human rights, trafficking and prostitution, assertions of national and even continental morality in the face of putative cultural invasions (same-sex sexuality being a high-profile example), and a site for the refashioning of identities and subjects.[2] None of this will come as a surprise to anyone familiar with Michel Foucault's (1978) claim that sexuality is a transfer point for power relations, especially in times of change when human subjects are intensively reformed and controlled.

This book takes its cues from queer theory, feminist scholarship, and the anthropology of sexuality and gender. These are all either avowedly critical approaches or, in the case of the latter, have the potential to be so. It contributes to a critique of the normative dimensions of sexuality and gender as they figure across a range of social and cultural settings, explicitly and implicitly. In particular, and in keeping with a queer theoretical focus, it interrogates heterosexist and heteronormative assumptions. Heterosexuality is much more than sexual practices. It is an identity, institutional arrangements, cultural frameworks, moral order, psychological regimes, legislation that confers rights and responsibilities – families, inheritance, custody of children, hospital visitation rights, immigration, monarchical succession, etc. – that variously impinge on individual practices. It is a major support of the gender order, including labour market relations, child rearing, and a multitude of gender appropriate practices, and it is a regime of violence: Heterosexuality is not only policed by legal demands, it is also enforced by practices ranging from heterosexist assumptions, through to homophobic violence and murder, as the above examples from Uganda and Russia illustrate. Precisely because it is all of these, heterosexism permeates a vast range of social and cultural phenomena. All the more so because the assumptions often go unnoticed; heterosexuality is rarely a marked category.

---

[2] See, Binnie 2004, Adamas and Pigg 2005, Rofel 2007, Hodzic 2009, *Ethnos* 2009: 3.

Since its appearance, queer theory has been made part of and in some respects emerged out of identity politics. It did not take long for the term queer to become a label deployed by those unhappy with the label 'gay'. This is ironic, as the thrust of queer theory, at least initially, was precisely to question the existence and need for such categorical identities. All too soon 'queer' became a badge, and indeed a form of symbolic capital with which to bludgeon sexological discourses and their adherents, including gays and lesbians. To my mind the identity dimensions of queer have largely run their course, often doing little more than adding yet another (commercially exploitable) category to the already numerous identities of late modern times. For this reason, I have intentionally held the topic of identity at arm's length. Instead, the book ranges across subjects as diverse as materiality and things, questions of embodiment and fieldwork, the senses, diversity discourses and speciation, gifts, commodities and gossip magazines.

This book is primarily anthropological and I have attempted to make it as accessible as possible for readers at all levels both within anthropology and outside the discipline. To this end, the introductory chapter contains a guide to queer theory for the uninitiated, but even readers well versed in it should find the parallels it draws between anthropology and queer theory useful.

Most of this book is newly written. However, small sections of Chapter 1 first appeared as 'Sexual Things', *GLQ* 10 (2): 299–303, 2004. Chapter 3 is a revised and expanded version of 'Queer Smells: Fragrances of Late-Capitalism or Scents of Subversion?' in *The Smell Culture Reader,* Jon Drobnick (ed.). Oxford: Berg, 2006. Chapter 6 is a revised and expanded version of 'The heterosexual tragedy: on myths and heterosexual failure in the mass media' (originally in Swedish) in *Queersverige*, Don Kulick (ed.), Stockholm: Natur och Kultur, 2005. I wish to thank Duke University Press, Berg Publishers (an imprint of Bloomsbury Publishing Plc), and Natur och Kultur respectively for permission to publish them here.

This book germinated over a long period of time, and developed in unexpected directions. The course it has taken has benefited from numerous people and institutions. I would like to thank in particular colleagues at the School of Sociology, the University of New South Wales, which provided me with a haven when I began to write the book, at Stockholm University, especially Lissa Nordin and Don Kulick, and the three anonymous reviewers of this manuscript for excellent suggestions. They are all absolved from responsibility for any shortcomings. I also thank Neil Jordan at Ashgate for his monumental and apparently inexhaustible slabs of patience and Pam Bertram for editing assistance. My thanks also go to The Swedish Foundation for International Cooperation in Research and Higher Education (STINT), and the Bank of Sweden Tercentenary Foundation for financial support that made the writing of parts of this book possible.

Introduction

'Until a few years ago sex was a subject usually avoided in anthropological monographs.'
Raymond Firth (1936)

'The traditional reserve with respect to sexual matters has, with a few notable exceptions, inhibited American scientists almost as strongly as laymen...It is most regrettable that an area of inquiry having such fundamental importance in both its practical and its theoretical aspects should have been so inadequately studied and so incompletely understood.'
Clellan Ford and Frank Beach (1952: 267)

'Anthropology as a field has been far from courageous or even adequate in its investigation of sexuality.'
Carole Vance (1991)

'Many people still believe that anthropology is largely about sex.'
Harriet Lyons and Andrew Lyons (2004)

The above opinions, expressed by anthropologists at different times over a period of almost 70 years, can easily leave a reader confused. Raymond Firth, Clellan Ford (with psychologist Frank Beach) and Carole Vance claim during a period spanning 55 years that anthropologists have been timid on the subject of sexuality, while according to the more recent claim of Harriet and Andrew Lyons, anthropologists write about nothing else, at least in the public mind. Can they all be correct? Are anthropologists both uninterested (and maybe afraid) of sexuality and yet at the same time also voyeurs of the sexual proclivities of people outside that region arbitrarily called the West?

Beginnings

Anthropological attention to human sexuality is as old as the discipline itself and was a significant concern of its earliest practitioners and predecessors. The anxieties of Christian missionaries about the sins of heathens, Victorian explorers like Richard Burton, theorists like Marx and Engels who speculated on origins, social reformers like Mayhew in England who fretted over the sexual mores of the poor, evolutionists like Bachofen, MacLennan and Frazer who ranked sexual behaviours on an evolutionary ladder, sexologists such as Havelock Ellis eager to catalogue human sexual practices, sometimes as part of a reformist mission, and, of course, the emerging field of psychoanalysis entranced by incest taboos, sexual jealousies and traumas, all interested themselves in human sexuality. Interlaced with their concerns were issues of where the human and animal kingdoms began and ended, colonial anxieties surrounding miscegenation and the degeneration of the European 'race', and the impact of Darwinian evolutionism on eugenics.

The ur-mothers and ur-fathers of modern anthropology, including Edvard Westermarck, W.H. Rivers, Bronislaw Malinowski, Margaret Mead and Ruth Benedict had well documented research interests in sexuality and there was two-way traffic between their work and that of other scholars who sought alternatives to the prevailing Victorian morality. Malinowski (one of Westermarck's pupils) drew on the earlier work of Ellis as well as Sigmund Freud, while his own work was in turn read by Ellis and Bertrand Russell (Lyons and Lyons 2004: 155). Malinowski (2001: 74–5) presented a somewhat idyllic version of especially adolescent sexuality which he compared favourably to modern European sexuality, with its deviant evils of sexual jealousy and homosexuality caused by the frustration of healthy heterosexual activity among young people.

Why, then, if this interest existed does Vance write of a lack of courage? The work and public career of Margaret Mead provides some answers. Mead's legacy is undeniable, even if admirers and detractors have never agreed on the exact (de)merits of her work. Over time her writings displayed some interesting shifts and inconsistencies moving from the Boasian cultural determinism of *Coming of Age in Samoa* (1928) to *Male and Female* (1949) two decades later in which she claims that there are inborn differences in temperament between men and women, including women's tendency to nurturance. Such claims left her open to criticism from feminists like Betty Friedan (1963) who accused Mead of helping to force women back into the home in conservative post-War America. Micaela di Leonardo (1998: 208) reaches a similar conclusion and argues that Mead's ambiguous position helped her to navigate the sexual anxieties of Cold War America (see also Walton 2001). The ambiguities in Mead's writing reflected her own professional worries about the consequences that might befall her if knowledge of her own bisexuality became public. She dared not appear too eager an advocate of sexual rights for 'deviant' populations and on occasion used the language of 'healthy' sexuality to describe American heterosexual relations. Some of the more radical implications of her attention to female sexuality were undercut by her reduction of women to maternity and motherhood, a move that according to Mead's own daughter, Mary Bateson (Bateson 1984), served as public confirmation of Mead's own sexual normality. The example of Mead illustrates how anthropology's potential to provide an

INTRODUCTION

alternative perspective on western sexual mores, including same-sex sexuality, and the sexual experience of women beyond the bounds of motherhood, was undermined, or at least diluted, by a fear of censure both from within and without the discipline.[1]

The period after World War Two until the 1970s is often seen as one during which the study of sexuality, at least within anthropology, was eclipsed or forced into publicly acceptable forms. The influence of structural-functionalism, which paid little attention to individuals and their emotional, let alone sexual, states undoubtedly played some part, as too did the climate of the times.[2] In an increasingly professionalised discipline, in which careers were not only being staked out but also at stake, sexuality and gender was considered a risky even suspect topic likely to block career prospects. Openly homophobic sentiments were expressed by some anthropologists, such as the following:

> Social approval of active homosexuality is tantamount to declaring that society has no interest in, or obligation to make well, the sociopsychologically deviant so as to prevent a disturbing behavior pattern from spreading in its midst – or that society is not concerned with its own survival! (Suggs and Marshall 1971: 326, quoted in Lyons and Lyons 2004: 275)

The quote is taken from the Epilogue to the edited volume *Human Sexual Behavior* (Suggs and Marshall 1971) and can be read as the culmination of a nervous, even shrill, reaction to the appearance of the permissive society, second-wave feminism, and the demands for gay and lesbian rights in the late 1960s.

Homophobia, or at the very least heterosexism, has a long history in anthropology. The self-evident even normative status of the conjugal couple

---

1 Other luminaries included Firth, whose *We, the Tikopia* (1936) contains a lengthy discussion of sexuality, Ian Hogbin's *Island of Menstruating Men* (1970), which reports a very relaxed attitude towards same-sex sexuality among the people of Wogeo Island off New Guinea in 1934 (1970: 90–91), and work by Isaac Schapera (1966 [1940]) and George Devereux (1937), but these works were not made part of an applied anthropology of sexuality (something Malinowski explicitly advocated). Ruth Benedict occupies an interesting position in that she relativises sexuality far more than her contemporaries, preferring to avoid 'explanations' for male homosexuality, such as a safety valve in the absence of female partners, or an expression of aggression and alcoholism. She also suggested that those who do not fit into the dominant cultural configuration may become innovators and drive cultural creativity rather than simply be marginalised (Lyons and Lyons 2004: 251–4).

2 Clellan Ford and Frank Beach did, however, publish *Patterns of Sexual Behavior* in 1951. It was a cross-cultural study that drew on the Human Relations Area Files. Based on data from 191 cultures, they concluded, among other things, that same-sex sexuality was a 'basic mammalian capacity', see also Lyons and Lyons 2004: 268–70.

is found in Malinowski who universalised the nuclear family, and it made its way into kinship studies via Morgan's genealogical method and Radcliffe-Brown. For the latter, social structure derives from heterosexual descent, the 'elementary family' consisting of a man and his wife and their child or children (1952: 51). In the work of Lévi-Strauss the exchange of women between men in accordance with the incest taboo initiates exogamy, heterosexual marriage, gender relations and nothing less than the inauguration of culture (Rubin 1975). The potential support Radcliffe-Brown's formulation can lend to normative gender, and heterosexism is perhaps obvious. It is still deeply indebted to the biological assumptions surrounding kinship so effectively critiqued by David Schneider (1968). Lévi-Strauss' contribution perhaps needs a little more explanation. His ideas were selectively deployed by anthropologists and others who disapproved of France's *Pacte Civil de Solidarité* (PACS), a civil partnership open to both other- and same-sex couples. (It was superseded in 2013 by legislation opening marriage to same-sex couples.) Briefly, Lévi-Strauss's ideas were cast as irrefutable 'proof' of the damaging, even 'unthinkable' nature of PACS. The source of the threat was traced to Lévi-Strauss' incest taboo, the unstable boundary marker between nature and culture. Incestuous relations produce the monstrous and bestial through the mixing of 'sameness' which the incest taboo prohibits. For anthropologists like Françoise Héritier incestuous acts are 'homosexual' because, according to her logic, they mix the 'same'; there is no sexual difference involved. Same-sex unions, in this interpretation, become another version of incest and therefore threaten the universal foundation of culture. Lévi-Strauss himself refused to lend his name to the arguments (see Fassin 2001). Héritier's reasoning misses, among other things, a fundamental principle of Lévi-Strauss' work, namely the importance of *relations* in the social rather than pre-existing objects and identities (Strong 2002: 414). Difference arises through relations rather than presupposing them.[3] It is relationality that enriches social life rather than sex differences.

The Return of the Repressed

A renewed interest in sexuality emerged within anthropology in the 1960s and 1970s as part of a wider questioning of accepted truths.[4] Same-sex sexuality, as well as other forms of non-normative and marginalised sexual practices, has attracted

---

3 For example, within Melanesian ethnography differences most be extracted from sameness and this requires work, they do not predate such work, (Gillison 1987, Strathern 1988: 128).

4 See the discussion between three of the American pioneers of this period, Louise Lamphere, Rayna Rapp and Gayle Rubin (2007: 408–26).

INTRODUCTION

increasing scholarly attention during the last two decades.[5] A great deal of this literature challenges the assumption that same-sex sexual practices coincide with what in Euro-American societies are called lesbian, gay, bisexual, transgendered, and most recently queer, or 'genderqueer' identities (Nestle et al. 2002).[6]

In response to transnational movements of people, sexual imagery and ideas throughout queer diasporas, incitements and prohibitions in the face of cultural and social changes, the impact of commodification, economic restructuring, nationalisms, and fundamentalisms, human rights demands, medical developments, health campaigns, and the impact of international development programmes on sexuality local sexualities are being reworked and seem guaranteed to proliferate, providing the supply of new material for the ethnocartographic project (Weston 1993).

My primary interest in this book, however, is not cartographic. I do not aim to add a new ethnographic case study of gender and sexuality to the existing literature. As it is deployed herein, queer theory is not primarily about sexual minorities. Rather, it is the 'study of those 'knowledges and social practices that organise "society" as a whole by sexualising – heterosexualising or homosexualising – bodies, desires, acts, identities, social relations, knowledges, culture, and social institutions' (Seidman 1997: 13). What follows is therefore a queer anthropology rather than an anthropology about queers. My starting point is very much *anthropological* concerns rather than the identities and subjectivities focus of the humanities. It seeks to move beyond attention to subjects and persons, in fact, for the most part, beyond sexuality as conventionally understood to address a more expansive set of themes. Elizabeth Povinelli's (2006) *The Empire of Love* which interrogates questions of identity and the othering of sexuality is an exemplary instance of this approach.

First, however, I need to say something about what queer means at least within the covers of this book.

Queer: A Brief Critical Summary for the Uninitiated Anthropologist

Queer theoretical ideas have a complex genealogy comprised of several currents of thought. As these have been extensively discussed by others elsewhere,[7] I

---

5 For reviews of this literature, see Weston 1993, Robertson 2005, Boellstorff 2007,

6 While the ethnographic record compiled by anthropologists challenges sexological categories, a perusal of introductory texts in anthropology reveals that their influence in the discipline as a whole remains strong (Graham 1997) once we leave the specialised fields of gender and sexuality research.

7 For general introductions, see Jagose 1996, Hall 2003, Sullivan 2003.

shall be brief and focus only on those aspects of the theory and its antecedents that are directly relevant for the chapters that follow.

At its simplest queer theory is a critical inquiry into the alignments of sex, gender and desire that are in the service of normative forms of heterosexuality, the heteronormative, that saturates the social and cultural order. Given its all pervasive nature, I want to introduce two related concepts not usually found in queer theory's attention to the heteronormative but which neatly summarise its character: implication and explication. In an implicate order,[8] all that is present exists in an overdetermined entanglement. This entanglement enables us to look at different phenomena from multiple angles because in a real sense everything *is* connected to everything else. This is not a difficult idea for anthropologists to grasp, accustomed as they are to seeking out the interconnections between phenomena – cultural, social, political, economic, aesthetic, and so on. Marcel Mauss referred to this as a 'total social fact', phenomena that contain a multiplicity of social and cultural dimensions.

In a heteronormative order sex, gender and sexuality/desire are tightly interwoven and implicate each other with normative results that are systematic, often systemic, frequently disadvantageous and sometimes lethal for those people who are not part of their normative weave, the loose ends. To explicate the (hetero)normative is to unfold the implications of this order across a range of social and cultural phenomena.

One of the qualities of an implicate order is that it performs a kind of origami that brings into propinquity phenomena that in the explicate order appear distant, unrelated and sometimes even antagonistic. There is therefore always a risk of complicity – another kind of fold – as critique skirts the edge of an adversarial abyss into which it risks falling. In particular, I have in mind strands of neoliberalism that insinuate themselves into queer theoretical work. This is perhaps unsurprising and maybe inevitable as we live in neoliberal times and queer theory developed at the present juncture. To expect a theory to escape fully from the context of its emergence is arguably to fall prey to the neoliberal tenet of unconstrained flexibility and freedom of choice. While I do not mean to argue that queer theory is merely a reflection or even a necessary ally of neoliberalism, we must be on our guard against complicity and interrogate possible manifestations of it.

---

8 The implicate, or enfolded, order is associated with physicist David Bohm (1980) and presupposes an explicate order. The latter is contained in the former. At the implicate level everything – although it is difficult to talk of separate things – is connected or entangled. It is out of this manifold that things are un-folded, made explicate. Bohm liked the example of an ink drop in water. If the fluid rotates very slowly, the drop is dispersed to the point of invisibility, yet if rotated in the opposite direction, the drop reforms. The dispersed ink drop in the fluid is implicate.

INTRODUCTION

Queer theory is also in the business of interrogating cultural assumptions surrounding 'natural' and self-evident practices. It is an old truism in anthropology that cultural norms generate their obverse, the tabooed, the monstrous, the troublesome, the inexplicable, that which subverts order, violates boundaries and threatens to turn the world upside-down. Hitherto queer theory has concerned itself primarily with sexual phenomena: the prostitute, the homosexual, the promiscuous girl, the john, the pimp, the transgender person, the paedophile. All, in their different ways and at different times, have acted as lightning rods for social and political unease (cf. Rubin 1984). They are the queer people who inspire fear and fascination, the people others are allowed to hate.[9] They mark the boundaries of the normal and provide vantage points from which to view the cultural and social centres. One of the questions queer theory has set itself from the start is how have these sexual subjects, indeed all subjects, come into existence?

The Subject of Queer

To be a subject in all known societies demands taking up a sexed and gendered position. How is this construction effected? The question takes us back at least to Freud and raises multiple issues surrounding sex, sexuality, gender, desires, fantasies and their mutual implications, questions of embodiment, the inauguration of the social and the acquisition of culture, inequalities between men and women, as well as the existence of human universals versus cultural particulars. Whatever theory of the subject we choose it has a great deal riding on it (see Moore 2007).

Michel Foucault's (1978) genealogical work on the history of sexuality has exercised a considerable influence on queer theory not least his work on sexual subjects. Foucault regarded the construction of sexuality as part of a process of subjectification effected through the elicitation and control of desire. More precisely, his argument that sexuality, conceived of as a recognisable phenomenon in itself, a thing almost, is an invention of the modern west was a frontal attack on the realist assumptions surrounding sexuality. According to Foucault, the categories of sexuality we take for granted, such as 'the homosexual', are not eternal verities but modern inventions of discourses that create the discursive object they purport simply to name and describe. The homosexual was constructed by sexological, medical, criminological and religious discourses as a specific type of person, a 'type of life'. In Foucault's famous words:

---

9 See Murray 2009 for contemporary ethnographies of homophobia.

> The nineteenth-century homosexual became a personage, a past, a case history, and a childhood, in addition to being a type of life, a life form...Nothing that went into his total composition was unaffected by his sexuality...The sodomite had been a temporary aberration; the homosexual was now a species. (Foucault 1978: 43)

The shift was from *acts* that define a person, such as the sodomite (anyone could become a sodomite through their actions) to an essential sexual *nature* that a person expresses.[10]

Since its appearance within the realist framework of sexology in the nineteenth century, the idea of a discrete, and possibly biologically determined, homosexual minority (along with a heterosexual majority) has dominated western discourses on sexuality even though no less a figure than Freud rejected the notion outright and there has long been ample ethnographic and historical evidence of the arbitrariness of a dichotomy that is much too precise and simply cannot account for the historical changes and cultural variation in how same-sex sexuality – female and male – is classified, understood, and practised (Greenberg 1988, Robertson 2005).

Queer theory reacts to this minoritarian assumption.[11] For queer critics, the gay and lesbian subject is at the endpoint of the sexological production of the modern homosexual, but one shorn of its more overtly medical and stigmatising associations with mainstream gays and lesbians demanding conformity to a respectable version of homosexuality (Simpson 1996, Warner 1999). The inadequacy of the sexological model, and not least its political perils, was revealed by the Aids crisis that emerged in the 1980s and the stigmatisation of an 'at risk' minority it exacerbated.

In order to dissolve minoritarian thinking, queer theory draws on post-structural ideas. Derrida's assault on the western metaphysics of presence – the assumption that categories, identities, and meanings refer to essences – has been highly influential. Derrida argues for the inherently relational character of meaning, the reliance of a term on what it is not. (Hegel's Master-Slave relationship is the prototype.) Thus there can be no category of the heterosexual

---

10 Alfred Kinsey's famous scale of 0 (totally heterosexual) to 6 (totally homosexual) illustrates essentially the same point: There are no distinct sexual types only a continuum on which you are placed depending on what you do. Kinsey first published his findings in the 1940s.

11 This is not a new reaction. Beginning in the 1970s, lesbian and gay activists began (seemingly paradoxically) to demand the end of the 'homosexual' (and by implication the 'heterosexual') (e.g. Altman 1993 [1971]). Their basic point was that these categories are arbitrary, constricting for everyone, and used to cement stigma and inequality. Queer theories are part of a critical project with a long pedigree.

without its necessary other, or constitutive outside, the homosexual, and vice-versa. A consequence of this theoretical heritage is that queer theory has become predominantly a critique of the heteronormative (Ruffolo 2009). There is a queer-heteronormative binary at its centre which it endlessly deconstructs. The result is oppositional and perhaps at times even paranoid (Sedgwick 2003).[12]

Along with Foucault and deconstruction, psychoanalytical models have also been influential, especially Lacan's account of how sexual and gendered subjects are formed. In Lacan's schema as the child develops it exits the Real, a pre-representational state of plenitude or unity with the m/other. This severance is traumatic but necessary to establish social relations outside the mother-child dyad.[13] Subjects emerge as the result of a cut internal to the Real. Desire emerges along with the subject. According to Lacan, we want to have whatever it takes to win the desire of an Other, mother who is now separated from us. Another Other, father, commands her desire because he possesses the penis and hence all children want the penis and shift their allegiance from mother to father and the world he controls beyond the mother.[14] However, any significant object can stand in for the penis and act as Freud's *das Ding*, that which we desire in order to be desired. Unfortunately, all the things — the *objet petit a* as Lacan calls them — belong to the empirical reality which is unable to satisfy the desires of our unconscious brewing in the Real. These insatiable desires condemn us to search throughout the cultural realm for things that can restore a wholeness forever out of reach.

At the mirror or Imaginary stage (aged anywhere from six to eighteen months) the child *imagines* itself to be a unified independent being, but this is a misrecognition because the acquisition of self requires internalisation of

---

12 In reaction to what are perceived to be the negative, even gloomy elements of queer theory's remorseless critique of the heteronormative some scholars have turned to the idea of 'queer optimism', see Snediker 2009.

13 It is traumatic in this version of the subject's development. But it is arguably more traumatic than necessary because it takes place within a patriarchical order in which woman is anti-social and the mother-child dyad must be severed. Ignoring the historical and cultural specificity of this trauma and making it into a universal feature of subject formation in which antagonism towards (m)others is foundational is both ethnocentric and self-serving of male domination, see Oliver 2001. In less patriarchal settings this trauma, which is made part of the subject's very foundation, is likely to be less.

14 For this reason, Lacan's Symbolic register is often considered to be phallogocentric, patriarchal and heterosexist (if not homophobic). Lacan claims that the phallus is a metaphor not the penis it symbolises (Lacan 1977: 281) but it never seems completely able to disengage itself from its association with the fleshy appendage. Feminists have debated the arbitrariness of their association extensively, see, for example, Campbell 2000.

an other, an *outsider*. A form of sympathetic mimicry engages the whole body and it remains contagious well beyond childhood: Once one person starts to scratch, everyone starts to itch. Moreover this imago is not only specular, it is also what others say about and expect of me, how I appear for them.

As the child is progressively socialised, it is subjected to the dictates of the cultural realm, the Symbolic. In return for the loss of mother, the father gives the child culture, gender, sexuality, and language along with a host of sexual prohibitions, exclusions and binaries (male and female). The Symbolic register predates us and is freighted with the intentions of others. It is made up of slippery chains of metaphors and metonyms like a language. When we communicate, we are obliged to use this borrowed and opaque system. Ironically, that which enables communication also erects an insurmountable wall of misunderstanding.

Things are not made easier by the Real, Lacan's third register and perhaps the most interesting from the perspective of queer theory. This original state of plenitude is also the remainder left behind by the internal cut that produces subjects, objects and desire. In his later work, Lacan places sexuality/desire in the unconscious realm of the Real. Importantly, he also severs any necessary connection between desire and a specific gender or genitalia. The Real no longer accommodates sexual identity or the homosexual/heterosexual binary (which belong to the Imaginary and Symbolic) and sexuality is freed from a genital heterosexual teleology (Dean 2000: 194–5). The Real also includes bodily pleasures not condoned by the Symbolic. The prime examples are unconscious homosexual and non-genital desires that evade and trouble the Imaginary and Symbolic registers. In short, bodies for Lacan tend to evade language and symbolisation, they are excessive.

The upshot of Lacan's tripartite model is that our ego formation is never more than a misrecognition of an Imaginary unity and self-control. We are continually at the mercy of the Symbolic's slippery and unstable signifiers. Despite all the efforts of culture and the social, there is always that which outruns our attempts to grasp ourselves and the world, the Real.[15] Processes of subjectification – Imaginary and Symbolic – do not reach everywhere. We are never totally socialised, never entirely puppets of social and cultural forces. Hence theories that attempt to provide a total picture of the subject will fail

---

15 One reason why Slavoj Žižek and other Lacanians who hail from the former Soviet bloc find Lacan appealing lies precisely in his promise that totalitarian regimes are unable to determine our being and eradicate opacity in human subjects. No amount of propaganda, social engineering, or maniacal control will succeed. The truths of ideology are continually undermined by the Real. The Real is not, of course, 'reality' which is but a comforting illusion. The Real is what gets left behind in all our attempts to make things meaningful. It is a 'place' from which challenges and promises are issued.

INTRODUCTION

because we are all riven by tensions and gaps that cannot be papered over by the cultural categories of gender and sexuality and the limited corpus of subject positions and identities they condone at any given time. The appeal of Lacanian ideas lies in their promise that the sexuality of the unconscious (the Real) challenges heteronormative dictates. It is this corrosion from within that holds out hope for the politics of sexuality/gender subversion and is embraced by many queer scholars, not least in the humanities.

The other pillar of the queer subject, the Foucauldian, also provides some relief from heteronormative *prohibitions*, which amount to a negative and repressive theory of the subject. The first volume of Foucault's *History of Sexuality*, which has been most influential in queer theory, is a rather bleak work in which the power of discourse thoroughly saturates the subjects it creates and from which there appears to be no escape. However, in his later work the hold of power is loosened. Here Foucault attends to how power provokes and initiates the very things it prohibits, and how the field of relationships power constitutes does not necessarily produce compatible outcomes. Foucault saw hope in the workings of power when it is perverse and exceeds attempts to channel it through predictable circuits. He writes, 'we must conceive discourse as a series of discontinuous segments whose tactical function is neither uniform nor stable' (1990: 100) and 'discourse transmits and produces power; it reinforces it, but also undermines and exposes it, renders it fragile and makes it possible to thwart it' (1990: 101). His claim that power gives rise to resistance also implies an oppositional response. However, given power's perversity this need not imply that resistance to power will simply follow the same vector only in reverse. (Something implied by his idea of 'reverse discourse'.) It may involve a deviant movement with unpredictable consequences.

Even though Foucault wrote against psychology and the more conservative versions of psychoanalysis, which he saw as the endpoint of the western history of incarceration, there is a degree of convergence between the instability emanating from the Real which Lacan finds lodged in the heart of the subject and Foucault's later writings on the unpredictability of power. Both Foucault and Lacan, and in the case of the latter sometimes almost in spite of himself, furnish us with ideas that undermine the realist account of gender and sexual types.

What in all of this is appealing to anthropologists? Personally, I am attracted to the later Foucault's attention to the subtleties of unpredictable power, and to the later Lacan's subversive Real, as well as the importance of bodies and things that are likely to evade social and cultural demands. All leave space for change and inject a strong dose of instability and the unexpected that troubles any seamless social and cultural reproduction. Taken together, their work also undermines heteronormative assumptions and steers us away from an overemphasis on sexual categories and identities. This makes queer theory, in my rendition of it, an ally of process philosophy which I introduce in the next chapter and on which I draw throughout this book.

Reification

The assumption that sexual types are objective facts, actually existing biological entities, or species (see Chapter 4), rather than historical and cultural constructs, is perhaps the most obvious example of the kind of reification that queer theory interrogates.

Simply put, reification involves the generation of phantom objectivity in which human creations, such as institutions, beliefs and concepts, take on the character of objects or forces that control us. Arguably, reification is an inevitable, indeed necessary, process. In order to represent the world to ourselves, we must perforce cut away most of it to create even a semblance of concreteness and provide ourselves with objects of thought. We cannot possibly cope with everything that precedes us, coincides with us, and will succeed us. Any attempt to do so would paralyse us. It is on this necessary amnesia that reification nurtures itself. Commodity fetishism is perhaps the best-known example of the forgetting of what lies behind appearances. In the version of Lukács (1971), the obviousness and solidity of the commodity can be penetrated by the proletariat which sees through the ruse fetishism perpetrates to the class exploitation it conceals. This liberation involves a move from facts to processes, from objects to relations, and from identity thinking to heterogeneity. The parallels to queer theoretical ambitions are obvious though rarely explored mainly because of the reliance of much queer theory on French post-structuralism rather than German Critical Theory.

Performative

Queer theory proffers its own preferred method for dissolving reified gender, performativity. In her highly influential statements about the 'heterosexual matrix', Judith Butler (1990) argues that repeated gendered performances (physical and speech acts) that 'cite' or 'reiterate' existing gender norms *do* something, like Austin's (1975) speech acts. They create the cultural categories of 'man' and 'woman', the two genders that relate to each other and ought only to relate to each other heterosexually (1990). When viewed from this angle, the concept of gender assumes and supports heterosexuality, heterosexism and homophobia. Monique Wittig's (1992) *The Straight Mind* is a pre-queer exemplar of this critique.

The result of this repetition, the materialisation of two sexes, argues Butler, is mistaken for the 'natural' cause of gender. But if what we are is the result of acts – like the sodomite – rather than the expression of an essence – like the homosexual – then change is an ever-present possibility. We can act – practise – ourselves out of our gendered identities. When we cite or reiterate existing gender norms, we also reproduce them, but because every new citation takes place in a new context there is always the risk – or hope – that it will, so to speak, be a bad citation and that gender will fail to materialise satisfactorily and thus be opened up to resignification. This sounds promising, but on occasion Butler makes functionalist claims about power's *modus operandi* which seem to set severe limits to the ability of performative reiteration to effect change when, for example, she writes of 'the law's uncanny capacity to produce only those rebellions that it can guarantee will – out of fidelity – defeat themselves and those subjects who, utterly subjected, have no choice but to reiterate the law of their genesis' (1990: 106, quoted in Kirby 2006: 41). The above claim that rebellions routinely defeat themselves would not be out of place in old structural-functional theories in anthropology that stressed that reproductive and conservative function of apparently subversive ritual practices (Gluckman 1954). Butler here relies on a juridical conception of the law as purposeful and intentional, rather than a Foucauldian conception that recognises power's suppleness and even 'stupidity' (Kirby 2006: 41). Butler's attention to the content of the 'rebellions' she mentions is actually quite minimal, beyond noting the inherent instability of the performative production of gendered subjects. So despite the appeals to the subject's inherent instability and contingency, regardless of how stable and permanent it might feel, the details of how to escape gender remain sketchy.

It helps little to locate change in indeterminate symbolic structures, individual mistakes in the rendering of gender norms and rather obscure psychic processes, when we recall that gender and heterosexuality are not only individual practices but also encompass a massive socio-cultural order. Performative approaches remain largely in the realm of sexual and gender identities and the reworking of symbols and meanings – resignification.

There is an important difference here between Foucault and queer theory. Whereas Foucault saw in the nineteenth-century proliferation of sexual categories ever more finely tuned and invasive tentacles of power that reached into and subjectified an ever broader range of sexual subjects, queer theory sees in the proliferation of sexualities and genders a performative destabilisation of the same. By bringing to light the genealogy of sexuality Foucault aspired to dislodge the process of subjectification itself. It is doubtful whether he succeeded or even could succeed. But that is not the point. While we might never live in a subjectless world, and it strikes me as unlikely, we can nonetheless see his work as a limit case or an invitation to explore the limits of subjectification (see Huffer 2009). Rather than undermining subjectification, per se, queer theory puts its faith in resignifying identities so that they escape the subject positions that enclose them. The problem here is that Foucault was a theorist of subjects and subjectification, not identities and identity politics, a North American phenomenon foreign to his French intellectual heritage (Huffer 2009: 70–71). This is another, more theoretical reason why I do not devote attention to identities and it ushers in a few cautionary words on the subject of neoliberalism.

Queer theory emerged in the context of neoliberal ascendency and has from the start questioned stable sexual identities and advocated theoretical and political opposition to them. An important question is whether this kind of politics is enabled by and even dependent on liberal capitalism which is relatively sympathetic to the demands for recognition and inclusion in identity politics, but less inclined to countenance an overhaul of the economic order. There is some truth in the accusation that queer theory neglects the material, socio-economic conditions of its own emergence and existence. According to critics, queer advocacy of the destabilisation and transgression of sexual and gender norms and the resignification of meaning fails to consider in any detail the political and economic contexts in which these resignifications and transgressions of gender and sexual norms take place. In fact, some commentators argue that it pursues an anti-normative line to the point where it has difficulty distinguishing between normative goods and normative bads. Queer theory, or at least its performative politics, is accused of being complicit in the reproduction of the very inequalities it claims to oppose (Ebert 1993, Nussbaum 1999, Hennessy 2000).[16] Readers ought to bear these criticisms in mind when reading this book.

It now remains for me to turn to the relationship between queer theory and anthropology. My main purpose here is to draw out the similarities, parallels and areas of overlap between both.

Queer by any other Name: Anthropology

Queer theoretical writings began with, and many still do, focus primarily on Euro-American societies and their sexual commonsense. Indeed, in some respects we can see queer theory and its critique of the normative as carrying out anthropological work by scrutinising the everyday sexual assumptions of

---

16 The relationship between queer theory and feminism has been and remains an awkward and sometimes hostile one. Perhaps the most frequent criticism directed at queer theory by feminist scholars is that queer theory privileges sexuality over gender, fails to appreciate the importance of patriarchy in sustaining heteronormative regimes and focuses on gay men but neglects lesbians. For illuminating and constructive recent discussions between feminist and queer scholars, see Richardson, McLaughlin and Casey 2006, see also Jackson 2006.

INTRODUCTION

Western cultures. As the discipline that has specialised in social and cultural worlds outside the Occident, anthropology has long had access to other kinds of commonsense surrounding gender and sexuality. Given the vast cultural and social variety anthropologists have encountered and documented, it would indeed have been strange if they had *not* been furnished with counter-examples that at least partly correspond to the alternatives thrown up by queer interrogations of Euro-American regimes of 'normal' sexuality.

Not surprisingly, then, some of the main themes and insights of queer theory resonate with and are already prefigured in anthropological writings. For example, the recognition that sex (bodies) and gender (culture) do not coincide with western expectations is an old truism that goes back to Mead and beyond. Examples include the *māhū* of Taihiti, the *xanith* of Oman, the *hejras* of India, the *'berdache'* of North America, the 'sworn virgins' of Albania, and the *tombois* of Indonesia.[17]

The central queer tenet of performativity, which understands gender to be the product of repetitive practices that materialise into a second nature, is prefigured in Bourdieu's (1977) habitus and in the earlier work of Mauss (1979) on techniques of the body. It even echoes the structural-functionalist emphasis on the unavoidable and obligatory performance of roles (Moore 1994: 24).

Queer theory's interrogation of the sexual subject parallels anthropology's assault on the western sovereign individual. In its place anthropology has given us dividuals, partible, dispersed and permeable persons, distributed agency, actor networks, and assemblages. The dividual subjects of anthropology resonate with the post-structural subjects buttressed by constitutive outsides and supplements that are the bedrock of queer theory. In addition, cultural models of the person, such as those found in Melanesia, that emphasise the combination of gendered substances that make up each individual body make it difficult to attribute an essential gender to a person, and it becomes even more difficult to accommodate within dominant western models when these substances are also understood to be transactable, such that the overall 'amount' of gendered substance making up a body and the relative amounts of male and female substances vary depending on the types of exchanges – sexual, economic, and ritual – in which the person engages (Strathern 1988, see also Gregor and Tuzin 2001).

There are theoretical differences too of course. For example, the wariness many anthropologists display toward psychoanalytical ideas. This is not to say that anthropology lacks a tradition of psychological and psychoanalytical work, but it has never occupied a place within anthropology comparable to that which it enjoys within much queer theory. The reliance of many queer writers on ideas

---

17 See respectively, Levy 1973, Wikan 1977, Nanda 1990, Roscoe 1998, Young 2000, Blackwood 2010.

derived from Lacan, for example, smacks of an ahistorical universalism and ethnocentrism to many anthropologists.

Yet while the language used by psychoanalysis is unfamiliar, not least its heavy reliance on a sexual vocabulary, there are parallels between anthropological concerns and Lacan's work. Earlier I pointed to the role of mimicry in the Imaginary constitution of the subject. Michael Taussig (1993) has made much of the faculty of mimicry drawing parallels between it and sympathetic magic. Then there is object *a*, forever elusive, unknown, and alien dwelling at the centre of our being. Numerous anthropologists have pointed to the importance of the incorporation of the radically other and even threatening for the well being of the social. Examples include the perspectivism of Amazonia (Vivieros de Castro 1998) and animist ontologies in which horizontal and egalitarian relationships prevail and a balance is maintained by means of inter-species transformations and movement between human and non-human worlds (Ingold 2006).

Another difference between queer theory and anthropology is the lack of sociological perspectives in much queer writing that emanates from the humanities which sits uneasily alongside anthropological empiricism and its emphasis on ethnographic description. But there is nothing in queer theory per se that excludes a stronger empirical focus more in keeping with anthropology.

Perhaps the critical thrust of queer theory also makes it less attractive, or at least problematic, for some anthropologists. Its anti-normative agenda is not always easy to reconcile with anthropology's mission to make what, in Euro-American eyes, are apparently bizarre, offensive or cruel actions incomprehensible when understood in their own local terms. Yet feminist anthropology has long faced a similar challenge as it balances between a critique of gender inequality outside Euro-American contexts while also trying to make sense of cultural others (Strathern 1987).

There are also differences between the disruptive and denaturalising approach of queer theory at home and anthropological use of the 'queer' label, which often refers to the sexual and gender subjects encountered 'elsewhere' that destabilise dominant Euro-American ideas about sexuality 'at home'. Why these are 'queer' examples in context (and what counts as queer is always contextual) is not always clear, as not all are especially disruptive of local understandings of sexuality and gender. On the contrary, examples like the *Hijra* of India (Nanda 1990), the *xanith* of Oman (Wikan 1977) and the *bissu* of Indonesia (Davis 2010) are embedded in local cultures and ascribed roles of their own. They are not especially subversive in context regardless of how they might be viewed from a Euro-American perspective.

There are then points of similarity and contrast between anthropology and queer theory but what they share is their capacity to place a question mark beside cherished assumptions. The remainder of this book charts out areas of mutual interest and points of fertile exchange between both of them.

INTRODUCTION

The Chapters in this Book

Central to all questions surrounding gender and sexuality is the relationship between the material of which the world, including our bodies, is composed and cultural expressions of appropriate gender practices for men and women. Chapter 1, 'Things', draws on process philosophy and the turn to ontology and materiality in recent anthropological and feminist scholarship to explore the dynamism of materiality right down to the level of quanta. Queer theory has often reduced matter to an effect of discourse. However, materiality, in whatever form, can no longer be understood as an inert backdrop or compliant surface for cultural inscription. The ideas presented in this chapter resurface throughout the book.

Chapter 2, 'Sexonomics', focuses on two types of things that have long been central to anthropology, commodities and gifts. It draws on Jean Baudrillard's argument that the structure of the commodity and the structure of the sign in capitalism mirror each other to argue that the structure of the logic of the heteronormative lies at the heart of the commodity. The chapter then turns to gifts and draws parallels between their contingency, risk, ambiguity, and superfluity and the queer materiality discussed in Chapter 1. It finishes on a note of caution. Providing matter with its due does not guarantee it will do as we wish.

Chapter 3, 'Smells', also draws on Baudrillard and his discussion of the value regimes of capitalism. The chapter provides a critical examination of scents that claim to transcend gender (and race and age) and that utilise a nomadic desire that appears to defy sexological categorisation. Scents are examples of queer matter on the loose that undermines and evades the subjects and sexualities it is supposed to reinforce.

Chapter 4, 'Species', addresses some of the implications of the 'species thinking' in Foucault's famous account of the emergence of the homosexual species. These include its minoritarian assumptions, its relationship to Darwinian ideas and neoliberal values, ecological arguments in management thinking, and arguments surrounding creative cities and valuable minorities. The chapter outlines a form of value that emphasises implication rather than position. Using turn-of-the-century Great Britain as an example, it reveals the species thinking behind policies for social cohesion but also some of the unintended queer implications of these policies meant to promote cultural creativity and value.

Chapter 5, 'Intersections', as its name suggests, examines the spatial metaphor of intersections and its theoretical application in intersectionality. It does so with the help of recent anthropological work on lines (Ingold 2007). The 'co-ordinated' assumptions behind the intersection metaphor, it argues, deserve critical scrutiny. The chapter goes on briefly to consider the experience of people diagnosed as inter-sexed to illustrate further some of the difficulties of the intersection metaphor.

Chapter 6, 'Failures' looks at a popular genre – gossip magazines and 'real life' soaps – and sees in it evidence of myth found in the work of Claude Lévi-Strauss and Bronislaw Malinowski. Despite their cultural prominence, the gossip magazines give only qualified support to the heteronormative, painting a picture of conflict even tragedy amidst the celebrity glamour. The chapter argues that performative theories of gender tend to ignore the banquet of heterosexual failures served on a daily basis, and that attention to failure in recent queer writings (e.g. Halberstam 2011) needs to be rethought in the light of failure not only as ubiquitous but as an ontological fact.

The final chapter, 'Explications', turns the lens of queer theory onto the source of anthropology itself, the body of anthropologist. It performs a deconstruction of the anthropologist as a fully constituted object through an exploration of how that object was put there, including metaphors, things, affects, visceral processes, and intuition.

Chapter 1
Things

'What is the Mind? No Matter. What is the Matter? Never Mind'

George Berkeley

One implication of Simone de Beauvoir's argument that one is not born a woman is that a male body might signify a woman. If Beauvoir is correct, then nothing in her argument demands that women are female or that men are male. Yet immediate resistance to this idea and appeals to the female body, whether direct or indirect, lead swiftly back to the biological 'facts' of sexual dimorphism. For example, Adrienne Rich's essay on compulsory heterosexuality, which in so many respects is a queer forerunner that troubles the category of 'lesbian', what we mean by sexuality, and not least the obviousness of heterosexuality, also appeals to 'motherhood' as a 'female experience' uniting all women (Rich 1983).

It was a central tenet of second-wave feminism that biology – bodies sexed as either male or female – does not exercise a determinate influence on gender, the appropriate local cultural expressions and actions associated with men and women (Oakley 1972). Gender became the terrain for feminist exploration while sex, the biological remainder, was surrendered to biologists and medics. It was not a fitting subject for feminism, being no more than a passive foundation upon which culture raised its gendered edifices.

In a path-breaking article, *A Critique of the Sex/Gender Distinction*, Moira Gatens (1996[1983]) points out that making gender into cultural representation leaves the biological/material ground that is represented intact and turns gender into ideality. It is the material-immaterial divide itself that needs to be questioned, not reinforced.[1] The sex-gender distinction, therefore, takes us

---

1 From within anthropology other examples include the work of Michelle Rosaldo (1974) and her distinction between a female private sphere and a male public sphere, and Sherry Ortner's (1974) equation of the natural with women and the feminine, and the cultural with men and the masculine. Arguably, while attempting to identify and explain women's subjugation these dualisms, and especially their emphasis on child-bearing and motherhood, served to reinforce what was already a pervasive cultural assumption about the 'natural' place of women and their determination by the material 'facts' of their biology. It did not take long for feminist anthropologists to recognise the ethnocentrism of these models and the inadequacy of the dualistic assumptions on which they rest (MacCormack and Strathern 1980). Within anthropology, Sylvia Yanagisako and Janet Collier (1987) pointed out the ethnocentrism of the divide as one that mirrors a nature-culture dichotomy. Other challenges include the classic ethnomethodological study by

directly into another area of research, one that, on the face of it, is not obviously queer but is of central importance nonetheless: the question of materiality. More precisely, it is the question of the nature of the materiality of bodies, and the realm of things and the part they play in producing gender, sexualities and desires. This is an area of inquiry that, as Stacey Alaimo and Susan Hekman (2008: 1) note, is 'an extraordinarily volatile site for feminist theory — so volatile, in fact, that the guiding rule of procedure for most contemporary feminisms requires that one distance oneself as much as possible from the tainted realm of materiality by taking refuge within culture, discourse, and language'. Materialist arguments are frequently assumed to imply biological determinism and the naturalisation of gender difference and as such are considered inexplicable, unintelligible, politically suspect and disqualified from the realm of the rational. Materiality, we might say, is a constitutive outside of much feminist theory. It is also an abject of queer theory which advocates denaturalisation of apparently 'natural' categories. Queer theory has neglected materiality as much as, if not more, than feminist thought. Yet, as I shall argue in this chapter, materiality displays characteristics that we can justifiably call queer and deserves closer attention than it has received (Graham 2010).

One reason for looking at materiality is to ask what it is about matter that makes it amenable to the imprint of sexing and gendering practices. There is nothing self-evident about this capacity. If matter is a remainder outside and barred from the cultural, how can we know anything about it? How can the cultural reach across the ontological divide towards nature and leave its imprint on it? Why should materiality be susceptible to what we refer to as the cultural? Why should it acquiesce to being sculpted by social and cultural imperatives? Why, in short, should the material of nature allow itself to be co-opted into the creation of sexed, gendered and sexual subjects? Its 'willingness' to comply is often simply assumed.

The division into a knowable culture and an unknowable nature is now being interrogated on several fronts. Work by feminist scholars such as Karen Barad, Elizabeth Grosz, Donna Haraway, Vicki Kirby, and Elisabeth Wilson, among others, argues for a nature that is part of the cultural, is semiotic, literate, and has agency. Indeed, Kirby (2008) goes so far as to ask whether culture wasn't nature all along, reversing the argument associated most recently with Butler that sex was gender from the start. These challenges to the nature/culture and sex/gender binary seek — if not always successfully (see Howson 2005) — to move feminist and related fields of scholarship away from too heavy a reliance on discourses, language and representations and toward greater attention to the

---

Suzanne Kessler and Wendy McKenna 1978, and somewhat later the work of historian Thomas Laqueur 1990, and philosopher Judith Butler 1990.

corporeal, the material, ontology and how the biological is inextricably tied up with the cultural and the social.

Yet, despite all the effort put into undermining biological essentialisms, biological determinism is still regarded as a legitimate explanation within patriarchal, homophobic, and racist discourses, partly because feminism has not paid sufficient attention to scrutinising and challenging dominant understandings of what nature/biology and materiality are. In short, more not less matter is needed, but more in the sense of a feminist counter-matter, or counter-biology that highlights the queerness of materiality. Mention of nature and materiality no longer automatically implies fixity and rigidity, nor a unilinear determination in the direction of sexist, homophobic or racist truths, but promises a far more dynamic, plural, and enigmatic materiality. But before we look at this queer materiality in more detail we must first visit the bathroom.

At Home with Grant, Andrew and Sarah

While doing an inventory of Grant's possessions, I discovered a small and obviously old can of Crisco vegetable oil in a cupboard in the guest bathroom of his apartment in Sydney.[2] Grant is a business executive in his early forties who works for an Australian multinational company. He was as surprised as I was to find the can there. It was rusty and had leaked leaving a stain on the shelf. The oil had never been used for cooking. The obvious place where he and I would have expected to find it was not in his guest bathroom or even kitchen but in the bottom drawer of his bedroom dresser, where he kept his pornography, his impressive collection of dildos, lubricants, poppers, handcuffs, and all his other sexual paraphernalia. He was a little concerned that his parents might have spotted the Crisco on one of their visits, but on reflection realised that they would have seen only a can of vegetable oil, whereas he saw a lubricant for hardcore sex. Since 1911, Crisco has been advertised as an element of American heterosexual family life, with Mom in her rightful place cooking in the kitchen, sometimes aided by her young daughter.[3] Among gay men, the brand is so well known that bars have been named after it in, among other places, Berlin, Florence and Stockholm. The can will open in either direction, which one depends on what is known about the thing and which of its uses eclipses the others: Baking or fist-fucking, conservative western femininity or hardcore gay male sexuality?

---

2 The material was gathered as part of a research project into materiality and sexuality. The fieldwork was carried out in Sydney in 2001, 2004, 2006 and 2009.

3 See www.crisco.com

Andrew is in his early fifties. Among his possessions are numerous religious items including rosary beads, an assortment of crucifixes, several bibles, and a book about the Roman Catholic School where he once taught. He also owns several ceremonial swords. He acquired them while he was serving in the armed forces apart from one that comes from an uncle who obtained it under suspicious circumstances in Japan at the end of World War Two. Military diplomas and testimonials from Rotary Club hang on his walls and a dress uniform he occasionally wears hangs in his closet along with a nun's habit. He has dozens of gay porn videos, and a bone china tea service decorated in gaudy pansies that he inherited from his grandmother. He also owns a sizeable collection of Hollywood musicals on video,[4] especially those featuring Judy Garland. Considering this small fragment of the total material assemblage that includes Andrew does not provide us with a clear and unambiguous picture of his sexuality. Gay porn sits uneasily alongside Roman Catholic rosaries, the Rotary club and things military.

The military, did, however, provide Andrew with his swords. He eagerly displays how to handle them as part of his seduction technique. They make him *feel* sexy, they do not simply signify his sexuality, and there is something erotic about the precision with which Andrew handles them. It is the fact that the swords are real, not theatrical props, that lends the display its sexiness. The nun's habit appears at parties and is a good showstopper and conversation starter. It too is part of his seduction technique. Martial Arts and Mother Superior, two very different genderings in pursuit of the same thing, sex, preferably with younger men. Andrew uses things to make social and sexual contacts, but the selfsame things connect him with institutions that, in Australia at least, either publicly condemn or are nervous about his sexuality.

What is the sexuality (or gender or sex) of the assemblage 'designer suit and woman'? The suit I have in mind (a jacket and skirt) is worn by Sarah a lesbian banker in Sydney. The power-dressing garment projects status, wealth, and success. Sarah always wears it at meetings where she needs to intimidate; on all other occasions she wears trousers. It was designed by a gay man (Giorgio Armani), and paraded down a catwalk by a woman who projects a version of heterosexual femininity. Aussie sheepshearers sheared the wool, men who are notorious for regularly announcing their heterosexuality and cursing women and queers. People about whose sexuality I know nothing wove the cloth on industrial looms. It was probably sewn together by underpaid female workers. The finished suit was advertised in women's magazines as sex appeal and professional success. The garment is the result of an entanglement of sexualities, sexes, genders, and social and material relations, raw materials (what,

---

4 A latecomer to technology, he has since upgraded to DVDs, CDs, iPods and iTunes.

for example, is the sex or gender of the wool?), and exploitative relations of production that are particularly disadvantageous for women. The finished product does not advertise them. There is no simple sexuality here anymore than there is an obvious gender, or nationality once we look beyond the body wearing the suit and also take into account the relations and materials condensed in it. If sexuality is often talked of as though it were a thing, it is also clearly dependent on things.

But what is a thing?

Things

The word 'thing' derives from the Germanic *thingan* and is related to the Gothic *theihs*, time. The thing was the appointed *time* for deliberation, accusation, judicial process, and decisions. It came to stand for the *place* where these proceedings occurred, such as the Icelandic parliament, the *Althing*, or an electioneering speech from an English husting. In English, a thing was the *subject* of discussion and it finally came to refer to an *object*. The word *thing* is thus a reification of time, place, process, deliberation and dispute.

Cutting is a term often used in connection with things. Henry James writes: 'What shall we call a thing anyhow? It seems quite arbitrary, for we carve out everything, just as we carve out constellations, to suit our human purposes' (quoted in Grosz 2009: 126). Henri Bergson is of a similar opinion but doubts that the cut is every entirely successful: 'The separation between a thing and its environment cannot be absolutely definite and clear-cut, there is a passage by insensible gradations from the one to the other' (quoted in Grosz 2009: 128).

There is also a cut involved in amputating things from the relations between people, places, materials and history that have produced them in order to create discrete objects as the above brief examples demonstrate. In this respect, making things also involves 'sexing' them. In making this claim, I do not mean that they are assigned a masculine or feminine gender, although many objects obviously are. Rather, I am playing on the possible origin of the word sex in the Latin *secare*, 'to cut'. This cut or 'sexing' differentiates things and conceals at least part of their history (Graham 2004). The gendering of Grant's can of vegetable oil occludes its sexuality. The sexuality of Sarah's suit is largely closeted and complicit in racial and gender hierarchies. Andrew's seductive use of ceremonial swords does not advertise that they are the spoils of war (although this may well make them sexy for some people).

But out of what are objects cut exactly? What is the matter from which materials emerge and out of which time do they appear? Few questions are more fundamental to the study of gender and sexuality and to the question of cultural influence on matter, and indeed whether a distinction between the two is even tenable.

Meta-Physics

To explore these questions I turn to metaphysics, more precisely to the work of Baruch Spinoza, Henri Bergson, Alfred North Whitehead, and Gilles Deleuze. These thinkers can all be grouped under the heading of process philosophy. This is a heady philosophical brew which I finish off with a dash of quantum physics.

My discussion of process philosophy sets the metaphysical tone for the book as a whole. Unlike queer theory's heavy reliance on a Hegelian and post-structuralist theoretical apparatus, I want to steer it towards process philosophy, which, it seems to me, is eminently queer in its implications. There are two main reasons for this. Firstly, it shifts attention away from the negative and reactive critique of the heteronormative which is in keeping with the overall goal of this book. For reasons that will become clear shortly, there is a pronounced vein of optimism in process philosophy influenced to some extent by Darwin's ideas on evolution. For many process philosophers, whatever is most recent and complex is also superior to what precedes it. While decay, decline and mortality are undeniable and inescapable they are more than compensated for by the novelty inherent to the world's becoming. While its modernist faith may be out of vogue, it does not diminish the insights of process philosophy as a whole. Secondly, it obliges us to take greater account of materiality because the speculative or metaphysical character of process philosophy is not about a transcendental realism but very much about the world we live in.

Baruch Spinoza's rationalist philosophy posits a unified universe in which everything that exists is 'a more or less active, more or less powerful or expressive facet of a single, unlimited power of existing and acting' (Hallward 2006: 10). There is only one substance and everything that exists is a modification of it. Spinoza dissolves any absolute distinction between mind and matter, culture and nature, real or imagined. His ideas exercised considerable influence over Bergson, Whitehead and through them Deleuze. Spinoza's universe is active and creative but it also congeals into objects – *naturans* becomes *naturata* – singular instances of the underlying universal substance.

For Henri Bergson, the ceaseless becoming of the world, what he calls Duration, is a seamless, forward and creative movement that continually produces the new and unexpected from within itself. This, in essence, is Bergson's élan vital, the impulse to differentiate and elaborate seen most clearly in living things and their continual evolution towards greater complexity as they proliferate in and beyond their life worlds.[5] Change, the emergence of difference, is inbuilt into the passage of time and unfolding of matter itself.

Time is integral to Bergson's ideas on novelty and creativity. The new continually emerges out of the past making the present a version of the past but not an exhaustive one. What becomes present is only a fraction of the past in the present. Importantly, for Bergson the present is not simply that which the past makes possible. This would make the present, or the 'Real' (not to be confused with Lacan's Real), nothing but a result or precipitation of what was already 'Possible'. The real, the present, would be predetermined, preformed in the past. This would leave no room for novelty or creativity. Indeed, all that is possible could theoretically be imagined and predicted before it even happened. Matter would simply be the concrete expression of what is already preformed. Likewise, the 'future cannot be contained in the present (not without reducing the future to the present) because it is an expansion or elaboration of the present rather than distillation, essence or inevitable consequence' (Grosz 2004: 196). For Bergson, therefore, the transition from the 'possible' to the 'real' is a misleading conceptualisation and he replaces it with the 'virtual' and the 'actual'. The actual appears by differentiating itself from the unity of the virtual, it is therefore no mere copy of the virtual, it is not a pre-existing possible, it differs from the virtual even as it is derived from it. In this respect, actualisation, the world's coming into being, is creative.

Human intellect, which for Bergson is of a practical inclination, tends to lag behind the process of differentiation because it recognises the familiar and the useful in the world in the form of stable, spatialised objects in which the creative impulse is switched off. Bergson writes that 'our needs, are then, so many search-lights which, directed upon the continuity of sensible qualities, single out in it distinct bodies. They cannot satisfy themselves except upon the condition that they carve out, within this continuity, a body which is to be their own, and then delimit other bodies with which the first can enter into a relation' (quoted in Hallward 2006: 60). The stability of the objects we cut out of duration is illusory. Change cannot be understood as a movement from object to object or state to state, such as in a conception of time as a succession of units – seconds, minutes, hours and so on. Duration is a *continuous* flow.

The philosopher Alfred North Whitehead defined life as a 'bid for freedom'. His phrasing expresses a central tenet of process philosophy with which his name is virtually synonymous.[6] Whitehead's philosophy is about becoming rather than being, change rather than stasis, relational processes rather than

---

5 The exuberance of biological matter continually enthrals us but can also spring unpleasant surprises, such as new viruses and invasive species.

6 On process philosophy, see Whitehead 1929, Gray 1982, Rescher 1996, Mesle 2008.

independent objects. Whitehead rejected what he saw as the illusion of 'simple location', the assumption that the world is compromised of discrete objects. The material world in process philosophy is an interconnected and manifold process that is always becoming. Like Bergson, Whitehead considers the world to be an innovative place characterised by 'appetition'[7] the bringing into realisation of the new. The world manifests what Whitehead calls 'concrescence' 'the name for the process in which the universe of many things acquires an individual unity' (quoted in Mesle 2008: 101). A basic tenet of process philosophy is that we are all part of this emerging world: 'interwoven with everything that is, a thread in the fabric of the same system of natural laws and interconnecting causes as everything else' (Mesle 2008: 20).[8]

Whitehead addresses an old philosophical problem: If matter is without consciousness (or a soul), then how can consciousness as found in beings like humans and animals ever emerge? Not it seems from inert matter which by definition lacks the capacity for consciousness. Instead, it must be added from the outside (usually by God in the western philosophical tradition), a non-material agency that turns inert matter into vital matter.[9] In this respect, matter is performative, it internalises norms, demands, and proscriptions. But it is also in this account largely pre-formative. The form matter takes is prefigured in the character of the external agent.

What if, unlike earlier philosophers who added consciousness to inert matter, we consider matter itself to be 'conscious'? Whitehead does indeed argue that 'consciousness' must be present in all matter to some extent. The material world experiences all the way down to the level of quanta. Whitehead employs here a vocabulary that is most usually applied to sentient beings. He stretches the meaning of everyday terms like 'experience', 'feeling' and 'emotion' in such a way that he seems to humanise matter (or perhaps make the human more material). The point, as I understand it, is to appreciate that these qualities are

---

7 The term is taken from Leibniz and refers to the inner drive that continually destabilises the monads, the bundles of activity that make up the world.

8 I return to these metaphors of weaving and threads in Chapter 5.

9 Similarly, Tim Ingold has recently criticised anthropological work on materials that regards matter as basically inert and in order to give them 'agency' sprinkles 'magical mind-dust' on them (2011: 28). The boundary between animate and inanimate becomes even less distinct in the latest animation techniques. These are available as software packages that employ mathematical models based on biological processes, such as growth and development. They have the dynamism of biology enfolded within them. Or, if you like, animated images are informed, in-tended, by life processes themselves (Kelty and Landecker 2004). The immense efforts and sums of money that have gone into transforming biological matter – DNA, proteins, stem cells, and so on – into information that can be stored, retrieved and commercialised also dismantle a nature-culture boundary while also tightly implicating the results into politics and ethics.

all matters of degree. For Whitehead, experience and feelings are not confined to consciousness (human or otherwise) or to bodies, but to matter all the way down.[10] Consciousness in humans only perceives a tiny fraction of the constant becoming of matter. Likewise our 'feelings' are only a fraction of all that is felt by our bodies in its continuous relations with itself and the surrounding world. The quantum phenomena of energy, fields, regularities and probabilities also 'experience'. So too do bacteria, cells in bodies and bodies. Mesle (2008: 37–8) again: 'If [experience] does go all the way down, it seems unsurprising that, as these elementary drops of feeling are organised into successively more complex forms, like molecules and cells and animal bodies, central nervous systems and brains, the complexity of those feelings will increase until it crosses a crucial threshold into conscious self-awareness such as you are having right now...Consciousness is only a tiny, but brilliant, flicker in the sea of experience that constitutes this world'.

Another philosopher, on whose work I draw quite extensively, Gilles Deleuze, is indebted to Spinoza, Bergson and to Whitehead. His ideas also place him within the process philosophy tradition. In recent years, the number of anthropologists making direct or indirect use of Deleuze has increased. The specifics of his thought that appeal to anthropologist include concepts like the 'nomad', the 'desiring machine', 'assemblages', 'rhizomes', and 'virtuality'. His ideas have been applied to the study of ritual (Kapferer 2006), time (Hodges 2008), personhood (Humphrey 2008), mental health (Biehl and Locke 2010), and violence and commemoration (Bar-On Cohen 2011). My own route to his thought passed through sexuality, gender and materiality.

Following Bergson, Deleuze accepts novelty as an ontological principle and difference and heterogeneity as his starting point rather than a unity that is then divided. He also refers to a virtual as that which subsists the actual. The latter emerges out of the former, a fraction of what could have been actualised from the virtual's teaming reservoir of potential. However, the virtual does not determine the form the actual takes. Again under Bergson's influence Deleuze does not see the real prefigured in the possible: 'It is not the real that resembles the possible, it is the possible that resembles the real, because it has been abstracted from the real once made' (Deleuze 1988/1966).

---

10 To experience demands an 'individual', a unity of some sort, whether an electron, atom, cell or single member of a species. It must have the capacity to register experience and the difference it makes. A book experiences only at the level of its atomic structure, the book itself cannot experience. Experience is then an organisational matter, or matter organised. All bodies are different and their experiences are different the more so the greater their degree of complexity or organisation. Complexity also eventually entails experience beyond immediate relations with the environment to include abstractions and fantasy. Exactly where the boundary goes for this capacity is a matter of debate.

Here we encounter a significant difference between process philosophy and the post-structuralism that informs queer theory. The Foucauldian dispositive sees bodies as consequences of power that imprints an external difference upon them. This reflects the Hegelian heritage that underlies much post-structuralism and the queer theory that draws on it in which differences in being arise in relation to another, an outside and external difference. While it is true that we do see ourselves and things in terms of contrasts, and there are numerous examples of this including gender, sexuality, racial and national ascriptions among them, this is not the whole story. For Deleuze, difference is not simply imposition of a dispositive or the citation of external norms, such as gender norms, no matter how many genders the norm legislates. The problem from Deleuze's perspective, again echoing Bergson, is that the performative reality thus created is already prefigured in the matrix of the possible – gender norms – and is therefore better termed the *pre*-formative than the performative. For Deleuze, difference cannot simply be equated with citation. Matter differs not only in relation to an outside, the negative Hegelian model of identity and becoming, but also from within in relation to itself, as Bergson and Whitehead both argue.

Like Whitehead and Bergson, Deleuze is also sceptical towards objects. What we perceive as solid form is but a temporary congealment, or 'stratification', of flux, the potential of the virtual. Deleuze distinguishes between 'molar' and 'molecular' phenomena. Molarity involves correlation or organisation of particulars, the imposition of form and a boundary. Molar objects are disciplined in accordance with dominant categories and social demands. Molecular processes have yet to be stratified in this way. However, molarity is only ever an approximation to the category, there can be no exact replication because differentiation and the emergence of differences are inherent to becoming. The distinction between molar and molecular, it is important to note, is qualitative not quantitative. It pertains to the degree of organisation. This means that molecular processes can be large scale, but also smaller, less structured processes at work within an encompassing molarity.

We have arrived at quantum physics, in several respects a support for and culmination of process philosophical ideas. Karen Barad (2007), whose work I summarise in this section, writes that: 'Existence is not an individual affair; it is about entanglements of ideas, practices, politics, ethics, apparatuses of production.' Barad's 'agential realism' is a fusion of ideas from feminism, quantum mechanics (most especially the writings of Niels Bohr), queer theory, post-structuralism and philosophies of science. Following Bohr, Barad argues that the world is not made up of individual objects awaiting our description: Knowledge is not, as in realist accounts, simply a matter of representation in which words and other forms of expression re-present already existing objects. Scientific practice, including its concepts, helps to *'produce'* those objects. Epistemology and ontology are not separable.[11] This is not a claim that discourses *create* matter. Barad's account is realist – there is a world out there independent of us – but how that matter *manifests* itself depends on the apparatuses we use, including the conceptual apparatus we employ. In classical Newtonian physics, the observer does not significantly affect the character of the observed, whereas in quantum physics the interaction between experimental apparatus and object is an *inseparable* part of scientific practice and the very nature of the physical world as it reveals itself to us. This inseparability is what Bohr calls 'quantum wholeness'. Physics is about the phenomena that are comprised of 'the observations obtained under specified circumstances, including an account of the whole experimental arrangement' (Bohr quoted in Barad 2007: 119). It is these phenomena, not objects, that are the primary ontological units of physics (2007: 141) and the basic building blocks with which knowledge is constructed.

The point to appreciate here is that the objects and the subjects that are part of an experiment crystallise out and are made 'determinate' in the moment of measurement broadly conceived, they do not precede that moment. Different measuring apparatuses will manifest different objects from within the phenomena. Barad calls the process one of '*intra*-action', rather than '*inter*-action', because the latter suggests objects that precede the experimental situation and then inter-act with each other. This is not what phenomena are about. They produce the objects from *within* – intra – themselves. Phrased slightly differently: 'A phenomenon is a specific *intra*-action of an "object" and the "measuring agencies", the "object" and the "measuring agencies" *emerge* from, rather than precede, the intra-action that produces them' (2007: 128, emphasis added). The process enacts what Barad calls an 'agential cut' that separates 'subject' and 'object' *within* the phenomenon. Prior to the cut matter is all ontological and semantic indeterminacy, an entanglement (2007: 334).

---

11 The anthropological literature on ontology has grown rapidly in recent years and I shall not attempt a summary here. Central themes include attention to the material practices that give rise to objects and concepts, including actor networks and assemblages; invitations to 'think through things' (Henare et al. 2007) which act as affordances in efforts to challenge and alter concepts, searching for the difference and becoming from *within* ideas and things, a task akin to the process philosophy considered here, and not only differences between cultural worlds. Some ontological approaches are more concerned with concepts and remain closer to epistemology, while others follow a more material avenue of inquiry and are closer to ontology as it is often understood. Common to both is attention to the shaping of the world, or perhaps more accurately how it manifests itself on its own terms rather than through anthropological representations of it. For some recent contributions, see Willerslev 2007, Blaser 2009, Jensen 2010, Candea 2011, *Ethnos* 2011, 76 (1), Holbraad 2012, Pedersen 2012, Scott 2013.

Continuing on the theme of the cut and in view of what quantum mechanics tells us it will come as no surprise when I write, following Whitehead, that matter makes decisions (Mesle 2008: 81). Decision here plays on the meaning of the word, de-cision, literally a 'cutting off'. The classic example is the electron. Depending on the experimental apparatus used, an electron can appear either as a particle with a location or as a wave. It cannot be observed as both at the same time because the apparatus needed to make a particle appear excludes the production of the wave, and vice-versa.[12] Decisions are part of the electron's incessant becoming as it de-cides whether to manifest itself as a wave or a particle. It is impossible to predict in advance what the decision will be. It is undetermined and only a probability, not a certainty. Moreover, the becoming is inseparable from the intra-action with the world. When the electron decides on a particle future, it does so in intra-action with others, such as the experimental situation. The becoming doesn't happen to isolated entities because this presupposes independent pre-existing objects, the atomistic model of the world, rather than phenomena. An electron's decision is not consciousness but the logic of cutting off options is the same as conscious decisions. Decisions manifest or actualise a future that is emerging. Even at the level of the electron there are options, nothing is decided in advance.

One immediate consequence of looking at phenomena is that the observer is not located outside them in some neutral space. In a very real sense the human agent with determinate corporeal boundaries is also part of the 'whole experimental situation' and is produced by the agential cut in the phenomenon along with the 'natural' objects (Barad 2007: 148, 160). Experimental apparatuses are open-ended practices. Hence Bohr's conventional piece of laboratory equipment is too narrow a definition of an apparatus. Where then should we draw the line when determining the boundary of an apparatus? Is it an instrument display, infrared interfaces, the laboratory scientists, printers, the paper in the printer, the journal in which experimental results are published, the readers of the article, universities, funding bodies, or government policies? Ought all to be included? There is no simple answer to this question that does not imply a degree of arbitrariness (2008: 134). Agential cuts are unavoidably selective; not everything can be made determinate and materialise at once,

---

12 Werner Heisenberg believed that the effect of the apparatus could be compensated for in calculations. Bohr objected that this leaves us with preexisting objects, electrons, whereas the electron is manifested within mutually exclusive phenomena by an agential cut that materialises it as *either* particle *or* wave. Bohr writes of *indeterminacy* that is integral to the nature of matter, an ontological indeterminacy, whereas Heisenberg's *uncertainty* is epistemological. Importantly, and unbeknownst to many, Heisenberg eventually agreed with Bohr and wrote a postscript to his famous paper on uncertainty to that effect (Barad 2008: 134).

because 'there is no outside to the universe, there is no way to describe the entire system, so that the description always occurs from within: *only part of the world can be made intelligible to itself at a time, because the other part of the world has to be the part that it makes a difference to*' (Barad 2007: 351, emphasis in original).[13]

The marriage of Bergson, Whitehead and Deleuze with quantum physics is not coincidental. Quantum discoveries lent strong support to central tenets of Bergson's and Whitehead's process metaphysics.[14] 'Twentieth-century physics has thus turned the tables on classical atomism. Instead of very small things (atoms) combining to produce standard processes (windstorms and such), modern physics envisions very small processes (quantum phenomena) combining in their modus operandi to produce standard things (ordinary macro-objects)' (Rescher 1996: 98).

From this several important points follow. The enactment of boundaries around things, including human subjects, concepts, and apparatuses entails exclusions for which we can be held accountable: Who/what did not materialise/ matter and why? But this partiality also leaves the universe open. There is no final completion, no things-in-themselves locked up with their essences. Matter, we might say, is always an open matter, not a simple matter of fact. Moreover, if matter is indeed a continual becoming and not a fixed state, then it would seem to be a poor candidate for a stable and invariant substrate capable of determining the essential nature of its own temporary configuration in the form of sexed, gendered and racialised bodies. This kind of materiality is far less attractive a stomping ground for misogynists, homophobes and racists who believe in eternal – that is purely 'natural' – 'truths' about the people whom they despise because said truths supposedly derive their indisputable character from the stable foundation of matter itself.

The Inscrutability of Things

Once we regard things as the result of agential cuts, implicated in all manner of inequalities, and in their thingness as harbouring disputes and contestations, and, if we follow Whitehead, feelings, consciousness, and even decision-making,

---

13 There are even resonances here with Lacan's ideas surrounding the cut internal to the Real that produces subjects and an outside to them, object *a*.

14 Another source of support was provided by the materiality of Darwinian evolution, which had a major impact on process philosophy. Biological matter for Darwin is continually in flux, evolving, never still. His successors have been faced with the challenge of reconciling species thinking, which assumes the existence of objects, with biological material that is forever undergoing changes. I return to this theme in Chapter 4 where I discuss 'sexual species'.

then they become very inscrutable indeed. It is this inscrutability that has often been overlooked in anthropology where material culture has frequently been assimilated to a Durkheimian sociology in which it is stable, compliant surfaces onto which social meanings are projected. This is not to suggest for one moment that material objects cannot have a stabilising function. For example, in his early work Jean Baudrillard writes of *'categories of objects* which quite tyrannically induce *categories of persons*. They undertake the policing of social meanings, and the significations they engender are controlled' (1988: 16–17, emphasis in original). Similarly, in *The World of Goods* Mary Douglas and Baron Isherwood (1979) argue that consumption uses goods 'to make firm and visible a particular set of judgements in the fluid processes of classifying persons and events' (ibid.: 67). Their argument relies on a Durkheimian theory of ritual in which goods are solidified, collective representations. There is certainly no shortage of ethnographic examples of how material things are employed to stabilise, or 'tyrannically induce', gender and sexuality. In her classic essay, *The Bow and the Burden Strap*, Harriet Whitehead (1981) describes how among the Yaruk of California the *wergen* displayed his gender preference through weaving baskets, wearing women's clothing and pounding acorns. Tests for children manifesting gender-crossing behaviour included a forced choice between implements that were gendered as either male or female. The object chosen determined which gender was attributed to the child.

More recently, Daniel Miller (2008), when summarising his viewpoint on the role of material things based on ethnography from 30 households in London, writes that every household is a 'tribe' that constructs a household cosmology out of its material culture, a cosmology that is 'holistic rather than fragmented', even if it contains contradictions (2008: 294). Material culture here provides 'the comfort that Durkheim associated with religion in society' (p. 295). Miller contends that people create relationships to people and things that 'give order, meaning and often moral adjudication to their lives; an order which, as it becomes familiar and repetitive, may also be a comfort to them' (p. 296). This is a perfectly legitimate way to summarise one aspect of material culture, but it is not the whole story and it reduces the material to stability, social relations and representations – order, structure and cosmology.

Yet whatever the stabilising uses to which they can be put, things remain material and, as we have seen, exceed linguistic and semiotic attempts to summarise what they 'really' are, not only because they are too complex but because materials are actively becoming different from themselves. It is certainly important to allow things a social life of their own, one that recognises their status transformations from, for example, a commodity to a singularised object (Kopytoff 1986), but it is not enough as this opens things up to even more social and cultural coding while still not taking their materiality fully into account. Without denying the importance of the insights of Appadurai (1986) and the other contributors to *The Social Life of Things*, we also need to recognise that things have 'inexplicable' and 'deceptive' qualities (Pinney 2005: 262).[15]

Tim Ingold (2011: 20), who makes use of Bergson, Whitehead and Deleuze, argues that in trying to understand 'materiality', anthropologists have often abandoned 'materials', the stuff in which and with which we live, materials that are inseparable from everything we do as embodied beings, as material creatures. He complains that anthropologists, in keeping with the neglect of materials, have tended to focus on the consumption of finished objects, rather than their production. Attention to the latter would bring anthropologists into closer contact with the materials that make up things and which have given them an inescapable dynamism. 'Far from being the inanimate stuff typically envisioned by modern thought, materials in this original sense are the active constituents of a world-in-formation. Wherever life is going on, they are relentlessly on the move – flowing, scraping, mixing and mutating' (Ingold 2011: 28). The 'original sense' he refers to is *mater* ('mother') the Latin root of material. Matter is a fecund becoming.[16]

The Fetish

Is there anywhere we can look for things that manifest enigma and ambiguity where entanglements are present? Is there a kind of thing in which the ontological and semantic are closely intertwined and which defies processes

---

15 Some readers may be wondering why I have not mentioned Bruno Latour or Actor Network Theory. Latour is known for his advocacy of a democratic symmetry between the human and non-human, the animate and inanimate. Actors, regardless of status, arise within networks and the differences to which they contribute and the creations they bring about. Latour insists on the relational character of the world in which there is no pure nature and no pure culture, these notions being but the delusions of modernity (Latour 1993). However, according to critics, despite his insistence on symmetry Latour nonetheless subordinates the non-human and inanimate to humans (Whatmore 2002). His rejection of a realm free from the human and outside culture results in a similar problem as that faced by performative theories of gender and matter, namely, that matter, the inanimate can only ever be approached as a sign. There is no room for an outside to the networks, or the independence of things. Yet most of what goes on 'out there' in the material world is indifferent and untouched by human culture.

16 Ingold also argues that people who hold animistic beliefs are united 'in a way of being that is alive and open to a world of continuous birth [that]…issues forth through a world-in-formation, along the lines of their relationships' (2006: 9). That is, they continually emerge out of ongoing processes, the flux of the world, rather than a matter of existing objects. In Ingold's rendering of the distinction, the animists are compatriots of process philosophy and agential realism.

of representation? What if any-thing troubles a human/non-human, subject/object binary and forces us to think in terms that do not uphold as separate nature and culture, matter and meaning? Perhaps it is the fetish.[17]

According to Peter Pels (1998) we ought to pay more heed to what he calls the 'untranscended materiality' of things, their capacity to exceed, avoid or subvert cultural coding. This capacity he sees exemplified in the fetish. The fetish, he argues, has the quality of 'generic singularity'. There is something about them that makes them unique in themselves. Fetishes are objects *sui generis* (like rarities, the odd objects we find difficult to categorise Pels 1998). This is not the singularity described by Igor Kopytoff (1986), which is the result of an object being excluded from commodity exchange because of its unique – singular – significance, such as a family heirloom, or the sentimental value of a childhood teddy bear. The singularity of the fetish is resistant to classification as anything other than itself. The fetish also retains its status as separate from the one over whom it asserts its power; it is not emotionally or socially assimilated as in the value of the teddy bear. It remains alien, yet it exercises influence. It is matter that 'strikes back' from a 'border' 'between' mind and matter, bodies and objects, self and other (Pels 1998: 102; Speyer 1998).

Fetishes saw the light of day as things that regulated trade between people in West Africa and Venetian, Dutch and Portuguese merchants and mariners in the Sixteenth and Seventeenth centuries (Pietz 1985, 1987, 1988). The fetish was the product of several traditions and the encounter between them. It was precisely the bringing together in the fetish of heterogeneous things and unlike materials that made its placement and representation difficult (Pietz 1985: 7–8). Fetishes appeared in a zone where much was up for grabs, where change was constant, relations fluid, and the rules unclear. If nothing is stable, categories obscure and relations ephemeral and constantly refashioned, it is difficult to re-present anything. From the earliest accounts of fetishes from the Dutch and Portuguese it is clear that the fetish did not represent anything, unlike an idol, which *stands in* for a god or spirit which it re-presents. Indeed, argues Pels, the fetish acts as a boundary marker or constitutive limit to classification and representation, where representation stands for a signifier that stands in for a signified.

---

17 According to Arjun Appadurai (1986), a degree of 'methodological fetishism' is usually involved in our study of things, we describe them as if they had a life of their own, even as we insist that this life is determined by social and cultural processes. Things may appear to have their own voices, but for Appadurai it is we, social actors, who have put them there. Peter Pels (1998) argues that Appadurai looks at the spirit in matter (a dualist model), rather than the spirit of matter. Ingold (2011) agrees with Pels but wants him to go even further. He detects a lingering mental-material distinction in 'the spirit of matter'.

Fetishes were in fact 'done', they were made rather like a deal when they were needed. The parties could 'drink' or 'eat' fetish. It was the equivalent of the business lunch. The practices and assumptions each party brought to the table were inadequate to guarantee outcomes. It was the fetish that guaranteed the terms of the exchanges. Failure to comply or renege on the deal risked punishment by the fetish.

I want to supplement the West African example with another from Brazil. Marcio Goldman (2009) argues that the deities, the *orixás* of *candomblé* religion – itself a mixture of influences from Native American cosmologies, Catholicism and western spiritualities – are 'made' in the process of initiation at the same time as the person they possess, 'the saint daughter', is 'made', a transformation known as 'making the saint'. 'Making' requires some careful qualification. The deities involved, the *orixás*, exist prior to their union with the saint daughter, which produces a specific instance of the *orixá*. The *orixá* is fixed in the initiate and in ritual objects, an *assentamento* (seat) that includes special stones (*otás*). These stones are not there by accident, they ask to be found and are able to do so because they belong to the same *orixá* as the initiate, and, like the saint daughter, they too are *destined* to become *orixás*. (Not all stones are so destined but all stones, like all initiates, belong to a specific *orixá*.) Both are, so to speak, cut out of the entanglements of which they are part in order to reveal what is already there, in the manner of cutting a diamond out of the potential in the uncut stone. Clearly, we are looking at a world in which everything is in some sense connected. It is also a world in which stones and initiates become, or are made into, what they 'already' are, by means of a kind of actualisation of a virtual, to employ the Deleuzian terminology which several scholars have used when considering these aspects of *candomblé*. The *assentamento* and the things that comprise it are, like a fetish, matter with its *own* creative potential that is involved in the making of the world.

The fetish is also a peculiar thing in that it departs from the everyday evaluation of objects, as use, exchange or sign value (see Chapter 2). A fetish may well be a commodity, a pair of patent leather boots, for example, but it maintains a value of its own that sets it apart from everyday objects and imbues it with a power that is difficult to assimilate to our relationships with 'ordinary' objects and hence difficult to control. This 'failure' to be subsumed by signification and value marks the fetish as suspect, an example of matter gone awry.

Fetishes bring us down to earth, back to our bodies and the material world, and away from idealist schemes of signification. Marx referred to fetishism as a 'religion of sensuous desire' (Pels 1998: 101). It is perhaps not surprising that the fetish is often associated with sexuality, rather than the religious objects of early West African fetishism. Sexuality in the Euro-American west is thing-like and yet not, a matter of embodiment *and* identity, completely colonised by history and culture yet felt as 'natural' and as emanating directly from the materiality of bodies independently of both historical and cultural determinations.

It is the refusal of the fetish to bow down to the past and respect its pedigree that makes it interesting not only from an anthropological but also a queer perspective. The difficulty of turning it into an epistemological object testifies to its stubborn thingness, as well as its elusive value. The fetish stands at the confluence of several traditions that are folded into it, it is a manifold that resists reduction and emerges out of connections. Anthropologists should be on the look out for fetishes. These are the things that take us to the limit of what we can represent. They oblige us to take an extra step into the inexpressible.

Final Matters

As I noted earlier, the turn to gender in feminism and the more recent turn to discourses and signification (Howson 2005) left the field of biology/nature to natural sciences and provided a flimsy bulwark against patriarchal and conservative claims about the 'true' nature of gender and sexuality, which are simply and directly the result of certain configurations of matter into sexed bodies. The removal of biology from feminist concerns was part of a necessary political project aimed at undermining the biological essentialisms that were deployed to justify women's subordination as natural, grounded in indisputable and universal biological facts that did not admit of anything but superficial social and cultural modification. However, the result was that the nature-culture dichotomy was left firmly in place. Nature, the female, remained the 'inert ground for the exploits of Man' (Alaimo and Hekman 2008: 4). Yet, as we have seen, this is no inert ground, far from it. For this reason, unless otherwise stated, throughout this book matter, materiality, will refer to things rather than objects. It will assume the capacity to change, to be creative, no matter how modest, it will not assume simple location or discrete entities. It will take as given that any definition of what a thing is must always be partial and leave a remainder, that representations never fully represent, that things are interconnected, parts of a manifold, that the division into subjects and objects is chimerical regardless of how self-evident it may seem, and that matter and mind are not easily if ever kept apart. It will also take as axiomatic the importance of the cut, of the necessary but arbitrary division of the world into objects, units, and that these cuts always have ethical implications. These are the qualities of matter I want to emphasise in keeping with process philosophy and the spirit of queer theory. In the next chapter, I consider two kinds of thing that have long been anthropological staples, gifts and commodities.

Chapter 2
Sexonomics

No eunuch flatters its despot more basely or uses more infamous means to revive his flagging capacity for pleasure, in order to win a surreptitious favour for himself, than does the eunuch of industry, the manufacturer, in order to sneak himself a silver penny or two or coax the gold from the pocket of his dearly beloved neighbour (Karl Marx, quoted in Slater 1997: 110).

Human economic activity has been understood with the help of more than its fair share of sexual metaphors. Long ago, Aristotle described interest *tokos* ("offspring") as 'the birthing of money from money [in which] the offspring resemble the parent. That is why', he concludes, 'of all modes of getting wealth this is the most unnatural' (1998, 1 10 1258b 5–7). Compare Aristotle's opprobrium with that of Karl Marx over 2000 years later in the above quotation on the subject of manufacturing industry. Here Marx resorts to sexual metaphors, in which a mutilated, sterile masculinity, which he obviously despises, persuades the hapless consumer to buy unnecessary wares. Even the goods themselves are not innocent. The culture of 'commodity aesthetics', the entire apparatus of signs, packaging, advertising, and design intended to make commodities appear desirable, has been referred to by Wolfgang Haug as a 'technology of *sensuality*' (1986: 45, emphasis added). Haug writes: 'Without discrimination, commodity aesthetics smiles invitingly on everyone, the soul of the commodity is as ingratiating as it is *promiscuous*' (ibid: 86, emphasis added). So effective was the 'ingratiating', 'promiscuous' commodity that kleptomania, in the form of shoplifting, reached epidemic proportions among the middle-class women who patronised the new department stores of late nineteenth- and early twentieth-century Europe and North America. Their thieving was diagnosed as a *sexual* malady brought on by the menopause or disorders of the womb and as such beyond their moral control, unlike working-class women whose thieving was simply that and landed them behind bars (Abelson 2000: 314).

As the above examples make clear, sex and the economy implicate each other and can be used to think each other. What is striking about these comparisons is the way in which the sexual metaphors are employed to decry practices the authors find abhorrent. Something about economic gain makes it morally dubious in a way that suggests sexual impropriety: Bad economics is bad sex.

In this chapter, I want to examine a less explicit sexual current within matters economic. I shall argue that the structure of the commodity displays striking homologies with that of the two main sexual types of modern western culture, heterosexual and homosexual, and that the gift bears all the hallmarks of queer materiality. The relevance of a queer analytical approach for the study of gifts and commodities may not be immediately apparent, until, that is, we recall that they are often understood in highly gendered dichotomous terms that coincide with and help to reinforce a number of others, among them primitive and modern, private and public, home and market (*oikos* and *agora*), romantic and rational, trivial and important, superfluous and necessary, and female and male. None of these binaries is neutral, as the two sides of the dichotomy are marked by significant differences in status, power, and resources, and none of them is stable, despite the ideological and material efforts that have gone into trying to make them so.

To ask questions about gifts, commodities and materiality in general is, then, to ask, indirectly, about sexuality. I start with the commodity.

The Commodity

Karl Marx was convinced that the urge to labour and produce was a transhistorical, universal and natural human imperative found at the very core of our 'species being'. His conviction was grounded in a romantic image of traditional societies as harmonious, communal, holistic, and free of ideological screens between humans and nature. In this prelapsarian world, people enjoyed a direct relation to the products of their labours, products they used to satisfy their 'natural' needs. Marx had little to say about the possible cultural determination of what constitutes needs themselves (Sahlins 1976), and thus as a result usefulness appears as distant from culture.

However, we cannot always produce the things we need and must on occasion turn to others to acquire them. We are obliged to exchange things for other goods where they realise their *exchange-value* and in capitalism a profit (their surplus-value) for the owners of the means of production. Despite the centrality of exchange-value in commodity culture, Marx insisted that use-value is the necessary bedrock upon which exchange-value rests. Exchange-value is therefore a step removed from this natural foundation and is a cultural phenomenon through and through. With the expansion of objective culture under capitalism, our 'natural' needs give way to the unbridled explosion of 'unnatural and imaginary appetites' (Marx 1975: 358), of which, as his choice of words suggests, Marx did not approve.

Not everyone shares Marx's productionist view of humanity. Jean Baudrillard (1981: 82), for one, argues that by depicting humans as essentially producers, Marx inadvertently completes the colonisation of our life world by the productionist ethos that political economy initiated. Marx's critique of political economy, Baudrillard argues, is implicated in too many of its ideological assumptions, not least his failure to realise that the idea of use-value is the product of a cultural system of needs (the demand for goods) created by capitalism in order to perpetuate the system of production. For Baudrillard, Marx's contention that use-value is the truth or essence of a thing prior to its entry into exchange is really no more than an idea derived from the reality of exchange-value. If all that Marx sees as exploitative in exchange-value is subtracted, then use-value emerges as the remainder and the true nature of things. The very idea of a use-value that precedes cultural 'interference' is in fact a product of the exchange of objects. Use-value, argues Baudrillard, is an 'alibi' that naturalises objects by presenting them as necessary, whether it be washing powder, the latest model of mobile phone, or a new chocolate bar. Our 'need' to consume them keeps the circulation of goods in motion.

Baudrillard contends that there are no fundamental human needs existing outside of the cultural realm (cf. Sahlins 1976). Rather, in contemporary consumer culture we do not consume use-values that satisfy our natural needs, but the cultural *representations* of functions and needs. Taken to its logical conclusion, this entails that we do not consume commodities that have use-values or even exchange-values, what we consume are *sign-values*. Just as use-value serves as an alibi for exchange value, exchange-value serves as an alibi for sign value.[1]

Following Veblen and Barthes, Baudrillard argues that goods make sense to us within a system of signs that denote and connote use, function, aesthetic properties, status, and so on. These signs derive their meaning (or value) from their relations to other signs within a system of objects (Baudrillard 2005). When we purchase something, we buy into the system of meanings which increasingly is about consuming a status expressed through an entire 'lifestyle' encompassing everything from clothes, to the food we eat, the car we drive, the homes we live in, and the holidays we take. These are all part of a code of social differentiation in which an object 'no longer gathers its meaning in the concrete relationship between two people. [Instead, i]t assumes its meaning in its differential relation to other signs' (1981: 66). Things do still have a function. A coffee-maker makes coffee, this is its *denotation*, its use-value, which is the alibi that justifies buying it, but it may also *connote* the best design, the most advanced technology, and the wealth and impeccable taste of its owner. Connotations, unlike denotations, are substitutable. You cannot make toast with a DVD

---

1 It is important to appreciate that regimes of value do not simply replace each other *in toto* as part of an historical sequence; they coexist. It is not therefore possible to reduce an entire historical conjuncture to one kind of value. What Baudrillard seeks to do is to identify the emergent and nascent forms of value that are making themselves felt but have not necessarily redefined how we understand our relationship to the objects around us.

player, but the toaster may carry the same connotations of sophistication as the DVD player. Consumption in advanced capitalism for Baudrillard is therefore about consuming signs in the form of the connotations of objects in pursuit of the social differences and distinctions they represent and create (cf. Bourdieu 1984).[2]

The Sign

Having identified the importance of sign-value, Baudrillard goes on to scrutinise the structure of the sign itself. He poses a question: If exchange-value creates the illusion of a fundamental truth to objects, namely, that their *real* nature lies in their use-value, and in so doing helps perpetuate the circulation of commodities, is the idea of the real itself complicit with the logic of capitalist production? Here we meet one of Baudrillard's arguments that is of special interest to queer theorising, his critique of the logic of signification.

Baudrillard argues that the structure of the logic of the commodity is at the heart of the structure of the sign in capitalism and that they are supportive of each other (1981: 146). Drawing on Roland Barthes, he focuses on the claim made by Ferdinand de Saussure that there is an equivalence between a signifier and a signified. The sign creates itself as a positive and complete value. One signifier (image, word) induces one signified (concept) which together constitute the sign. The real (the referent) is produced as the effect of the sign, but this is only part of the story. It is the equation of one signifier to one signified that Baudrillard finds problematic. 'The sign', Baudrillard argues, 'is a discriminant: it structures itself through exclusion…All virtualities of meaning are shorn in the cut of structure' (1981: 149). In making this observation, Baudrillard again follows Barthes who argued that Saussure's sign only describes a process of denotation, but that this is not exhaustive as there are additional 'virtualities of meaning', or connotations, present. It is these 'mythical' connotations that insinuate themselves into the psyche of the consumer behind the screen of denotation. It is precisely because denotation conceals the connotative level of objects that Baudrillard writes: 'Far from being the objective term to which connotation is opposed as an ideological term, denotation is thus (since it naturalises the very process of ideology) *the most ideological term*' (1981: 159, emphasis in original). Denotation – the 'real', 'convention', 'fixed meanings' – is therefore only ever the result, or ghost, of connotations which the structure

---

2 Sign-value is not the endpoint of this progression from use (natural), exchange (commodity), and sign (structural) value. There is a fourth, the positive fractal stage of value which I shall look at in more detail in later chapters.

of the sign suppresses but which are nonetheless integral to the objects we consume.

To summarise: It is 'secondary' exchange-value that produces 'primary' use-value, the 'secondary' connotations that produce 'primary' denotation, and the sign that produces the real rather than the other way round. The structure of the commodity and the sign coincide with each other.

Subjects and Objects

From the notion that there is an *object* that has use-values that can be exchanged follows the notion of the *subject* that produces and exchanges the object. Although Marx critiqued the relations of production that underlie capitalism and capitalist exploitation, including the occlusions of the production process and the ideology of commodity fetishism, he did not critique use-value nor did he critique the fundamentals of production itself. On the contrary, he viewed history as a succession of modes of *production*. Once all past societies are viewed through a productionist lens, production becomes universal and transhistorical. Indeed in the *Mirror of Production* (1975) Baudrillard points to the productionist ideas that have colonised consciousness in the Lacanian-style mirror in which we imagine ourselves as a productive imago.

The logic of capitalist production is to produce objects with a positive identity that enter the domain of exchange. The structure of identity and difference serves to codify objects as having values that can be compared with other objects in the form of equivalences, literally 'equal value': one leg of lamb is equivalent to five loaves of bread. The 'economic' in classical and neoclassical economics arises when the object is believed to have an essence, when its value is obtained with respect to an abstract code that enables the objects relation to other objects to be ascertained through a logic of equivalences – its exchange-value – with this value justified through appeals to the object's use value – grounded in nature. Victoria Grace summarises Baudrillard thus:

> The object-that-is-'produced' is the object-to-be-consumed, is the object that has an 'identity'. To have an identity means that it *is* something (albeit deferring any absolute meaning): its ontology is fixed within a semiology structured in accordance with the dichotomy of identity/difference, in other words it cannot be both this and not this at the same time. The construction of objects (and subjects) as identifiable within this semiological structure creates the possibility of 'production'. (2000: 17, emphasis in original)

The individual emerges as subject in relation to a world of objects, and the relationship between them is justified by the myth of needs (and after psychoanalysis desires). Subjects too eventually believe that they have essences – the inner self of the bourgeoisie – in need of cultivation.

> In the process of satisfaction, he valorises and makes fruitful his own potentialities; he 'realises' and manages, to the best of his ability, his own 'faculty' of pleasure, treated literally like a productive force. Isn't this what all of humanist ethics is based on – the 'proper use' of oneself? (Baudrillard 1981: 136)

Among these needs and their 'proper use' are sexual needs and the demand for sexual satisfaction. An economy of sex, the production of sexual subjects, is instituted as part of the productive economy. The logic of equivalence and identity that marks the world of objects is therefore not confined to the economy, it is central to sex and gender.

The logic of the economy is evident in a patriarchal gender order. Gender is not located in what people do, in actions that may and often do traverse gender categories, but in biology, the presence or absence of specific sexual organs that act as a natural referent for the signifier. As Grace makes clear, Baudrillard's alternative is not Freud's bisexuality, because understanding sex as either an either/or, or a proliferation of sexes leaves intact a logic of binaries or units that can be multiplied. Either way we have a standard of sex against which its 'opposite' or a multitude of 'different from' are evaluated. We are still within the logic of the economy. In a patriarchal order it is the phallus (actually the penis) that acts as the benchmark, the 'one', against which all sexual possibilities are evaluated (the master signifier in the early Lacanian Symbolic). Baudrillard's point is that we need to understand sexual differences within the system of values structuring the economy. As the natural referent loses its sway and the economy of sign-value expands, we would expect a similar expansion in the signs of sexual differences. Rather than the binary of identity (male)/difference (female), in which women are denied an identity as true subjects, Baudrillard argues that signs multiply (though they certainly do not completely displace a heterosexual binary) into a proliferation of positives where all signs stand for themselves. A multitude of positives leaves no room over for ambivalence, all spaces are covered by a mosaic of positive identities. In the words of the song, 'I am what I am, I am my own special creation'. A more succinct statement of pure positivity, self-identity, self-ownership, and self-production is hard to imagine. The song is taken from the musical production of *La Cage aux Folles* and was a huge hit for Gloria Gaynor in 1984. It became something of a gay anthem because of its message that lesbian, gay, bisexual and transgender people need not evaluate themselves with reference to straight norms, but produce – perform – themselves into being.

I want to develop the ideas of Baudrillard and commentators like Grace on the mutual interrelatedness of the economy, the sign, gender and sexuality. As we have seen, patriarchy in Baudrillard's schema goes well beyond the dichotomy male-female and masculine-feminine, it is found in the very system of values – axiology – and the system of signification – semiology – that underlies the logic of identity/difference, either/or, self/other and its integration into hierarchical distinctions. Likewise, as I shall argue, the hierarchical binary of hetero-homo can be interrogated with the help of some of the analytical tools Baudrillard provides.

The scene is now set and the players are autonomous subjects with value, essences and identities and objects, also with value. We can now begin to see why, from the perspective of queer theory, there are some striking parallels to be drawn out from the ideas of Marx and from Baudrillard's critique of them between the logic of the commodity, the structure of the sign, and the logic of heteronormative culture. They include the notion of use, of the real, the idea of an original and a copy, and the processes of denotation and connotation.

First, the idea of use.

Use

Appeals to nature and the natural are one of the commonest ideological devices in that they exempt certain phenomena from social and cultural determination and thereby place them beyond the influence of human agency. The claim that an object has a natural use-value prior to cultural interference and its transformation into exchange-value has an obvious parallel in the meanings often attributed to 'sex' and 'gender'. The former, as the previous chapter noted, was long considered to be a natural, biological entity of little interest to anthropologists and feminist scholars who concentrated on socially and culturally variable gender. Sex was present, but its relevance was minimal and it remained an undertheorised 'matter', rather like Marx's use-value. Yet, as anthropologists have long pointed out, the idea of 'nature' is itself a cultural construct (MacCormack and Strathern 1980).

Another parallel to be drawn is with the heteronormative ideology of the body that manifests itself in ideas about 'natural' or 'correct' usage. Not least the genitals are 'naturally' intended for some uses, while others are deemed 'unnatural', perversions, or not the 'real thing'. Their use-value lies in biological reproduction to be precise.[3] In the politics of sexuality and gender, this is one of the most frequent claims heard from those who wish to maintain the

---

3 Within the spermatic economy of western Christian tradition the issue of sperm ought to eventuate in fertilisation and biological reproduction, all else being a waste of seed, Barker-Benfield 1976.

heteronormative status quo. In a telling passage, dealing with the use-value of objects, Marx, quoting William Petty, writes that 'labour is its father and the earth its mother' (Marx 1995: 53). Use-value, which enjoys Marx's approval, is depicted as the product of a heterosexual union in the form of active male labour and passive female earth. Nature is the ground against which the subject, man the producer, emerges, and once man is the subject the remainder is woman the object.

Real Objects

The historically and culturally specific categories of 'heterosexual' and 'homosexual' purport to denote real objects that pre-exist and are entirely independent of their cultural and historical enunciation. The correspondence between heterosexual signifier, heterosexual signified and heterosexual referent (living, breathing people classified as heterosexual) does not, however, express a naturally existing type. Part of the process of producing this exclusive type involved the evacuation of negative meanings and associations from the category heterosexual, which, originally, was used to refer to an exaggerated and pathological interest in sex with almost any partner (Katz 1995). Eventually, however, it came to refer to genital sexuality between persons of the 'opposite sex' (itself a relatively recent Western notion, see Laqueur 1990) and was harnessed to ideals of romantic love, commitment, monogamy and biological and social reproduction. By contrast, homosexuality – sexual relations between persons of the same sex – came increasingly to refer to all manner of sexual 'perversions' and disorders incompatible with the emerging category of normative heterosexuality. In effect, the labour put into the creation of the homosexual produced the heterosexual as 'real' sexuality.

However, as Baudrillard argues, the real arises through a process of exclusion that bars ambivalence and *indeterminate*[4] value rather than poly- or multi-valence. Yet ambivalence can never be fully excluded. Consequently, the 'white light of denotation is only the play of the spectrum – the chromatic ghost – of the connotations' (1981: 158). Likewise, we can argue that heterosexuality is the 'white light' that emerges from the sexual connotations it eclipses. Its blinding obviousness, at least in modern Euro-American societies, is only possible because it exists at the intersection of a spectrum of references to what it is not – behind it lies a rainbow of differences.

---

4 Indeterminate value is a defining feature of what Baudrillard (1993) calls 'symbolic exchange'.

Original and Copy

Historically, homosexuality is the original category (the term was minted first, in 1869 to be precise), and normative heterosexuality is the derivative.[5] However, in the ideology of a heteronormative regime, which insists on its status as the primary category, alternative forms of sexuality are viewed through the lens it provides where they appear as copies, fakes or counterfeits of the heterosexual 'original' (Butler 1990: 138). The logical operation involved corresponds to that employed by Marx when he claims that use-value is primary and exchange-value secondary, and to Saussure's real that precedes the sign. In all three cases, historical and logical priority is reversed.

Just as use-value is not an original, but is in fact a derivative of exchange-value and an ideology of needs created by capitalism, the category of heterosexuality is the derivative of the blocked connotations that threaten the hegemony of normative forms of other-sex sexuality.

Connotations

Connotation has been termed the signifying practice of homosexuality (Miller 1988). Within a cultural system built around what Eve Sedgwick (1990) calls the 'epistemology of the closet', same-sex sexuality is often not permitted to advertise its presence openly through denotation, but instead must rely on connotation. This concealment does for homosexuality what 'eclipse', to use Marilyn Strathern's (1988) term, does for the commodity by concealing the relations that went into the creation of the latter and along with them the agency and cultural significance of those who created it. This is but one example of the more general 'secrecy' of commodities which as a rule conceal their histories and the social and material processes that are congealed in them, histories and processes which studies of commodity chains reveal (egs. Mintz 1985; Haugerud et al. 2000; Collins 2003).

In the light of the above observations, we can add an additional claim to Baudrillard's own critique of signification and the commodity: The structure of the logic of the heteronormative lies at the heart of the sign and the commodity.

But what about the gift?

---

5 Queer theorists like to mention this reverse priority, but it leaves intact the logic of sexual subjectification that Foucault was attempting to subvert.

The Gift

If the commodity seems to be waging a constant battle against connotations, the threat of ambivalence and a lack of stability, the gift seems to revel in them. The title of Frederick Bailey's (1971) book *Gifts and Poison* plays on the overlapping etymologies of the words 'gift', in German meaning poison and in English a present or donation. The very idea of 'poisonous presents' alerts us to something about gifts which makes them oxymoronic and difficult to categorise. As Marcel Mauss (1990: 3) observed, gifts, as examples of implicate 'total social facts', encompass a wide range of social and cultural domains, and precisely because of this transcend closed categories and invite multiple understandings. Gifts continually gesture beyond what we take them 'really' to be about at any given moment.[6] In short, they court ambiguity.

As an example of this ambiguity, consider the well documented role of gifts in establishing social relations. Famously, Claude Lévi-Strauss posits a primordial scene in which the genesis of culture is the outcome of men exchanging women (the greatest of 'gifts') with each other (Lévi-Strauss 1969), a claim that did not go unchallenged from feminist anthropologists (Rubin 1975). For Alvin Gouldner (1973), reciprocity initiates relationships and stabilises them through reciprocal exchanges. Marshall Sahlins (1972) suggested that different forms of reciprocity characterise relations between near and distant others. For Strathern (1988: 139), giving and receiving involve becoming 'enchained', as giving establishes links to another and we become more not less than we were.

Yet the sociality of gifts is ambiguous and the feelings surrounding them ambivalent. Mauss saw the gifts that create social bonds as imbued with generosity *and* a threat of violence. At the end of *The Elementary Structures of Kinship* (1969: 497), Lévi-Strauss writes that 'mankind' dreams of evading the law of exchange in a world where 'one could gain without losing, enjoy without sharing', and 'in which one might keep to oneself'. The nature of this sociality appears even more complicated if we consider George Devereux's (1978) psychoanalytically informed supplement to Lévi-Strauss, in which he argues that the brothers-in-law who exchange are vicarious lovers whose attraction is forbidden but is nonetheless 'expressed', here we might say connoted rather than denoted, in the marriages that result from their symmetrical exchange of sisters.[7]

---

6 It also enables them to challenge disciplinarity. For example, as Callari (2002) explains, the gift calls into question the viability of a pure economics which is unable to explain many aspects of gift exchange, including its affective dimension. Something about gifts makes them unruly, even disrespectful of discipline(s).

7 For a similar, but later claim from a precursor of queer theory, see Sedgwick (1985), who explicitly draws on Lévi-Strauss.

According to Pierre Bourdieu (1977), whatever ambiguity we discern in the gift is the result of strategic calculation concealed behind apparently disinterested exchanges (1977: 6). He makes this point very effectively in his discussion of the importance of time to gift exchanges (1977: 6–9). It is the temporal delay between giving and receiving that allows what is basically an economic motive to be 'misrecognised' as disinterested or altruistic. Bourdieu's position, in common with many other accounts of gift giving, is economistic: the *true* nature of the gift, (appearances to the contrary) lies in calculation or the creation of forms of contractual relations between the parties to the exchange. The 'disinterested' nature of the gift is only ever 'real' at the moment of giving, which also paradoxically creates the obligation to reciprocate thus immediately nullifying the altruism of the free or pure gift. In other words, the gift is never 'really' a gift, but is what Jonathan Parry (1986) calls 'the Indian gift', a donation burdened with the expectation of a return. In a sense, then, Malinowski (1922: 177–80) was right, there is a free gift, but only for an impossibly short moment before the demands for a return gift make themselves felt however subtly.[8] This is Jacques Derrida's point when he writes that 'there is no gift without bond, without bind, without obligation or ligature; but on the other hand, there is no gift that does not have to untie itself from obligations, from debt, contract, exchange, and thus from the bind' (1992: 27).[9] Derrida's 'solution' to the puzzle is to see the gift as risky, spontaneous and uncertain precisely because it rests on what he regards as a logical paradox. He therefore restates, if in needlessly elaborate language, what Mauss himself recognised much earlier, namely, that gifts are ambiguous. However, unlike philosophers, most people who give and receive gifts seem to tolerate the 'paradox' without problem, whereas theorists like Derrida demand a logical consistency from gifts which is inappropriate to social praxis.

Exchanging gifts proceeds according to the rules and produces the system of gift giving on which it seems to draw, but, like gender, it might fail to produce the correct effects. Understandably, perhaps, Stephen Gudeman regards gifts as 'probes into uncertainty' (2001: 467). There are no guarantees what will happen or that the results will be as intended. To some extent, this may even explain the pleasures of gift giving, which lie not in meticulous calculation or even in the expectation of return, but in the openness and uncertainty of the exchange.

---

8 Malinowski later recognised the problem, pointed out by Mauss (Malinowski 1926: 40–41).

9 In view of Derrida's comments here it is all the more surprising to find his ideas being used to support a version of gift giving as asymmetrical reciprocity. Iris Marion Young (1997: 54–5) draws on Derrida and presents gift giving as an economy not based on the obligations demanded by contractual exchanges. Her claims ignore the substantial literature that clearly shows the obligation, even compulsion, to reciprocate.

In middle-class Britain, gifts ought to be a delightful surprise, and also be self-effacing: 'Oh, it's just a little something I thought you might like'. Yet the mere trifle ought to be accepted with effusive comments: 'It's marvellous! Just what I wanted!' In truth, it is often the last thing you really wanted. It is in fact entirely superfluous to your needs, and may even offend your sense of taste. Indeed, Mark Osteen concludes that: 'We might tentatively propose, then, that the essence of the gift is superfluity itself' (2002: 26). In fact, a poorly chosen gift can make someone unhappy, such as a book on train crashes given to someone who has just lost a relative in one.

Contingency, risk, the unexpected, surprise, ambiguity, superfluity and even inappropriateness are part and parcel of gifts and space must be made for them in any theoretical statement of what gifts 'really' are.[10]

Excess

George Bataille (1985: 117) gives us a somewhat different version of the gift than Mauss who emphasised its constructive dimensions in a micro-sociological counterpart to Durkheim's conscience collective. Bataille argues that, in what he calls the 'restricted economy' of western, bourgeois capitalism, economic transactions are governed by a logic of acquisition which demands that all expenditure must result in a return or profit. In sharp contrast, gambling, festivals, artistic activity and especially sacrifice, free us from the compulsion to save and acquire. For Bataille, it is not gain and productive expenditure, but non-productive expenditure and loss that form the basis for human sociality in the non-productive destruction of wealth. Gifts, too, belong to this 'general economy' (Bataille 1988), which exists outside the actions and meanings that dominate the restricted economy which looks askance on the excessive and superfluous. It is no coincidence that Bataille drew inspiration from Mauss' *The Gift* (Clifford 1988: 126) for he believed that gifts, especially as expressed in the potlatch, escape the obligation to accumulate endlessly (Bataille 1985: 121).[11] He also believed that they thereby avoided the social and libidinal economy

---

10 If the ambiguity of the gift is abolished in order to expose what it 'really' is, then the thing given ceases to be a gift. Privileging one aspect of the gift over the other – disinterested or interested – has immediate social and physical repercussions. Not only does the gift become a transaction if the obligation to return is foregrounded, the very bodies of donor and recipient alter as the emotional dynamics and their physical counterparts to gifting shift. See my intra-active analysis of gift exchanges Graham 2010.

11 Bataille chose to emphasise this aspect of gift-giving, its competitive logic. Mauss tended to emphasise its creative and stabilising effects, as does Bourdieu whose analysis of gifts ignores the competitive dynamics of potlatch-style exchanges.

of bourgeois capitalism. Bataille contends that what he calls 'perverse sexual activity' escapes the 'genital finality' of familial sexuality which is in the service of a (re)productive unit that works for the benefit of capitalist accumulation and the atomised world of bourgeois individualism (ibid.: 118).

Bataille's argument faces a problem. The potlatches on which he bases his claims were in all likelihood not typical exchanges. Their excessive form was a direct result of disease, famine, population decline and the incursion of European goods and markets, which together had inflationary effects on the performances (Layton 1997: 112–13). Waste and excess are better understood as central to capitalism, which demands endless consumption in the destructive sense of the word to 'consume', goods are bought but discarded quickly either thrown away or forgotten and new goods bought to replace them. The restricted economy certainly demands savings, investment and growth but it also needs the profligate waste of the general economy based on the galloping obsolescence of yesterday's commodities. Living in a capitalist society means taking part in potlatches, even if we might not like to admit it.[12]

Despite these qualifications, we can retain Bataille's point that gifts are not easily assimilated to the demands for accumulation and profit that are characteristics of capitalism, and his insistence on the sexual side to the economy.

Bataille's ideas made a strong impression on Baudrillard, who draws on them to develop his critique of Marx's claim that our productionist ethos rests on natural needs which are satisfied by the products of our labours. Bodies are present in Marx's theory, as we saw earlier, in the form of the use-values created by the active 'father' labouring on the passive 'mother'. Baudrillard takes this sexual metaphor to mean that the genesis of wealth and of production involves 'the genital combination of labour…a normal schema of production and reproduction…The metaphor is that of genital, reproductive sexuality and not at all that of corporeal expenditure for the sake of enjoyment' (1981:

---

12 Waste too is sexual. There is an entire ovarian and spermatic economy surrounding sexuality. In it lesbian women are 'wasted' on other women, gay men are 'wasted' on other men. Neither, and perhaps especially lesbians in the Euro-American context, fulfil their potential defined as sexual reproduction as part of the restricted economy's (biological) investment in the future. Stereotypes of shopaholic gay men, and increasingly of wealthy lesbians, also fit neatly into the general economy of waste and profligacy. They do not even possess use-value if the usefulness of a person is measured by the performance of reproductive duty (we can ignore all the gay and lesbian parents). Nowadays, however, it is the wastefulness of queers, understood as their spending power, that makes them *attractive* on the urban scene where their presence can be marketed and sold, and where they acquire exchange-value as part of urban regeneration. I return to this theme in Chapter 4.

32).[13] In Baudrillard's view, Marx's economy of production is not guided by pleasure, but by the 'rational domestication of sexuality', or a 'productive Eros' (cf. Foucault 1978) which channels labour into productivity rather than *jouissance* (Baudrillard 1981: 38). At the heart of Marx's critique of bourgeois capitalism lies a bourgeois sexual morality.

Baudrillard also extends his critique of the concept of value – use-value, exchange-value and sign-value – and argues that all three are alibis which conceal the true foundation of human sociality, 'symbolic exchange', which lies outside the order of value itself (Baudrillard 1993). Baudrillard bases his notion of symbolic exchange on Bataille's idea of general economy, Mauss' analysis of the gift, and Sahlins (1976) on reciprocity. He writes: 'the kula and potlatch have disappeared, but not their principle, which we will retain as the basis of a sociological theory of objects' (Baudrillard 1981: 30–31). The principle he has in mind is the cyclical reciprocity of ritual gift exchanges, rather than the linear logic of capitalist production, accumulation, profit and growth. Symbolic exchange, for Baudrillard, is based on the logic of sacrifice and reversibility. Moreover, in symbolic exchange there are no objects, like commodities, that are separate from the relationships in which they figure. Neither are they produced in the service of capitalist production. The embeddedness of things in social relations prevents them from becoming part of a system of autonomous objects – commodities with exchange-values – and it also prevents a subject-object distinction from emerging as it does under capitalism. Baudrillard writes that 'only when objects are autonomised as differential signs and thereby rendered systematisable can one speak of consumption and objects of consumption' (1981: 66). Mauss made the same point about non-capitalist societies in which persons and things are tightly implicated in each other.

---

13 Even if the ideas of Bataille and Baudrillard are undoubtedly highly suggestive and contain many insights, there are nonetheless problems with the position staked out in their writings. Theirs is a rather non-material reading of the things which are given as gifts. Furthermore, both Bataille and Baudrillard present a one-sided version – not to say caricature – of 'heterosexuality'. Other-sex sexuality in capitalism is not exclusively the bourgeois nuclear family and even within it there is more going on than a productionist ethos of biological reproduction. If this were not the case, Freud would never have made a living. While the libidinal economy they castigate certainly involves both social and psychic repression, it is difficult to envisage any kind of human sexuality that does not do so, even if it were not to insist on a reproductive teleology for all sex.

Divergent Things

Yet whatever the differences between them gift giving and commodity exchange are not separated by an unbridgeable chasm. As Maurice Bloch and Jonathan Parry argue, the opposition between gifts and commodities that anthropology helped to construct (but has also worked to dismantle) 'derives in part, we believe, from the fact that *our* ideology of the gift has been constructed in anti-thesis to market exchange' (1989: 9). Assumptions about the truth of the gift are therefore reliant on that which it ought not to be. One of the commonest contrasts, as we have seen, is between impersonal, alienated commodities and personal, social gifts that establish bonds between people. Yet, as we have noted, Lévi-Strauss argues that we also wish to escape from these bonds and the obligation to give and receive. The notion of the pure gift unfettered by any constraints or hidden calculations is not without problems either. In effect, it portrays the donor as disinterested. Yet a disinterested, autonomous giver strongly resembles the autonomous individuals of western economic theory. Gifts begin to resemble commodities in their effects when the social ties they forge do not extend beyond the duration of the transaction. The autonomous economic actor (or something rather similar) is, it seems, readmitted through the backdoor (Carrier 1995: 149).

While there may not be an absolute distinction to be made between commodities and gifts, I do not wish to deny that differences exist between them. Certainly, when seen through the lens of sexuality employed here, contrasts emerge between the respective logics of the two categories of things. I have already pointed out some of the parallels between heteronormative ideology and the theory of the commodity privileged by Marx and its attendant sign form, not least the 'truth' of use-value and the 'falsity' of exchange-value, the real versus the ideological, and the notion of an original and a copy. These allow the structure of the commodity to coincide with the logic underlying the sexual dichotomy of modernity, heterosexual-homosexual. For the gift, it is its ambiguity and its 'superfluous' nature, its instability and opacity that align it with queer theory (Graham 2010). We might phrase the distinction thus: The structure of the commodity recapitulates the modernist binary of heterosexual-homosexual and its vain attempt to maintain a clear distinction between them. The gift, on the one hand, has all the hallmarks of a queer ontology in which no such binary is sustainable and indeterminacy is the rule. The former rests on the apparently self-evident character of the object while the latter suggests the indeterminacy of things. Both start with the excessiveness of material things but follow divergent trajectories. The logic of the commodity involves the progressive erection of ideological screens that obscure its material and social complexity and history, and the cutting way of connotations in pursuit of a univocal object, an endpoint of actualisation. Gifts, on the other hand, with their ambiguity, contingency, unpredictability and superfluous character, point to the sheer excess of the material. At the risk of another dichotomy: in the former we witness the actualisation of the virtual and in the latter the virtualisation of the actual.

The Return of the Gift?

Moving now from the more traditional concern of anthropology with gifts, I want to conclude the discussion of material things in this and the previous chapter with a warning flag as a necessary counterweight to any overly 'optimistic' portrayal. I do so through a selective borrowing of the ideas of Scott Lash and Celia Lury (Lash and Lury 2007, Lash 2010) on the subject of what they call the 'Global Culture Industry'.

Lash and Lury (2007) proffer their ideas as an extension into the present of Max Horkheimer and Theodor Adorno's (1997) thesis in *Dialectic of Enlightenment*. Very simply, for the Frankfurt School, the subjugation of the masses was effected through predictable standardisation and the equivalences of extensive dead commodities whereas in the Global Culture Industry subjugation is effected by inequivalence and intensive things.

What Lash and Lury want to highlight is how goods have become 'media-things', commodities that are examples of transcendental empiricism, mind and matter combined, the substance of Spinoza, Bergson, Whitehead and Deleuze and good deal of recent anthropological work (e.g. Ingold 2011). This has happened because, as Lash and Lury argue, the cultural superstructure has collapsed into the material base, 'goods become informational, work becomes affective, property becomes intellectual and the economy more generally becomes cultural' (2007: 7). This differs from the commodification of *representation* or culture critiqued by Horkheimer and Adorno. Instead, culture is *industrialised*, it becomes media-things that we encounter everywhere. Not only the things themselves, so to speak, but also the settings in which we purchase, enjoy, and interact with them are all part of the experience.

Part of the power of media-things is derived from brands. Brands are singular, they mark a difference. Here Lash and Lury recapitulate Baudrillard's tripartite schema: 'A good works for me through my hands-on use of it [use-value]. It works as a commodity in terms of how much money I bought or will sell it for [exchange-value]. The brand functions as a sign-value through its and my difference' (2007: 7). Brands are not only singular – differences – they are also abstract, they transcend any concrete product that bears their mark. The brand is, if you will, the spirit of the product, the soul of the company that manufactures it or provides the service. The brand is the virtual, the products are its actual avatars: clothes, electronics, pens, shoes, mugs, cigarette lighters, financial services, you name it. Lash and Lury argue that we as consumers encounter actual differences – the objects – but that we experience the virtual brand. It is this 'living' quality of the brand in the commodity that makes it intensive, informs the product and enables it to install itself in the heart of the consumer. It is the *hau* of the commodity.

The saturation effected by these intensive media-things is inescapable. In the Global Culture Industry our relationships to goods become increasingly ontological rather than distanced epistemological appreciation of them. We interact with them, touch them, taste them, wear them, exchange them and collect them, encounter them in media all around us, and increasingly get hooked up to them. Lash and Lury emphasise our playful relationship to them in the sense of spontaneous, impulsive and improvisational play rather than the rule-governed play of organised games of sport – *paida* rather than *ludens*. Yet, at the same time, the spontaneity and not least creativity of this kind of playful relationship enables media-things to colonise our life worlds, not only stimulate us, and is central to capital accumulation. Indeed, capital nowadays generates considerable profits through the control of the *creative* culture industries.

We need therefore to be very careful before extolling creativity and the potential of material things within the conjuncture Lash and Lury describe. Intensive media-things are both liberating *and* captivating, and I use captivating in the sense of enchantment and imprisonment. As informational matter coded through and through and not simply vessels to be filled, they can effect a colonisation of the life world more insidious than the classic commodity.

I have reservations about some aspects of Lash and Lury's argument. None of what they write about intensive goods is exactly news to anthropologists who are familiar with things that are not purely representations – for example, the fetish – that have souls, spirits, wills of their own, and that are persons even if not humans. There is ample evidence of ontological and intensive relationships to things prior to the Global Culture Industry, as any anthropologist can attest. They also rely on the base superstructure dichotomy, which has always been suspect and they neglect relations of production almost entirely. The actual use of goods receives short shrift despite their emphasis on getting ontological with things. Nor do they fully demonstrate the *global* reach of all their arguments. Nonetheless, in the light of what I wrote in Chapter 1 and this chapter the final paragraph of their introductory chapter gives pause for thought:

> Horkheimer and Adorno's culture industry was dialectical. We are today, perhaps, less dialectical than *metaphysical*. Dialectical presumes ontological difference: between spirit and matter, being and beings, superstructure and base, same and other, friend and foe. Metaphysics is instead a monism, an immanence of spirit-matter, of superstructure-base. The ontological difference of dialectics is displaced by metaphysics' ontology of difference...The *Weltanschauung*,

> the *episteme* of global culture industry, is no longer that of dialectical but of metaphysical materialism...matter is multiplicity, matter not as identity but as difference. (Lash and Lury 2007: 15)

This shift to a 'metaphysical materialism' recalls the work of process philosophy from Chapter 1, and it points to the ambiguous character of material things. The commodities Lash and Lury discuss bear strong resemblances to aspects of the gift. Gifts have tended to receive a good press in anthropology where anthropological economics, has been dominated by the critique of capitalism (Carrier and Miller 1999: 33). But as I noted earlier, gifts are ambiguous, the flipside of peaceful exchange is violence, they compel a response, and like fetishes they too can strike back in unexpected ways. There is no guarantee that matter, given its full due, will do as we tell it.

This could be read as a normative piece of anti-hegemonic advice to beware of mediated culture, and it is, but it should also be read methodologically. If things have re-emerged in their transcendental empirical, intensive, fetish and animistic splendour, then who better to explore them than anthropologists? We have puzzled over animism, totems, fetishes, gifts and commodities for well over a century. Intensive objects are profoundly ambiguous, both creative and part of capitalist accumulation. It is this ambiguity, their ability to unfold or explicate in all manner of directions that demands the fine-grained attention of ethnography to do them justice.

In this chapter and in Chapter 1, I have pointed to the sexuality of things and the thingness of sexuality as part of a queer theoretical approach to things in general, and commodities, gifts and fetishes in particular. In doing so, I have pointed to how ideas aligned with a heteronormative logic (usually concealed) permeate our understanding of matter itself and undergird normative ideas surrounding sexuality. This ought to come as no surprise given the use of traditional gendered metaphors and the heterosexist assumptions they entail. The normative support is all the more effective because largely unrecognised. Yet we have also seen how things, rather than simply providing us with a stable foundation on which to rest cultural models of sexuality and gender, can also pull the mat(ter) out from under them.

Chapter 3
Smells

The metaphysics of presence has long been the guiding philosophy of the perfume industry. Convinced that there are essences to be found and sold at an exorbitant profit, the intangibles of attraction, lust and romance have been distilled and bottled as liquids that promise to unleash desire. From a queer perspective this is reification with a vengeance and worthy of attention.

To smell something you must inhale it and thus literally incorporate it into your own body. If vision, in some formulations, is the modernist sense par excellence (Levin 1993), then smell, by contrast, is the sense of the postmodern (Classen et al. 1994: 203–5). It is the sense that confuses categories and challenges boundaries. Smells are difficult to localise, hard to contain and have the character of flux and transitoriness. If this is the case, then some interesting affinities appear between the character of smells and queer theory's suspicion of fixed categories.

If smell is indeed the sense of the postmodern, then perhaps it also reflects something of the character of late-capitalism, the historical, social and economic juncture that has produced postmodern and queer theories. In particular, the tendency of capitalism to dissolve distinctions, to fragment subjectivity, to encourage and even require flux and change in the interests of economic growth and profits (Mandel 1975; Jameson 1984). If smells and the understanding of them seem to be in tune with the postmodern and late-capitalism, then it seems reasonable to ask whether they are also complicit in its logic. When, for example, the perfume industry, which has been built on pedalling essences of heterosexual man and heterosexual woman for many years, appears, at least partly, to have abandoned its heteronormative bias, just how radical are queer theories themselves?

Queer Smells

In some advertisements for scents decidedly queer things can happen. In one advertisement for Lynx (1996) for men, a young woman borrows her boyfriend's cologne. Once outside, a woman who passes her on the stairs is transfixed by her scent. Later, when riding the bus, three teenage girls stare longingly at her. Back home, and none too pleased about her experiences, she angrily returns the body spray to her boyfriend who laughs with amusement.

In another television advertisement for AXE (1998), a handsome young man in a lift sprays himself with the cologne while buttoning up his shirt. As he leaves the lift, another young but less attractive man enters it. He shares the lift with a succession of women, who, judging by his state of disarray every time the lift doors open, all ravish him between floors. His irresistibility is thanks to the lingering scent of AXE. On his final journey, the doors are about to close when they are suddenly forced open by a male hand wearing a fingerless leather glove. The hand belongs to a large, hirsute leather queen who lecherously eyes the man in the lift. Aware of what he is in for the young man swallows nervously and the rest is left to the imagination. Having been reduced by the power of the scent to a sexual toy for the female passengers, his ultimate degradation is to become the sexual plaything of a gay leather clone.

What can be said about the logic of desire operating in these advertisements? Lynx, the body spray for men, makes the woman that wears it desirable to those people attracted to the male gender. In the advertisement, this is restricted to heterosexual women, but homosexual men ought also to be swayed by the scent. The AXE advertisement depicts this with the help of a dubious stereotype of a predatory gay man, who, at the level of the olfactory, is positioned as a woman. By the same logic, the scent that makes a woman irresistible to heterosexual men should also make her the object of lesbian desire. As far as I am aware, no advertisement portrays lesbian desire like this. Neither do I know of any advertisement in which a heterosexual man mistakenly uses a woman's cologne. If he were to do so, he would presumably become attractive to other heterosexual men and lesbians, but unattractive to gay men and heterosexual women. The transformation of the male heterosexual into an object of attraction for other heterosexual men is, it seems, still too daring for the industry. But whatever the combination of genders involved, desire that conforms exclusively to heterosexual demands appears to have been derailed.

Smelly Genders

Many smells are gendered in that they are classed as masculine or feminine. But what if gender is not only ascribed to smells but is itself considered to be a smell? In Melanesia, for example, some aspects of personhood are relational matters that involve the flow of tangible and intangible elements between persons, persons and animals, and persons and other beings such as ancestors (Strathern 1988). Gender in this cultural context is not understood as an immutable essence or difference. Rather, it is continually created and transformed along with the flow of substances – blood, semen, mother's milk, foods, gifts, odours – between persons. Among the Hua of New Guinea, the odours of menstruation are considered to be harmful to men who should avoid inhaling in the presence of menstruating women (Meigs 1984). The reason for the various taboos is that the Hua define aspects of gender in terms of fluids and scents. In other words, gender-determining substances are considered to be transactable. They can be passed on between persons and can alter the gender of whoever gives and receives them. However, a shift in gender among the Hua does not automatically translate into a shift in desire. The man who inhales in the presence of a menstruating woman does not thereby start to desire other men. Desire among the Hua is still expected to follow gender, even if gender is not wholly understood as determined by anatomy. Nonetheless, what the Hua example shows is that models of gender need neither assume the coincidence of sex and gender nor rely as heavily on visual models of gender difference and essentialist notions of male and female gender as those found in Euro-American societies (see Howes 2003). Developments in the perfume industry point to similar ideas present within Western consumer culture.

The Heteronormative Odour

The queer tinkerings with how scents are normally marketed are relatively few and go against the grain of the industry as a whole. Perfumes are still more often sold with the promise that they will bolster or awaken heterosexual desire. In advertising, scents are associated with typically masculine or feminine characteristics and pursuits. Boss for Men has been advertised as a 'commanding fragrance.' Could it perhaps be fifty millilitres of patriarchal authority? Givenchy Gentleman suggests that the buyer think of it as 'investment spending.' Is it bottled business acumen? Bijan manufactures DNA for men. It is sold in a bottle shaped like a DNA strand. The suggestion is that the scent contains the building blocks of masculinity. The product description is cryptic: 'DNA fragrances do not contain deoxyribonucleic acid (DNA) except as included in the ingredient list on product packaging' (Classen et al. 1994: 191). In one of the advertisements for DNA, from 1993, the designer Bijan is shown holding his baby son in his arms while his young daughter kisses the baby's knee. The top caption in the advertisement reads: 'DNA it's the reason you have your father's eyes, your mother's smile Bijan's perfume.' The bottom caption reads: 'Bijan with *his* DNA son Nicolas and daughter Alexandra.' The message here is once again cryptic, and perhaps one shouldn't expect too much exactitude from a perfume advertisement as the genre is notable for its vagueness. What the caption seems to be suggesting is that the scent is somehow an essential expression of who you are in the same way as Bijan's own children are genetic expressions of who he is (although no more than fifty percent). DNA is a product that derives its character from vague similarities to heterosexual reproduction.

The claim, however implicit, that scents supplement the gender of heterosexual men and women and awaken or reinforce their desirability for each 'other' is one that raises some troubling questions for a heteronormative model of desire. Marketing strategies that sell scents as substances able to enhance and supplement a gender that is inadequate admit that the aspects of gender that are sexually desirable are at least partially constructed. Much advertising presents men and women in conventionally gendered behaviours and settings at the same time as their gendering appears to be constantly in need of supplementation in the form of consumer durables. Heteronormative gender is portrayed as a precarious accomplishment, one that can never be taken for granted, and one that is never finished: Lack haunts it perpetually.

One very simple and perhaps reassuring way to explain this lack is to attribute it to chemical imbalance. Herbal Sensations is a preparation that is said to work by travelling throughout the body freeing testosterone. Testosterone, the Internet advertisement for the substance explains, stimulates sexual activity in men and women, but with advancing age it becomes bound to various compounds in the body and sexual stimulation declines. Among its effects Herbal Sensations counts firmer erections for men, more multiple orgasms and climaxes, solving impotency problems, restoring women's interest in sex, lowering cholesterol, and relieving pre-menstrual tension and prostate problems.[1] An earlier version of the same website came with the following reassurance: '[A v]ery important point for women is that it FREES UP, and does not ADD testosterone to the body. So you maintain your natural balance and [do] not have to worry about becoming masculine! (The difference is YOU may be pursuing HIM!).' Herbal sensation locates sexual drive in testosterone, a substance locked inside the body but one that can alter gendered behaviour – women become more sexually predatory. As the advertising hastens to assure potential buyers, the sexuality remains firmly within heteronormative bounds. But what of other preparations that are said to be capable of influencing desire in ways that dispense with gender and sexual preference altogether?

Bottled Gay: INTENSE, the Homonormative 'Scent'

INTENSE, 'The World's First Gay Pheromone Product,' is advertised as 'the scent of a man.' INTENSE is supposed to contain the 'gay pheromone' N10Z. It is a 'pheromone splash' developed exclusively for 10% PRODUCTIONS (www.10percent.com), an Internet retailer of goods aimed at the gay and lesbian market. The advertising leaflet that accompanies the 'scent' explains that some people are mysteriously more attractive than others and that this has

---

[1] www.libb.com/Herbal_Sensation/

been shown to be caused by the power of pheromones, natural attractants that send airborne signals from the body to other people. The pheromones work by stimulating the vomeronasal organ (VNO) which is found in humans a few centimetres inside the nose in the form of a small pit. Some scientists claim that it is connected to the hypothalamus, the gland in the brain which triggers the chemicals responsible for emotions and desire. Other scientists argue that there are no neural connections between the VNO and the brain and that it may only be a vestigial organ (see Taylor 1997). As much as that may be, scientists at the Human Pheromone Science Institute, the leaflet informs us, have discovered 'the proper chemical mixture of human pheromones that can result in same-sex attraction between men.' INTENSE, readers are told, 'is designed for gay men who want to spice up their social life, improve their self-confidence and make themselves mysteriously irresistible.' The majority of people is odourblind for pheromones, although I have heard INTENSE described by someone who can smell them as reminiscent of a 'rancid armpit.' Its lack of odour allows men to wear it without masking the scent of their favourite cologne. To the question 'Does INTENSE work?' the leaflet answers 'Yes.' 'Respondents in consumer studies have reported overwhelmingly that INTENSE has made them feel more "romantic, alluring, more confident in social situations", and noticed that people tended to cluster around them more.' There is 'significant evidence,' the leaflet claims, from studies carried out at the Chemical Senses Center in Philadelphia PA, the University of Utah School of Medicine and other research centres that pheromones affect the behaviours of those exposed to them. Researchers at the University of Kentucky, it adds, 'discovered that subjects exposed to pictures of men that were sprayed with the human pheromones found these pictures more sexually attractive than pictures of men that were not sprayed with pheromones.' In England, a test was done on national television – although the programme is not named – using twin brothers. One brother was sprayed with the pheromone and then both brothers were introduced to test subjects. The sprayed twin was found to be more attractive than the unsprayed. And, finally, a chair in a dentist's waiting room that had been sprayed with pheromones was the one most likely to be chosen by patients. However, whatever the promises made by INTENSE the leaflet is careful to point out that the 'splash' is *not* an aphrodisiac: 'INTENSE simply adds more pheromones to your body which increases the chance that someone will receive and be stimulated by them.'

Apparent in the advertising leaflet for INTENSE is a notion of essentialism. The sexual desire of men for men can quite literally be bottled in the form of INTENSE.[2] This goes very much against the grain of queer theoretical

---

2 The claims border on a form of sexual species thinking for which sexual orientation coincides with biological categories. I discuss species thinking in the next chapter.

critiques of sexological types and the necessary coincidence of sex, genders and desires that are part of heteronormative and indeed homonormative regimes. INTENSE appears to be a homonormative scent. But what is also apparent from the advertising blurb is that the desires elicited by INTENSE and other pheromone combinations need not be confined to relations between gay men, or even humans; a dentist's chair has the potential to become desirable.

At first glance, it seems that INTENSE contains a specific 'gay pheromone,' N10Z, but a careful reading of the advertising leaflet makes it clear that INTENSE contains 'the proper chemical mixture of human pheromones that can result in same-sex attraction between men.' This would suggest that a skilled chemist could concoct all manner of pheromone combinations able to stimulate sexual attraction between every conceivable gender and sexual mix: heterosexual males for homosexual males, heterosexual females for homosexual females who have been doused in the pheromones of a heterosexual male, transsexual M2F for F2M, M2F for M2F, and so on. The combinatorial possibilities are many.

Possessed: The Lesbian Aroma

Women who wish to attract other women can wear Possess, a 'lesbian pheromone formula'.[3] This concoction is based on research in Sweden, so we are told in the advertising blurb, which scanned the brains of lesbians as they were exposed to different human pheromones. 'Lesbian women's pleasure centres activated when exposed to the pheromones of young, healthy straight females'. Just why they had to be *straight* young and healthy is not explained. Given that lesbians tend to have sexual relations with other lesbians, meet them at lesbian bars or other sites of socialising, wouldn't a pheromone from young, healthy lesbians have been more appropriate? The blurb omits such considerations. It claims that 'Possess features a complex pheromone formula with multiple human pheromones.' Like INTENSE, we are looking at a mixture rather than purified 'essence of lesbian'. Again the combinatorial possibilities are hinted at. Unlike Intense, Possess is a perfume: "'Possess is too HOT!" A seductive and exotic scent with notes of raspberry, melon and citrus, and a slight floral note. Not to mention the intense and erotic pheromone blend'. It is a 'Pheromone Perfume for the Feminine Lesbian'. Presumably the 'floral tone' is what makes it feminine.

There are other lesbian alternatives such as Nude, an unscented human pheromone combination, again based on the same Swedish research. It

---

3 www.pheromonesperfume and cologne.com/possessforwomentoattractwomen.html

contains a 'complex multi pheromone blend', this time lesbian brains activate in response to 'dominant healthy straight females'. Again, why straight women are of sexual interest rather than other lesbians remains unsaid and what exactly 'dominant' refers to is unclear. Nude promises that 'you will appear more attractive to lesbian and bisexual women than you actually are', and 'Women will bond with you on a deep level and they won't be able to understand why'. The advertisement also contains the following:

> A message for heterosexual men: as there is a high likelihood that straight men will be asking if this product can be used by them to seduce lesbian women. The answer is yes, it can, but humans are complicated and your odds are going to be lower than a lesbian woman trying to attract women...but it does work sometimes.

Here there is explicit, if guarded, recognition of the combinatorial chaos these concoctions are supposedly capable of unleashing. As well as an admission that they might not be as effective as promised.

Nomadic Desire

Pheromone preparations for heterosexuals are also commercially available. One such product is APC for Men. APC stands for Androstenone Pheromone Concentrate. The e-mail that brought this product to my attention introduced it with a promise: 'Be a magnet that ONLY ATTRACTS WOMEN!!' (www.apcformen.com). This reassurance suggests some degree of nervousness about who will be magnetised by the concentrate. Who else but women does it have in mind? The advertising does not say, but it does provide some interesting examples from the animal kingdom to illustrate the potency of pheromones. 'Scientists have long known that certain hormones, called pheromones, trigger strong sexual desire in animals. This is the reason that male dogs are driven crazy by a female in heat.' And: 'In animals and insects this "chemical compound" is irresistible. For example, when a glass rod is doused with pheromones from a female cockroach, the males go crazy and actually try to mate with the rod.' APC promises to be the 'quick and easy way for men like you to attract the women you've always dreamed about. *Beautiful women, that up until now, were out of reach.*' Why were they out of reach? The advertisement provides the answer: 'until now, you used to need exotic [sic] cars and good looks to attract certain women, *the women we really want.*' But according to the advertisement appearances – good looks and the right car – are no longer necessary. The chemicals will do the job as women 'subconsciously detect the pheromones and suddenly find you more sexually attractive.'

The nervous assurances about only attracting women, together with the implicit understanding that it will not attract other men, and the use of crude zoological comparisons between heterosexual attraction and rutting dogs and cockroaches cannot save these advertisements, and also the advertisements for INTENSE, Possess and Nude from a dilemma. They have admitted one of the main arguments of queer theory: Desire does *not* necessarily follow gendered persons. Desire in the form of a smell is understood to be a quality in its own right. It is a force of attraction, that can be congealed into an object – in this case a 'scent' – and enjoy a life of its own. This receives comic expression in an AXE (2002) television advertisement for men's cologne. In it a young man in a Mexican bar sprays himself with the scent and immediately becomes attractive to women. He is bitten on the chest by a mosquito – it too finds him irresistible – which is eaten by a frog. The frog then immediately goes on to mate with another frog. The unfortunate amphibian is caught in a net and served as frog's legs at a French restaurant where the old man who eats them immediately attracts the attention of a beautiful young woman. They are about to consummate their passion when he dies of heart failure. In his grave the worms eat him and one of them ends up in a tequila bottle. A young man in a Mexican bar swallows the worm along with his tequila and immediately attracts the attention of the women in the bar . . .

Even if this saga of nomadic desire is a product of the advertiser's fantasy, it points nonetheless to a theory of attraction that is at variance with Western heteronormative regimes in which sex, gender and desire ought all to coincide. (There are even examples of cross-species sexual attraction present.) Although intended to effect just such a coincidence, the logic in the advertisements in fact ensures its disruption (assuming that the scents work), because desire is located in the fragrance, not in the consumer who uses it. Hence, the attraction the cologne elicits bears no necessary relationship to the sex, gender or any other characteristic of the person wearing it. The genie of desire has been let out of the perfume bottle and is on the loose.

A World without Gender: The Unisex Scent

In 1994, Calvin Klein released CKOne, the company's first unisex fragrance. The scent is described as 'clear, pure and contemporary with a refreshingly new point of view.' Two years later Calvin Klein released another unisex fragrance, CKBe. This time: 'Calvin Klein takes a closer look at who we are within this ageless, raceless, genderless world.' It does more: 'It invites us to take risks, make mistakes, be unpredictable. It invites us to close our eyes, to open our minds, and to dream'.[4]

The advertising text for CKBe is particularly striking for its utopian and disembodied description of the world as one without age, race or gender. Business rhetoric that extols the virtues of diversity argues that discrimination on the grounds of age, race and gender is detrimental to global capitalist production. Companies that want to survive in a competitive market require a diverse workforce to ensure their flexibility and ability to innovate. They must be able to sell their goods and services to a diverse range of consumers who want to feel recognised, not exploited or ignored, by corporate businesses. But the new production processes of global capitalism have not abolished class (Harvey 1996). On the contrary, new forms of class inequality and injustice have appeared in their wake in the lowest levels of the Western service sectors and in developing countries. It is surely significant that the advertisement for CKBe does not claim that the world is classless. Moreover, the dream of disembodiment, it is important to recall, has been a fantasy of the male Western philosophical tradition for millennia (Bordo 1993). The apparently positive message of the advertising – that our desire not be constrained by gender, age or race – rests, therefore, on some problematic silences and assumptions about class, gender and the body.

The two scents from Calvin Klein are by no means the only unisex scents on the market, other, more recent, examples include Cartier's L'Heure Mysterieuse, Van Cleef's Cologne Noir, and Tom Ford's White Suede. The desire these scents are supposed to elicit does not operate within the neatly dichotomised channels of a heteronormative gender system. Its direction is unclear and its form protean.[5] In the case of CKBe, it seems that no differences are necessary at all in order to drive desire, and one is left wondering how desire ever gets started in the first place.

This short, fragrant journey started with conventional heteronormative scents, continued on past homonormative scents and finished with unisex scents. For heteronormative scents, desire is essentialised as part of a two-sexed and two-gendered world and occurs *between* two sexes and two genders, although the heteronormative scents do occasionally acknowledge, albeit nervously, that desire may be independent of gender and sex. In the case of INTENSE,

---

4 www.scentagious.com

5 However, the scent Back to Black Aphrodisiac by Kilian comes with this reassurance from its maker: 'On my skin, I smell the woods and tobacco, but on my female staffers, the honey takes over. I almost don't recognize it'. The desire itself remains firmly within heteronormative gender norms, 'masculine' tobacco for men and 'feminine' honey for women. http://www.marieclaire.com/hair-beauty/trends/unisex-fragrances#slide-1

Possess and Nude, all homonormative scents, desire is also essentialised and enhanced *within* the same sex and gender. But INTENSE is marketed as a chemical that can be bottled, and that has the capacity to elicit desire for objects that are not sexed or gendered in any conventional sense. Indeed, the object of desire may even be inanimate. The unisex scents elicit desire that can be both between and within sexes and genders. In fact, it is not always clear if there are sexes and genders in this 'genderless' world. These latter fragrances are scents for a generalised humanity without essences. To varying degrees all three kinds of scent loosen the ties between sex, gender and desire. And in all three cases, desire can or does break free of a two-sex/two-gender order. In the case of unisex scents, sex and gender fade in an androgynous world and it is unclear if sexual desire persists at all.

Flexible Fragrances

Why is it that such apparently innocuous commodities as perfumes and colognes, which, if anything, have been used to bolster heteronormative sexuality, have been resignified as desire that is free-floating from any natural, that is to say anatomical, substrate? If the perfume industry has been willing to dispense with gender as part of a marketing experiment at about the same time as queer theories of gender performativity took off, then just how radical are these theories?

According to the advertising for CKBe, the consumers of unisex fragrances are without age, race or gender. They are blank slates on which desire can be sprayed. These unisex fragrances can be worn by anyone and, as such, are flexible fragrances capable of producing desiring effects among any combination of people independently of the qualities of the object of desire. The 'flexibility' of unisex scents does clearly resonate with the characteristics of late-capitalist production in which workers are exhorted and forced to be flexible, and adaptable to the shifting demands of the production process.

Rosemary Hennessy (2000), while not wanting to abandon the critical take on heteronormativity afforded by queer theoretical approaches, sees them as complicit with commodification and consumer culture. Flexible gender codes, fluid sexualities, and sexual identities, she argues, resonate and are compatible with the mobility and adaptability required of service workers, and the new fluid forms of the commodity (2000: 108–9). Employing a similar materialist critique, Max Kirsch (2000) sees elements of queer theory as promoting individualism and the fragmentation of working-class struggle. In short, according to these authors there is nothing in queer approaches to sexuality and gender to disrupt capitalism, even if it may challenge some aspects of the heteronormative order.

In *The Transparency of Evil* (1990a), Jean Baudrillard argues that contemporary existence occurs in a 'trans'-world. This is a world marked by a confusion of boundaries, a promiscuous intersecting of states and a loss of specificity in a world of movement in which everything is always *trans*itional. Baudrillard himself uses the term 'transsexual' to refer to what he sees as the breakdown of the categories of gender and sex. He also argues that this transsexual state of affairs extends to the breakdown of boundaries between the economic, the political, and the aesthetic domains. Baudrillard's vision is that of an actual and potential world in which signifiers are cut adrift from signifieds, and 'race,' 'class' and 'gender' no longer unambiguously denote any object. Subjects in this world do not express a natural substrate, their biology, nor do they arise within a post-structural logic of relations of positive and negative value. Rather, the identities of subjects are not straightforwardly relative to anything. In such a world, where there are no clear relations between things, value is difficult to assign.

According to Baudrillard, the value that has displaced that of the natural use, commodity exchange and structural sign logics (see Chapter 2) is that of positive fractal value (1990a: 5). The fractal repeats itself. It generates itself from within itself and not in relation to others against which it must be defined as difference. A plurality there is, but each identity or position can be labelled, packaged and sold for what it 'is', its very own essence.

Gender performativity aspires to split the signifier from the signified in order to evade the tyranny of the label that conjures up its own essence. In practice, this has meant a proliferation of genders performatively produced. Baudrillard employs an unpleasant medical term to characterise this proliferation: a metastasis of value, which, he argues, is highly in tune with the axiology and semiology of contemporary political economy. Baudrillard writes: 'We have conquered otherness with difference, and in its turn, difference has succumbed to the logic of the same and of indifference' (quoted in Grace 2000: 137).

Does such a world have its own distinctive odour? What fragrance would *one* choose if *one* simply wants to *be* what *one* is while escaping insertion into an invidious system of gender and sex distinctions? If the advertisers are to be believed, CKOne and CKBe would seem to be good choices. They belong to a world lacking in basic distinctions between age, race and gender. In short, they exist in a world of positives. Yet in the form of nomadic and imprecise scents they point beyond even self-contained positives. It is no coincidence that the advertising for CKBe 'invites us to close our eyes, to open our minds, and to dream.' Once again, a parallel with Melanesia can be drawn. As Alfred Gell points out, among the Umeda of New Guinea, the word for 'dream' (*yinugwi*) is close to that for 'smell' (*nugwi*). For the Umeda, smells are like dreams in which things usually hidden, that is to say unavailable to vision, are revealed (Gell 1977: 32). Closing down the visual shuts out the greatest device for making clear-cut distinctions. How unlike it is the sense of smell and the shifting, fluctuating and imprecise qualities of its objects, odours.

It is the transient and elusive qualities of fragrances and aromas that lend them their appeal. Scents are often described in a language remarkable for its lack of precision. Adjectives like 'mysterious,' 'evocative', 'suggestive', 'enigmatic', and 'ineffable' abound. Just think of the language of wine connoisseurs as they struggle to find words to describe a wine's bouquet (Lehrer 1983). Some perfume advertisements dispense with words entirely. It is only a small step from this to abolishing the scent altogether to maximise its mystery and ineffability. Try to describe an odourless scent. And yet this odourless 'scent' now exists in the form of INTENSE, Nude and other pheromone products, and, moreover, they are meant to be the most seductive of them all and the most mysterious and discreet in the way they weave their magic.

A smell also links the person who senses the odour or scent with its source. Smells act as a tangible bridge between persons and the material world around them for the smell that enters your nostrils *is* the object that emits the smell. The smell of another person cannot be ignored short of refusing to breathe. One can close one's eyes against offending sights and efforts can be made to reduce noise, but smells, and especially offensive odours, are insistent and unavoidable. In short, olfaction confuses and violates boundaries. It has been noted that odours are very often present in rites of passage (Howes 1987) where they are employed to symbolise transitions and shifts in status (Gell 1977: 27). The ability of smells to transcend boundaries is exploited in the use of incense in rituals. Inhaling the incense binds together the congregation and makes everyone olfactory participants in the proceedings, whether they like it or not.

If gender and desire can be understood as free-floating qualities that can occur in different combinations, whether it be the gendered fluids and smells of the Hua or lesbian pheromones, is there something about smells that makes them suitable for the task of embodying these qualities? Is the olfactory the queerest of the senses? The question is intriguing, but my main aim here is not to award the prize for the queerest sense. The extent to which different senses lend themselves to a queer project is historically and culturally variable. Rather, I want to argue that the queer sensorium should be broadened to include senses other than the visual.

Expanding the Queer Sensorium

The ocularcentrism of Western cultures extends into models of gender, sex and desire and queer theories have not freed themselves from it. Appearance is held up as one of the cornerstones of desire in psychoanalysis. Freud locates one of the decisive moments in the development of infant sexuality in the dis-cover-y that the mother lacks the penis/phallus. And although this scene of reve(a)lation is not supposed to be taken too literally, its visual bias is clear enough. This ocularcentrism is even more apparent in Lacan's writings, for whom the ego is precipitated through its imaginary recognition of itself in the mirror, the 'theatre' of the ego's emergence in which it is able to view (*thea*) itself (Borch-Jacobsen 1991: 43–71). The dominance of the visual in Freud's and Lacan's work is inseparable from the subsequent gendering of the subject and how it is channelled into the correct form of object choice, heterosexual desire. How ironic, then, that smell, often considered to be the 'lowest' of the senses in the Euro-American west, is presented as capable of undermining this, the highest stage of sexual development, at least in a heteronormative order.[6]

Starting with Butler's own attention to drag (Butler 1990: 136–9) the theatrical dimension of the 'performative' is evident in the choice of examples (see, for example, Smith 1999). Ocularcentrism is part of Euro-American cultural common sense and it informs the theoretical sense too.[7] If the 'common sense' senses are examined with a mind to broadening the 'theoretical sense' (cf. Herzfeld 1997: 305), then a deeper understanding of one's own ethnocentrism in the field of gender, sexuality and desire may be provided. There is no room here to speculate about what touches, pressures or caresses might count as queer. Or to ask which tastes blended into sweet or sour, smooth and mellow, or sharp and tangy combinations can send taste buds into queer spasms. This is still largely uncharted territory. A few attempts have, however, been made within musicology to identify queerness in sound.

Of Schubert's *Unfinished Symphony*, Susan McClary writes that 'the opening theme becomes a pretext for deflection and exploration,' and that 'it invites us to forgo the security of centred, stable tonality, and, instead to experience – and even enjoy – a flexible sense of self.' 'Schubert's movement,' she writes, 'resembles uncannily some of the narrative structures that gay writers and critics are exploring today' (1994: 215, 233).[8] The falsetto, excessive vibrato and trill in singing have all at one time or another been seen as unnatural, or even degenerate forms of vocal expression. Why the fuss? Virtuoso singers were denounced in 1755 for their 'monstrous inversion of things' and because 'they over do, confound and disfigure every thing' (Kostenbaum 1993: 165, 168,

---

6 For an alternative sensorium of sexuality, one that builds heavily on the olfactory, see David Howes's discussion of smells among in the Trobriand islands (Howes 2003: 175–203).

7 The senses are also political. See Trnka, Dureau and Park 2013.

8 If MacClary is right, Schubert's *Unfinished Symphony*, with its invitation to enjoy a 'flexible sense of self', sounds like the perfect musical accompaniment to the flexible workers of late-capitalism.

184).[9] They did not conform to a structure and were difficult to classify. They 'deviated' and were too flexible. It would seem that their voices were like smells.

Ambiguous Aromas

Some of the more egregious results of a simplistic voluntarist theory of desire, when placed at the service of commodity capitalism, are evident in the utopian promise made by scents like CKBe: Becoming an object of desire requires no more effort than choosing your eau de cologne. These scents promise the wearer identity choices that are divorced from structural inequalities of class and race, and a genderless world that echoes male fantasies of disembodiment. Such fantasies are parasitic on a visualism that supports the illusion of a distant and disengaged regard, rather than embodied, sensual involvement with others in the often messy and frequently unjust particularities of life.[10] Yet the voluntarism these consumer choices imply, and of which performative theories of gender are sometimes accused, challenges the heteronormative and homonormative alignment of sex, gender and desire. They evoke an alternative olfactory imaginary that is at least suggestive of other gender and sexual possibilities, even if we are not always convinced of the power of the scents.

Another lesson to be drawn out of these scents is that senses and the subject need not coincide. Smells, scents and odours are but emanations, the distilled vapours of material things, and things sometimes misbehave. The queerness of smells lies in the affective states they arouse and evoke which can work to undermine identity and the sensible assumptions of a centred and transparent subject. Instead, we have unpredictable processes of a molecular kind, and literally so, that are not necessarily supportive of molar realities. They remind us that our bodies lead their own lives independently of subjective consciousness. We may confuse vision with an insight that provides reliable knowledge, but smells can lead us down other redolent pathways.

The gender-bending of the 1960s onwards was very much about visual culture. It is, therefore, perhaps not surprising that the initial attention of performative and queer theories has largely been to visual phenomena.

---

9 See also Peraino 2006, on 'queer music'.

10 Not everyone agrees that vision separates and objectifies. For Merleau-Ponty 'Vision is the place where our continuity with the world conceals itself, the place where we mistake our contact for distance, imagining that seeing is a substitute for, rather than a mode of touching' (Melville 1996: 109, quoted in Oliver 2001: 203). Similarly, Ingold (2000: 243–87) maintains that the dominant Euro-American model of vision is misleading. Vision he argues is 'auditory', like sound, it surrounds us but in light rather than vibrations in the air.

Manufacturers are offering nomadic desires in a bottle and theories of gender performativity need to explore the implications. Once more it may be time for The Owl of Minerva to fly off into the dusk – only this time to the strains of Schubert's *Unfinished Symphony* and reeking of CKBe.

Chapter 4
Species

One of the most quoted texts on sexuality written during the last 40 years is Foucault's description of the appearance of a homosexual 'species'. His argument has been discussed endlessly. Is it really true to say that homosexuals did not exist prior to their sexological invention, that 'they' did not have a clear idea of themselves as a separate category of people, or had nothing approaching what we today would call an identity, centred firmly on their sexuality as Foucault, or at least a common interpretation of his words, implies? Or is it the case that although the term homosexual is relatively new an awareness of belonging to a sexual type pre-existed modern medical and sexological discourses, perhaps by centuries? The other side of the couplet, the 'species', has not received anything like the attention devoted to the 'homosexual'. Indeed, it is probably true to say that it has been largely ignored, a self-evident term whose meaning is clear and whose implications, of essence, fixity and the ontological status of a discrete biological group everyone understands.

In current scholarship almost everyone under the influence of Foucauldian ideas, post-structuralism, much of feminism and queer theory is agreed that species-thinking, usually understood as some form of biologism or essentialism, is a bad thing best avoided. According to its detractors, species-thinking undergirds the misguided notion that 'homosexuals' are a separate sexual population. It suggests, mistakenly, that there are mental and physical characteristics specific to homosexuals that distinguish them from heterosexuals, and that these characteristics are rarely if ever presented as positive, empowering or free from stigma. Species thinking also perpetuates the biological and medical naturalisation of a minority status and the pathologisation of same-sex sexuality as an aberration or a 'mistake' of nature in need of human 'correction'.

Others greet the species idea with enthusiasm and relief. It vindicates arguments that homosexuality is 'natural', a 'fact' of nature, and part of its wondrous biological diversity, like butterflies, giraffes and bottlenose dolphins. It helps to discredit attacks on the unnaturalness and sinfulness of homosexuality qua moral failing or perverse choice by pointing to the inevitability of homosexuality for the individual member of the species, who is merely doing what nature, or the divine, intended.

There is undoubtedly a lot of truth in the criticism that species thinking naturalises same-sex sexuality and contributes to a *minoritising* discourse. But there is more to it than that. Species thinking quickly runs into other difficulties once we look more closely at the species concept itself, and not only at its supposed implications for the homosexual species. Species thinking is problematic once it becomes part of *diversity* management discourses that stress the *value* of certain kinds of subjects and notions of worth, and even the presence of biovalue in the general population.

At first glance, then, species would appear to be yet another unwelcome visitor from the tainted realm of biological matter. Such a suspicion would not be entirely without foundation. But what I want to do in this chapter is, if not to disprove these arguments, then at least to complicate them and some of the misconceptions that underlie the uses to which biological models are put. The species concept provides a portal onto Charles Darwin's thinking that might reveal some surprises. After a consideration of Darwin's ideas I then turn to the UK in the first decade of the century and to the policies of New Labour. Specifically, I consider the government's stance on diversity and its policy of community cohesion. The Labour government walked a tightrope between the essentialist assumptions surrounding sexuality and the queer implications of the post-multicultural goals that inform its community cohesion policy.

Darwin's Legacy

First, a striking fact: Biologists are unable to provide a definition of species on which all practitioners of the discipline can agree and which is able to account for the kinds of entities described in the best biological theories (Wheeler and Meier 2000, Hey 2001: 109, Ereshefsky 2010). Jody Hey (2001) outlines the development of the species concept thus. From its origins in the philosophies of Plato and Aristotle, genus (*genos*) and species (*eidos*) respectively referred to a major category and narrower subcategories within it. In the eighteenth century, Carl Linnaeus gave these terms a more rigid meaning within a formal system of logic in which the categories were mutually exclusive and arranged in a tree-like hierarchy. Each genus had its own essence and corresponded to a kind of organism. In the nineteenth century, Darwin overturned this static model. For Darwin, despite the title of his epoch-making *The Origin of Species*, there were no distinct species apart from subspecies and variations. There were grades of distinction for the simple (but revolutionary) reason that species continually evolve, they were not and could not be separate logical categories as in the Linnaean scheme.

For Darwin, 'what evolves are not individuals or even species, which are forms of relative fixity or stability, but oscillations of difference...that can consolidate themselves, more or less temporarily, into cohesive groupings' (Grosz 2004: 24). As to the differences between species and sub-species and varieties, Darwin writes that 'these differences blend into each other by an insensible series; and a series impresses the mind with the idea of an actual passage' (quoted in Grosz 2004: 24). Natural selection involves 'the passage from one stage of difference to another' (quoted in Grosz 2004: 25). Darwin reasons that 'From these remarks, it will be seen that I look at the term species as one arbitrarily given, for the sake of convenience, to a set of individuals closely resembling each other, and that it does not essentially differ from the term variety' (quoted in Grosz 2004: 25). Strictly speaking, there can be no *origin* of species if origin is understood to mean a unity, entity, object or point in time out of which difference emerges. There is only difference and differentiating from the start. There are no discrete and fixed entities preceding new species, just grades of variation between closely related but not absolutely distinct organisms.[1]

The problem for biologists is that while they accept Darwin's ideas on evolution (with some modifications), he failed to convince them on the matter of species and they still cling to a model of organisms grouped into distinct kinds. As Hey (2001: 9) puts it: 'Darwin has left us stranded on a word, and modern biologists are semantic castaways, trapped with a word of little common meaning, struggling to fix the situation by puzzling their way out of it'. Despite the best efforts put into formulating an acceptable and workable definition of species the lack of consensus remains. One of the problems biologists face is that 'there may be an effectively infinite number of patterns that we might recognise and that might seem useful' (Hey 2001: 187). In short, there is a degree of arbitrariness in the identification and enumeration of biological taxa simply and inevitably because the categories in use are human cultural constructions. This is not a conclusion likely to surprise anthropologists.

One reason why biologists nonetheless persist in counting is the demand placed on them by governments, development agencies, and NGOs, for the names and number of species as an index of biological diversity. The results can be confusing. For example, the Global Biodiversity Assessment provided a figure of 1.75 million species worldwide in 1995, whereas the American Congressional Research Service estimated between five to 100 million in 2000 (Hey 2001: 188). Such a massive discrepancy points to a serious problem of definition. As Hey argues: 'Real evolutionary processes have given rise to unknown, albeit vast, numbers of DNAs, cells, and organisms, and our growing familiarity with their diversity could lead us to recognise an unending, effectively infinite, tally of patterns among them. It is silly to ponder just how many species taxa we might generate if we could see all of biodiversity' (2001: 189).[2]

---

1 All these aspects of Darwin's thought made it very attractive to the process philosophers like Bergson and Whitehead I discussed in Chapter 1.

2 As Jeffries (2006: 6–11) notes, the emphasis in major works on biodiversity has moved from the total number of species to genetics and systems (Reakka-Kudla 1997).

One response to the difficulty of defining species in line with what Hey writes is to shift attention away from species, qua 'objects', and look instead at the formative *processes* behind the emergence of species. 'It is not *form* (species) as mere morphology, but the *formative* (speciating) process that humans ought to preserve, although the process cannot be preserved without its products. Neither should humans want to protect labels they use, but the living process in the environment' (Rolston 1985: 722). For Holmes Rolston, it is the 'dynamic form' of evolution that must be preserved as it maintains the evolutionary process itself. An emphasis on emergent and formative processes shifts attention to the becoming or doing of biological matter rather than objectified results, the species. To identify a species demands actualising the virtual of biological matter – the teeming potential of biological process. Like the apparent stability of the gendered subject (and 'gender' is after all related to 'genus', one of the static and problematic features of the Aristotelian and Linnaean systems), a species is continually morphing and the direction it takes is not fully determined in advance.

As I argued earlier in Chapter 1, the performative version of matter found in work on gender can have preformative implications when gender answers to an *external* demand. Species thinking too relies primarily on a preformative version of matter rather than Darwin's creative performative ontology. For example, the 'survival of the fittest' is one of the ideas associated most readily with Darwin (although it was coined by Herbert Spencer and is not fully compatible with Darwin's 'natural selection'). It is in circumstances of extreme selective pressures that the survivalist thesis is most applicable. In such circumstances matter is preformative, it internalises an external dictate. It in-volves. The internal creative capacities of matter are relatively subordinated to external environmental pressures. Under less trying circumstances the internalisation of external pressure becomes less of an imperative. Instead, matter e-volves when its own internal differentiation plays a greater part.

From Species to Diversity

Up until the 1990s, species loss was seen as regrettable but endurable. Pollution was judged to be the greater threat. The UN Convention on Biodiversity, adopted at Rio de Janeiro in 1992, shifted the focus onto the conservation and protection of ecosystems their species and genetic diversity. Their conservation was identified as necessary for humankind's well being.

Several different arguments are put forward in favour of biodiversity. Economic arguments stress the importance of preserving enough genetic variety to produce food, medicines and support ecotourism. The economic value of the world's biodiversity is calculated to USD 33,000,000,000,000

(Jeffries 2005: 3). Moral arguments emphasise that humans do not have the right to wipe out other species. Precautionary arguments warn that we lack sufficient understanding of the effects species disappearance can have on ecosystems. For example, the importance of biodiversity is not always readily apparent. A specific function in one area may be reliant on considerable biodiversity elsewhere, such as the pollination of a local monocrop by an insect that lives in distant fields and meadows.

Another impetus to species-thinking is its close relation, diversity-thinking. Diversity has been seen as a necessary precondition for humanity's development for some time. Back in 1925, Alfred North Whitehead wrote:

> The differences between the nations and races of mankind are required to preserve the conditions under which higher development is possible…A diversification among human communities is essential for the provision of the incentive and the material for the Odyssey of the human spirit. Other nations of different habits are not enemies: they are godsends. Men require of their neighbors something sufficiently akin to be understood, something sufficiently different to provoke attention, and something great enough to command admiration. (quoted in Harmon 2001: 64)

It may seem churlish to scrutinise the sentiments of Whitehead and his insistence on the necessity and indeed foundational status of diversity. He appears motivated by the noblest of sentiments. Nonetheless, traces of the species problem and the seeds of some of the less welcome implications of diversity discourses are present. The idea of 'preserving' differences between entities like nations and races, which are taken to exist as objects, raises a host of issues that are easy to identify, among them the risk of reification. Whitehead's talk of 'incentives' might be a faint precursor of current management and business philosophies that extol the growth potential of diversity and use it as a spur to abandon outdated, monocultural, homogenous workplaces in the pursuit of profits or perish like the dodo (Kirton and Green 2005, Mor-Barak 2005). There is a palpable sense of entitlement in the notion of 'godsends'. Sent for whom? Although Whitehead seems to be addressing everyone, or at least all 'men', his is a cosmopolitan perspective that presupposes access to knowledge of 'other nations'. Not everyone enjoys that privilege, not even nine decades later. And finally, the description of the ideal neighbour as similar enough not to leave us bewildered (or afraid) and different enough to be interesting and in possession of something admirable (perhaps a quality we find lacking among our own kind) reads almost like an early advertisement for commercialised diversity.

Management Ecology

Diversity management business strategies do not shy away from using biological analogies. Take the following example from the *Harvard Business Review* (Iansiti and Levien 2004). The authors of the article in question, which is entitled *Strategy as Ecology*, are sensitive to the criticism that the biological analogies employed by them might be inappropriate but argue that 'we feel strongly that the analogy between evolved biological systems and networks of business entities is too often misunderstood. A sophisticated examination of this analogy is essential to improving our understanding about how such networks operate' (ibid: 76). 'Like an individual species in a biological ecosystem, each member of a business ecosystem ultimately shares the fate of the network as a whole, regardless of that member's apparent strength' (Iansiti and Levien 2004: 69). A network here refers to the links between suppliers, distributors, manufacturers, service providers and so on; the entire 'ecosystem' on which a company is reliant. 'Each of these ecosystems today numbers thousands of firms and millions of people, giving them a scale many orders of magnitude larger than the companies themselves and an advantage over smaller, competing ecosystems' (ibid: 70). The article goes on to outline a framework for assessing the 'health' of company ecosystems. Somewhat surprisingly the authors inform us that 'drawing the precise boundaries of an ecosystem is an impossible and, in any case, academic exercise. Rather, you should try to systematically identify the organizations with which your future is most closely intertwined and determine the dependencies that are most critical to your business.' (ibid: 71). However, this caveat does not stop the authors from making very explicit comparisons between the business world and the biology of ecosystems. For example: 'Productivity. The most important measure of a biological ecosystem's health is its ability to effectively convert non-biological inputs, such as sunlight and mineral nutrients, into living outputs – populations of organisms, or biomass. The business equivalent is a network's ability to consistently transform technology and other raw materials of innovation into lower costs and new products' (ibid: 72). And: 'Robustness. To provide durable benefits to the species that depend on it, a biological ecosystem must persist in the face of environmental changes. Similarly, a business ecosystem should be capable of surviving disruptions such as unforeseen technological change' (ibid: 72). Apart from productivity and robustness, the 'ecological literature indicates that it is also important that these systems exhibit variety, the ability to support a diversity of species' (ibid: 73). The authors also write of 'keystones', organisations that 'increase ecosystem productivity by simplifying the complex task of connecting network participants' (ibid: 73). 'As in biological ecosystems, keystones exercise a system-wide role despite being only a small part of their ecosystems' mass' (ibid: 74). They provide an example of keystones from the natural world: 'Like keystones in business networks, sea otters represent only a small part of the biomass of their community but exert tremendous influence. Note too, that, as in business ecosystems, some individual members of the community – the sea urchins that get eaten by the otters – suffer as a result of the keystone's behavior, but the community as a whole benefits' (ibid: 76).

Ecological thinking also, if obliquely, informs the arguments made by authors such as Richard Florida, which have been eagerly picked up by the planners of urban regeneration. The presence of a large, urban, middle-class, gay and lesbian population centred on visible consumption and entertainment, is according to Florida a positive measure of diversity and a very reliable indicator of creativity, tolerance and the global competitiveness of cities (Florida 2002, 2005). Florida's 'creative cities' are all about the survival of the fittest in the global capitalist market. His arguments employ metaphors that are strikingly reminiscent of earlier writings on urban ecology, specifically the Chicago School's mosaic of neighbourhoods and ideas of ethnic succession that were derived from biology. In Florida's scenario, transforming residential neighbourhoods or parts of the city is the work of the gay and lesbian vanguard. It paves the way for gentrification. Florida completely ignores the very real risks of physical harm and abuse faced by the 'pioneers'. He even quotes another researcher, Gary Gates, who likens lesbians and gays to canaries sent in to test the atmosphere (Florida 2002: 256). We all know what happens to the canaries when the atmosphere turns out to be hostile. There is a degree of cynicism in the model, both in terms of its neglect of risks, but also in how it ignores some of the consequences of gentrification that squeeze out existing residents and then eventually squeeze out the gay and lesbian settlers as wealthy, middle-class heterosexual families move in forcing up the house prices.

Florida is of course not alone in extolling the virtues of a visible lesbian and gay minority on the urban scene.

Cool Britannia

Britain's success in the global market was understood by the (New) Labour government (1997–2011) to require general acceptance of neo-liberal economic doctrine: a flexible and competitive labour force, creativity, innovation, individual choice, deregulation, and the exploitation of Britain's social and cultural diversity to this end, including its lesbian and gay citizens. Britain under New Labour in the first decade of the Millennium provides a useful test case of how queer ideas fare in the politics of the state and business.

Community Cohesion

The decade did not start well. In 2001, riots broke out in the northern towns of Burnley, Oldham and Bradford, which had strong racial and ethnic overtones. According to government and other reports written in the wake of the riots, Britain's larger cities are a mosaic of ethnic communities whose members live 'parallel lives' with little or no meaningful contact outside their own cultural and social enclaves (Ouseley 2001, Cantle 2001, Commission for Racial Equality 2004). In response, the government embarked upon a strategy of 'community cohesion' (Cantle 2005)[3] that aims to transform defensive ethnic and racial categories and groups into open 'communities' with meaningful relations to other sections of the population. Although initially about racial and ethnic divisions, the range of community cohesion was extended to include lesbians and gays, the disabled, and the elderly by none other than its main architect, Ted Cantle (2005: 159). He writes:

> The recent fractures in western democracies have generally been along ethnic and faith fault lines. However, the aim of community cohesion is to tackle the 'fear of difference' more generally and to enable people to be more comfortable with all areas of difference, including those based on sexual orientation, disability, social class and age...Community cohesion programmes must clearly, therefore, embrace all parts of the country and not just those with high proportions of ethnic or other minority populations. (Cantle 2005: 159)

The shift towards community cohesion is a step along the course Labour charted away from multiculturalism, a term which has fallen out of favour in many circles in Britain (Phillips 2004), towards integration. In its place we find Labour's cosmopolitanism, which sought to disrupt defensive and even hostile communities formed in response to racist, Islamophobic and also homophobic attitudes and actions, as well as the identities associated with them. Community attachments, if monolithic and traditionalist, are obstacles in the way of creating a New Britain integrated by shared values distilled from the diversity of cultural and social groups that comprise the nation. Rather than rely on 'inherited' cultures from the past, a future-oriented and emergent citizenship was advocated (McGhee 2008: 101–2).

Breaking down the boundaries between minorities was in keeping with the other major strand in New Labour's policy, the emphasis on the individual. Citizens, rather than identity groups and especially ethnic identity groups, were to be integrated into a framework consisting of local government, the public

---

3 An Institute for Community Cohesion was has recently been incorporated into the Centre for Social Relations, www.cohesioninstitute.org.uk

authorities, and through voluntary sector and other institutions, into 'civil society' (a term authors like Anthony Giddens (2001), one of the sociological architects of Labour's Third Way politics, prefers over community). Community members take *responsibility* for their individual actions, and resolve their conflicts and those of 'their' community and adjacent communities. Ultimately, it is active *individual* citizens who are to be accountable for themselves. In short, communities become part of a reformed British governance.

There is a palpable tension in New Labour's policy (one that has largely continued into the present coalition government of Conservatives and Liberal Democrats) between collectives and individuals. The demand for individuals as part of a neo-liberal philosophy coexists alongside the impulse to place people into the categories of diversity. In this process of interpellation (Althusser 1971) people are meant to exercise an *individual* agency that nonetheless refers them to their respective *collective* positions.[4]

The competing demands and expectations associated with these imperatives are clearly visible in how sexual minorities – 'lesbians and gays' – are positioned within diverse Britain. In species thinking at this neoliberal juncture, collectives and individuals are both countable and accountable. They are commonly understood to be a distinct numerical minority with some kind of lifestyle or cultural capacity, and ought to have a clear sense of their own responsibilities not only their rights. It is to this 'minority' I now turn. Firstly, through consideration of its supposed creative individualism and then, secondly, through attention to its reification into a biological type, a species.

Minority Fixations

Lesbians and gays occupy an interesting position in relation to the individualistic thrust of New Labour's philosophy. Because sexual orientation is not expressed phenotypically, lesbians and gays are in the unusual position of being brought up by parents who do not recognise or even understand a vital part of who their children are. As a result, young gay people, even in countries where same-sex sexuality has won some level of recognition and legal equality, are not provided with a cultural script that takes account of their sexuality and the particular needs and problems they face. Even if parents are supportive, it is not certain

---

4 Some of the official language used to describe categories of people who face discrimination is strongly reminiscent of ecological thinking and uses the language of the nature reserve. The British government's White Paper *Fairness for All* (2004), which outlined the responsibilities of the new Commission for Equality and Human Rights (CEHR) refers to 'protected groups', that is groups that need to be shielded by anti-discrimination legislation. Yet, as we have already seen, the government also emphasised the need to dissolve group and community boundaries.

that they can provide advice on how to live life as a gay man or lesbian. There is, then, a social and cultural disjuncture between generations.[5] This distinguishes them from many young heterosexuals, who, regardless of whatever problems they may have with parents and peers, do not face the same stigma because of their sexual orientation and who have access to a gigantic cultural and social apparatus supportive of their heterosexuality when expressed in the culturally appropriate forms.

The experience of cultural rupture brings lesbians and gays, and other queer youth, into step, albeit in an unforeseen form, with the community cohesion policy's suspicion of the cultural succession of generations. It also positions them within a broader set of developments in the culture of late modernity located in the affluent sections of western countries (but by no means only there) where the making of identity is increasingly claimed to be a matter of self-definition and self-creation as individuals choose from among

---

5 It is instructive to compare lesbian and gay experience with the UK Black population. Both have been demonised in the past, yet both are also an index of creative urban cultures, and for similar reasons. They both share cultural disjuncture. Britain's Black, or Afro-Caribbean, population (which originates mainly in the West Indies) arrived from small, island communities transformed by British colonialism into plantation economies and transplanted versions of British institutions and culture. As a result the West Indian first generation did not bring with them the kind of 'compulsory institutions' (Cohen 1974: xvii-xviii) that organised kinship, religion and marriage found among first generation, south west Asian immigrants (mainly from India and Pakistan). The latter arrived in Britain with a social and cultural heritage largely intact, despite British colonialism. By contrast, West Indian cultures were not distinct enough from white British culture to allow clear cultural boundaries to develop because cultural creolisation – including several African, as well as British, French and Spanish elements – was a central aspect of the region's history (Mintz 1974). The result was a 'cultural division of labour' (Hechter 1978) in which the imperial centre considered West Indian cultural heritages to be no better than second-rate versions, or poor copies, of the dominant culture. As a consequence, the first generation of West Indian immigrants to Britain was unable to offer its second generation the kind of relatively distinct cultural and social heritage possessed by the Asian first generation, which, even if rejected by its second generation, nonetheless offered them a coherent set of cultural materials and institutions with which to work. In the absence of a distinct alternative to British culture, there was a greater reliance on cultural materials drawn from an individual's own cultural sources (Bentley 1987, Graham 1992), rather than on the cultural stockpile of one's ethnic community. This made second generation Black British identity exploratory in a manner similar (but, of course, not identical) to that of gays and lesbians. It is the second and third generations of British Blacks who embody one face of Cool Britannia. Yet, like gays and lesbians, they too were demonised in the past (and in some quarters still are) as threats to the nation (Smith 1994) but now see their cultural flair valorised and celebrated as part of British diversity.

the raw materials furnished by consumer culture and stitch together their own biographies. Identity is presented as a matter of individual choices (for those who can afford it), of self-fashioning (for those who choose the appropriate self), and of reflexive awareness (e.g. Giddens 1991, Beck, Giddens and Lash 1994).[6]

Five Percent and Counting

Numerous actors have contributed to the perception of gays and lesbians as a distinct minority in the context of stressing the business advantages sexual diversity can provide. In the UK, the most successful contributor in this respect is without doubt the professional lobby organisation Stonewall,[7] which was founded in 1989 in the struggle against Section 28 of the Local Government Act (Stacey 1991).[8] One of Stonewall's initiatives is Diversity Champions, which was launched in 2001 as a forum in which employers can work with Stonewall to promote diversity in the workplace. The scheme runs workshops, seminars, regular conferences, lectures, and exchange of best practices between participating companies and organisations. Endorsements from major companies that have taken part include those from IBM, Barclays Bank, and Goldman Sachs.

A brochure describing the work of Diversity Champions points out the human costs to staff affected by prejudice and discrimination, and the costs for employers. Losing talented staff through harassment or discrimination entails extra costs in recruiting, inducting and training new staff. Stress-related absenteeism, the brochure points out, will be one cause of the £10.2 billion lost to British employers a year through staff sickness. On the other hand, robust diversity policies and practices create a healthier workplace, attract talented lesbian, gay and bisexual staff, and, as a member of Stonewall pointed out when I interviewed him, open-minded and talented heterosexuals who dislike a homophobic and discriminatory environment.

Stonewall further quantifies the benefits of sexual diversity at work through the use of statistics, even if it has difficulty providing exact figures, as do all who

---

6 For an incisive critical discussion of these kinds of claims and the often unacknowledged middle-class perspectives that inform them, see Skeggs 2004.

7 www.stonewall.org.uk

8 Passed by the Conservative government of Margaret Thatcher on May 24, 1988, Section 28 states that a local authority 'shall not intentionally promote homosexuality or publish material with the intention of promoting homosexuality', or 'promote the teaching in any maintained school of the acceptability of homosexuality as a pretended family relationship'. The legislation was eventually repealed in 2000 by the Labour government.

attempt to quantify sexual populations. 'Lesbians and gay men make up around 5% of the population. This represents a figure of 3 million potential customers and the numbers are growing as the barriers of discrimination come down', states the Diversity Champions brochure (Stonewall 2003: 5). Referring to a government report it also estimates the figure at 6 per cent of the population (Stonewall n.d.: 7). The figure comes in particularly useful when estimating the size of the gay consumer market and the profits to be made there, especially if, as the first quotation seems to suggest, the number of gay and lesbian consumers is *growing*. According to Stonewall, 'The latest data on the pink pound suggests that lesbian and gay couples without children are able to enjoy a young adult lifestyle for longer and will spend more on eating out, entertaining, holidays and leisure activities than their heterosexual counterparts' (Stonewall 2005: 5). The stereotypical content of these claims is common enough within discourses of business diversity that stress the profits to be made by flirting with gay and lesbian consumers with purchasing power.[9] What these economic arguments amount to is a minoritising discourse, that is primarily cultural, a 'young adult *lifestyle*'. But the process has not stopped with culture.

Facts of Nature

The biological 'causes' of homosexuality have been 'found' in brain structure, the hypothalamus, 'gay genes' (although nothing even approaching such a gene has been identified), and hormonal stimulation of the foetus (e.g. Le Vay 1993, Hamer and Copeland 1994). The findings of these researchers need not detain us. Suffice it to say that there are numerous and serious problems with them, including difficulties replicating findings, low statistical correlation between explanatory factors, the way that a vaguely defined influence is misconstrued – whether by researchers or the mass media – as a causal link, and the general failure to recognise that the binary of heterosexual-homosexual that guides the research is historically and culturally specific, not a natural fact of nature, see Fausto-Sterling 1985, Murphy 1997, Lancaster 2003, Roughgarden 2004.

Yet close attention to how the aetiology of sexuality is popularly understood points to a more dynamic conception of biology than a rigid sexual species model suggests. Ideologies that appeal to (or assume) 'nature' – genes, chromosomes, blood, or 'race' – understood as some form of causal mechanism that underlies and gives rise to socio-cultural differences in the service of creating and maintaining inequality, often rest on assumptions about biology in which the latter need not be fixed. So, for example, naturalisation ideas may allow the possibility that someone *becomes* a kind of person.[10] This may

---

9 See Chasin 2000, Badgett 2001.
10 For a discussion of the term 'naturalisation' and its implications, see Wade 2002.

involve biological causes but it may also refer to social practices that become a part of a person's 'nature', or 'second nature'. On occasion, it also extends to ideas of contamination, expressed, for example, in one of the commonest 'explanations' for homosexuality, namely that a young person was 'recruited' by older homosexuals. Homosexuality is here a learned behaviour, but once in place difficult and maybe impossible to change. It has become an essential part of a person's nature, one that cannot be altered. This is a dynamic view of biological matter indeed a performative explanation of sexuality combined with a static deterministic view with both in the service of heterosexist and homophobic ideologies.

The naturalisation of difference, understood as biologically predetermined sexual orientation, lent support to British legislation on the equalisation of the age of sexual consent in England, Wales and Scotland in 2000. (It took longer in Northern Ireland, Jersey, Guernsey and the Isle of Man.) Medical opinion was cited by gay and lesbian activists to 'prove' that sexual orientation is fixed at an early age and that granting homosexuals the same age of consent as heterosexuals would not lead to an increased prevalence of homosexuality. This assurance was precisely what the government, Members of Parliament, and the heterosexual general public wanted to hear. What the argument amounts to is a 'rationale of containment' (Waites 2005) in which equal rights are only granted if the heterosexual-homosexual binary is not only kept intact but even appears to be strengthened by biomedical 'facts'.

I have pointed to at least three strands within the cultural essentialisation and naturalisation of homosexuality: representations of a gay and lesbian community that puts it in the cultural (or at least consumer) vanguard of urban development; the inclusion within community cohesion of lesbians and gays as a separate category of the population on a par with ethnic minorities; and finally, an explicitly naturalising and minoritising discourse that draws on dubious medical findings and opinion in which gay men and lesbians constitute Foucault's sexual species. I want now to look more closely at some of the implications of these two strands in species and diversity thinking: the biological collective and culturally creative individual.

Genealogy and Autology

Elizabeth Povinelli (2006) discusses love, intimacy and sexuality and the tensions and demands made by what she calls 'genealogical society' and the 'autological self'.[11] The former contains ascriptions and legacies, such as kinship obligations,

---

11 She bases the contrast on her ethnography of aboriginal society in Belyuen in Australia's Northern Territory, and the Radical Faeries movement in the USA.

custom and tradition that set limits on the autonomy of the individual. By contrast, the latter resembles the self-fashioning, liberal individual unfettered by heritage.

The Enlightenment, Povinelli argues, drove Europeans slowly but surely to extricate themselves from the demands of a genealogical society and the dictates of tradition. Central to this process, according to none other than Jürgen Habermas, was self-recognition made possible by the acknowledgement of an other, which is basically a Hegelian argument about the emergence of the self. Habermas situates this selfhood within the conjugal household of heterosexual marriage. It is here that one's 'true self' could be found and confirmed. This 'intimate event', as Povinelli terms it, basically means falling in love heteronormative-European-style. It frees us from social and cultural encumbrances, 'love leaves people as they were in the Garden of Eden, merely men and women' (Povinelli 2006: 191). As Povinelli phrases it, a process of 'social strip-down and interpersonal lock-up' took place. Except that the intimate event was not available to all. 'Other cultures' outside the European tradition were unable to escape the genealogical constraints of ethnicity, race and gender. At the other extreme, we find the autological self roaming beyond the limits imposed by the conjugal couple and practising 'stranger sociality' (read non-conjugal and sometimes promiscuous forms of sexuality). (It is this autological self, in sanitised packaging, that is the darling of creative cities.) But the intimate event has a trick up its sleeve. The unencumbered, sovereign self is inserted into a social pyramid 'at the top of which is a self-governed "I", followed by the self-governing couplet of "I-thou" and the unity of "we" that unfolds out of this couplet, followed in turn by various levels of social organisation — say, our "family", "nation", "race", "culture", "religion." The truth and right of self-reflexive sovereignty means that social value runs in a specific direction along this pyramid of self-determination: I should determine I, We determine Ourselves, Races themselves, Cultures themselves, Religions themselves, but Religions should not determine cultures, cultures should not determine us, and we should not determine I' (Povinelli 2006: 192). These levels implicate and provide mutual support for each other.

New Labour's community cohesion strategy combines genealogical and autological understandings. We find inchoate ideas circulating around two principles, a genealogical/biological and an autological/cultural that interfere with each other. The autological self generates an innovative *culture*, a cosmopolitan outlook and lifestyle that are the results of the stranger sociality that provides a space in which the new can flourish. But might this innovation also be the result of an innovative *biology*? Beliefs that homosexuality is a biological fact easily conflate 'gay' innovation with gay genes. Creativity is a consequence of gene-alogy rather than its absence.

But what exactly does creativity and innovation mean in the UK?

The UK government has targeted creativity as a tool for economic survival (Leach 2004: 153). Creativity involves recombinations of elements derived from different sources, namely, the social and cultural diversity of Britain. Creative recombination is located in *individual* minds and intentions, rather than understood as collective and distributed process. This kind of recombination is a form of bricolage that emerges out of an existing culture and system of signification. The creations of the bricoleur, at least in Lévi-Strauss' formulations, if not backward-looking are certainly presentist. This kind of creativity stands in a tense relationship with some of the tenets of community cohesion, specifically that the hold of traditions – the multi-cultures – ought to weaken. Community individuals can choose amongst and recombine cultural materials in novel ways but should not be prisoners of their cultural heritage. Community attention ought instead to be focused on the future rather than the past. What we end up with is a creativity poised somewhere between a past unable completely to determine the present out of which emerges an open future. Although this is not creation ex nihilo, it is suggestive of autological selves and also Baudrillard's positive sign values released from any concrete anchorage or point of reference. If pushed to the limit, the logic of the creative autological self leads to Baudrillard's metastasis of fractal positives.

What about the genealogical selves? They are useful and of value to themselves within their own communities, but until their cultural stuff can be exchanged 'between' communities in the diversity marketplace it remains useless from the perspective of Cool Britannia. Indeed, it may even be labelled pathological and dangerous when it is not simply considered backward.

The anti-genealogical demands of community cohesion propel us in the direction of a performative culture in the expectation that it will produce novelty. Change and development in the 'correct' direction demand ruptures with the past rather than the seamless reproduction of those cultural heritages the government deems problematic. Without realising it, New Labour in its policy of Community Cohesion pursued a rather queer performative policy on matters of culture and community. The community cohesion strategy puts an emphasis on exchanges, relations, interactions and 'active mixing' (Cantle 2005: 157), which are meant to dismantle the barriers between Black and Minority Ethnic communities and the majority. This at least implies that self and other are not mutually exclusive, even if there was little to suggest that this ambition encompass the heterosexual-homosexual binary.[12] Nonetheless, the explicit logic

---

12 Just how cohesion and social order are to emerge from this greater fluidity of interaction is unclear and remains largely at the level of statements about shared norms and values (Cantle 2005: 147–50). The aim appears to be the creation of some kind of dialogical ethics (Benhabib 1992) and the promotion of social capital. More specifically, this is to be achieved through the creation of bridging capital (Putnam 1993, 2000) to

of the community cohesion strategy – that categories ought not to be reified and social boundaries ought to be permeable – is a queer kind of ambition. Properly performed these communities will not only undermine themselves but will somehow contribute towards a diverse UK that is cohesive, harmonious, innovative and not least of economic value in the competitive global market.

Values

David Graeber (2001) argues that anthropological theories of value have largely followed two options. Either they espouse theories of exchange value in which a thing is worth whatever someone is willing to give for it (a formalist or neoclassical model of value), or a Saussurean theory in which the value of a thing is conferred by its position within a field of relations, a meaningful difference between terms. Both approaches, he argues, are basically static: either reified commodities (objects) and acts of exchange, or the structure or code of Saussure's structuralism, a *langue* outside of time and action altogether.

Graeber identifies an alternative to these regnant anthropological models in Nancy Munn's (1986) work on the Gawa Islands, Papua New Guinea. Munn argues that for Gawans 'value may be characterised in terms of an act's relative capacity to extend or expand what I call *intersubjective spacetime* – a spacetime of self-other relationships formed in and through acts and practices. The general value of an act or practice is specified in terms of its *level* of potency, that is, what I sum up here as the relative expansive capacities of the spacetime formed' (1986: 9, emphasis in original). For Munn, value is about *creating* social relations, it is the recognition of an existing *potential* to form relations in 'spacetime'. Items exchanged are the medium through which the value of acts of giving is made manifest. Manifest is the operative word here; there must be an audience. Value demands recognition, or what Munn calls 'fame'.

Graeber finds Munn's approach attractive because he wants a theory of value that is not about the evaluation of objects, but of actions, a theory of value that is about potential, process, events, of becoming rather than is. Some form of recognition is probably unavoidable in the apportionment of value. However in whatever form it takes recognition can only ever be partial, in some sense a misrecognition as the complexity of persons is subsumed under

---

establish links between hitherto isolated and even antagonistic groups in pursuit of something resembling Iris Marion Young's cosmopolitan city life (Young 1990: 237). Critics of these efforts call for more attention to redistributive policies and greater responsibility for the majority society rather than attention to 'minorities'.

manageable evaluations.[13] I take this also to be Graeber's point that recognition of actions is precisely that a re-cognition that re-presents value in existing terms. He writes: 'Rather than value being the process of public *recognition* itself, already suspended in social relations, it is the way people who *could* do almost anything (including, in the right circumstances, creating entirely new sorts of social relations) assess the importance of what they do, in fact, do, as they are doing it' (2001: 47, emphasis in original). What Graeber seems to be suggesting here, at least in my reading, is that we will glimpse beyond the action's apparent meaning an alternative or implicate significance and potential, value that is something virtual or immanent perhaps, more intuitive than concrete.

Graeber and Munn move towards value in action, in practices, which positions them in the vicinity of use value. Writing of class evaluations in Britain, Beverley Skeggs (2004) also pleads for attention to use-value rather than exchange value. The latter is monopolised by members of the middle class who pilfer ('asset strip') what they perceive as the edgy and exciting parts of working-class culture to enhance their own 'prosthetic' selves. The cultural capital so obtained is then converted into economic and symbolic capital often with the help of the requisite social capital (the right connections). The working class must be closely identified with the culture extracted from them (which when it remains in their hands, however, is negatively valued), in order for that culture to appear authentic and possess exchange-value when appropriated by the middle class. The status and mobility accrued by the middle class in this manner rest and are dependent on working class fixity and immobility. Skeggs calls for use-value rather than exchange-value precisely to avoid these kinds of appropriation and devaluation. Use-value can only be known in the doing. Its value lies in actions rather than fixed positions. It is specific, local and equivalences between use-values are hard to impose unlike the equivalences on which exchange-value is based.

There are then parallels between Graeber, Munn and Skeggs. All three in their different ways seek to avoid forms of fixity that cement people and categories into positions from which they derive value. Species thinking and diversity discourses tend to do just that, they position social or cultural categories in relation to each other as part of a largely urban tableau of valuable (and entertaining and commercially exploitable) positive *differences*. The creation of positives within diversity discourses and policies, the biological population of homosexuals whose value is literally encoded in their 'genes' as biovalue (Pálsson 2007: 33–4) and develops accordingly as self-enclosed 'individuals',

---

13 In less socially differentiated settings there is likely to be a limitation on what is recognisable and considered worthy of recognition. There is a degree of consensus on what counts as valuable. In more differentiated settings value is likely to be contested, poly-valent.

and 'communities' or 'minorities', accords well with a value logic based on fixed objects. It is in stark contrast to Munn's potency. The latter is social, open, reaches beyond itself and connects to others. This going beyond – her intersubjective spacetime – cannot be fixed or static, 'heavy' is the derogatory term used by Gawans themselves; it cannot be self-absorbed.

Value in this form is a matter of implication, it indicates beyond itself, it points to potential. Munn writes of 'potency'. Value as implication avoids fixed position and equivalences. Its content can be derived from the several meanings of implication. Things, including people and ideas, implicate by involving others, by bringing them into the fold, so to speak. They implicate in the sense of attributing responsibilities and apportioning com-*pli*-city, whether innocence or guilt, and are therefore moral phenomena. They are temporal; they draw on a particular past that is implicated in what they are now and what they might become, but does not totally determine value. They also imply in the sense of pointing beyond themselves, of suggesting more than we can ever capture in our descriptions of them simply because they are implicate.

An anthropology of value then would also be an anthropology of implication. It would be inescapably ethical in its attention to past, present and future implications. It would ask why certain avenues were closed while others remained open. It would see or attempt to discern the emergence of the new in actions and events and what they imply. It would not only be an anthropology of what is but also of what might be and what could have been. To be so it would also need to be intensely empirical.

The End of the Species?

It is time to return to species. Implicate value eschews fixed objects – Whitehead's fallacy of simple location – in favour of process and concrescence. Its forward-looking momentum aligns it with autological selves, and once again there are insinuations of a neoliberal hue. However, its implicate character disallows any total rupture with the past, as in the more extreme versions of neoliberal choice and the New Labour visions of community cohesion, because the past in the present contributes to its value but cannot fully determine it. As we have seen, species thinking is preoccupied with the value or worth of things, such as a sexual or any other minority that is the source of creativity that can be encouraged, rewarded, located and 'kindly' exploited. Species thinking in Darwin's spirit resists any simple localisation because tracing a boundary around the species is a difficult if not impossible task. Implication too undermines any straightforward boundary between a creative agent and its environment; the two are implicated in each other making it hard to locate a single source or point of origin. The creativity of implication cannot only refer to processes that are traceable to our favoured objects, whether individuals, minorities, or species, it can have other addressees that include more molecular processes. Creativity is the property of assemblages, dispersed, elusive but still open to ethnographic description. This endows creativity with decidedly queer characteristics once a unified source, or species, out of which creativity and its creatures emerge gives way to difference all the way down, the starting point of process philosophy. Simple objects are simply not creative and nor are they valuable from the queer implicate point of view.

Needless to say this is not what the purveyors of diversity and species thinking want to hear. They crave objects and value with coordinates. It makes the job of identifying and exploiting creativity so much harder when extensive objects that can be grasped from the outside are replaced by intensive exploration of processes and connections from within. Perhaps this undermines species-thinking in any shape or form entirely. If so, we are simply back with Darwin's conundrum and the eternal challenge of how to capture flux with blunt instruments.

Chapter 5
Intersections

Oppression and injustice always take place somewhere, they have a whereabouts. During the last few decades feminist scholars have tracked them down to their lair, the intersection. It was the recognition by feminist scholars that the unitary categories of 'women' and 'gender' were clumsy tools with which to grasp the complexities of discrimination and injustice that led them to the 'intersection', the place where formations of class, race, and gender coincide.[1]

Intersectionality is now a broad theoretical church with its own internal dissenters and debates. There is, for example, no shortage of scholars practising intersectional analysis who are uneasy about or reject the crossroads metaphor because of what they perceive to be its overly spatialised and static character.[2] They prefer alternative terms such as 'dimension', 'field', 'configuration', or 'systems' (Davis 2011) that better capture the dynamics of discrimination. The exact object of intersectional analysis is also contested. Does intersectionality refer to individual experience and identity, or to structural phenomena irreducible to individual experience but nonetheless manifested in individual practices and their conditions of possibility (Yuval-Davis 2006)? Other scholars are concerned about reifying the categories of intersectional analysis and call for 'intra-categorical' or 'transversal' approaches (McCall 2005).[3] Yet others see

---

1 The literature is now very large and growing, but see, for example, Spelman 1988, Crenshaw 1991, Anthias and Yuval-Davis 1992, Collins 1998, McCall 2005, *European Journal of Women's Studies* 2006, Lykke 2010, Lutz et al. 2011.

2 The original intersection in intersectionality is a traffic intersection as described by Kimberlé Crenshaw (1989: 149):

Consider an analogy to traffic in an intersection, coming and going in all four directions. Discrimination, like traffic through an intersection, may flow in one direction, and it may flow in another. If an accident happens in an intersection, it can be caused by cars travelling in any number of directions and, sometimes, from all of them. Similarly, if a Black woman is harmed because she is in an intersection, her injury could result from sex discrimination or race discrimination...Sometimes the skid marks and the injuries simply indicate that they occurred simultaneously, frustrating efforts to determine which driver caused the harm.

3 The move away from categories in theory displays an interesting convergence with a similar policy move. The British Labour government adopted a policy on social integration and cohesion (discussed in Chapter 4) which attempted to break down communities and groups into individuals with multiple identifications who suffer

the proliferation of intersectional categories of discrimination as a problem and wonder how many categories there are. Is the number limitless especially if we include every nuance of identity as a potential candidate for inclusion? They ask at what point does inclusivity undermine theoretical power and trivialise the more 'fundamental' differences of class, race, and gender (Knapp 2005, Ludwig 2006)?

I do not pretend to have the answers to all these questions. My aim in this chapter is to perform a queer dis-location or dis-alignment of the intersection metaphor qua spatial location well aware as I do so that it has already been critically interrogated from multiple angles by practitioners of intersectionality. However, rather than eschew the crossroads metaphor, as others have done, I explore it from within in some detail to find out where it leads. To aid me I draw on recent anthropological work on lines.

The goal of this exploration is not an attempt to deliver a final adjudication on the merits of an intersectional approach. I sympathise with the ambition to provide as comprehensive a description and understanding as possible of the multiple factors that impinge on all our lives and the role they play in creating and maintaining inequality and injustice. I regard such an ambition as integral to any critical social theory and it is not my intention to derail such a project. This does not, however, alleviate some misgivings I have on the details of intersection. Whether what follows amounts to a rejection of intersectionality, a cautionary note or an elaboration of it, I leave to others to decide.

First we need to ask what exactly intersects.

Sections

Race, gender, class, religion, sexuality, age, disability, regional belonging, nationality, cigarette smokers, which of these subject positions, characteristics, practices, and in some cases identities qualifies as a 'section'? Intersectionality has for the most part concentrated on race, gender and class, other 'sections' have received rather less attention. One thing is immediately apparent, the sections most frequently found in intersectional texts refer to subjugated people, the disadvantaged, the marginalised and the despised. Not everyone is a

---

discrimination on multiple rather than group-specific grounds (McGhee 2008: 116). While attempts to reformulate intersectionality do not intend to individualise the facts of discrimination, in part by paying less attention to identities, the policy example from the UK points clearly in this direction. Attempts to deconstruct categories, especially perhaps in a neoliberal environment, face the challenge of how to avoid individuation and fragmentation, and perhaps even Baudrillard's metastasis.

member of the intersectional club.[4] The middle-class, white, male (and female), able-bodied, gender and sexually normative person is not the first to spring to mind when talk is of intersectionality. It therefore behooves any theory that deals primarily with the marginalised and subordinated to look with extra care at the implications of its theoretical terms for the people who are its object of study. Well-meaning theory can have unfortunate normative consequences. A first question we need to ask is: Where do these sections come from?

As Wendy Brown (2005: 122–30) argues, subjects are *created* through different modalities of power and not only oppressed, a Foucauldian point sometimes neglected in intersectional studies. But subjects that have gender, sexuality, 'race', and class are not the result of the same processes. They have different histories, and are the products of different institutional complexes that seize upon bodies in different ways, make different demands on subjects, and regulate them accordingly. Brown draws on legal studies to illustrate her claim. For example, sodomy statutes constitute a legal subject – the homosexual – that is a potential criminal from the start. By contrast, gender, race and class do not construct peoples as criminal for what are assumed to be inherent characteristics. Issues of maternity, such as freedom from discrimination for pregnant women, are not obviously class or racial matters. The regulation of workers in the workplace, access to the means of production, the right to join a union, and the right to strike, are not the result of the same modalities of power that shape sexuality. Fantasies of the elimination of 'gay' foetuses or the aborting of female foetuses in preference for male are not in any obvious ways about the production of class subjects. The debates about whether same-sex sexual orientation is a lifestyle choice or biological destiny and the political and legal consequences that flow from these would never be applied to race. Despite the recognition that subjects are produced through different formations of power, the respective contributions of these different formations do not take place in the form of separate and discrete units (cf. Walby 2007). Analysis may demand their disentanglement, but the perspective this theoretical lens provides does not correspond to living subjectivities.

Take 'transgender', a possible addition to the intersectional catalogue, as an example. In his conceptual ethnography, David Valentine (2007) has studied the appearance and usage of the term in New York in the 1990s among a range of social actors including people who identify themselves as transsexuals, pressure groups, and medics.

Like all categories, transgender has a history, a particular genealogy that can help us understand why it appeared at a certain juncture in time. Valentine argues that, at least in his fieldwork context, it emerged at a moment when private, respectable, gay identities became the property of white middle-class

---

4 On whether or not cigarette smokers count as an oppressed category of people, see Davina Cooper 2004: 40–67.

gays and lesbians in a political move intended to win social acceptance for the 'correct' forms of homosexuality.[5] Thus white, male, gay-identified men, he argues, rejected the feminine label attached to male homosexuality, which they found demeaning, and coded gay as gender normative. In all respects other than sexual preferences and practices gay men were, or ought to be, indistinguishable from other men. In effect, then, (homo)sexuality and gender were divided from each other and lived 'separately', sexuality does not automatically demand a particular form of gender and vice-versa.

Valentine wonders whether our linguistic categories encourage the impression that 'gender' and 'sexuality' are indeed distinct objects, experientially, epistemologically, and ontologically. The question he asks is: Just how can they be experienced separately? How are we to account for the experiences of transgendered and transsexual people who do not feel that their lives are lived in accordance with these categories? Or, for that matter, anyone who at one time or another has had occasion to wonder about what it means for them personally to be/do a woman or a man, or be/do gender in whatever form. Is the 'failure' to recognise oneself in the available categories – popular and academic – one of conceptual confusion on the part of the person concerned or the inability of those self-same categories to capture the complexity of how this person lives her life? Are our categories able to accommodate a Latino, cross-dressing sex worker who has had breast implants, but who has not undergone sex reassignment surgery, insists that she has always been a woman and calls herself 'gay'. The question can just as easily be applied to the members of other sections.

I shall return to this and related questions later. But first we turn to a specific intersection as an introduction to some of the themes I want to discuss.

Intersection

I take as my example one of the most famous intersections in the world. Gravelly Hill Interchange is junction 6 of the M6 motorway where it meets the

---

5 Valentine's argument closely resembles that of Beverley Skeggs and colleagues (Skeggs 2004, Moran et al. 2004) in the UK context, although he does not refer to their work. 'Propriety', Skeggs argues, is tied to 'property' and specific places such as the regenerated inner city of Manchester and its 'Gay Village', where those of the correct class who display the 'proper' gender and sexuality – a respectable, largely white, gay male variety – are welcome as representatives of the middle-class, cosmopolitan (and profitable) urban gay culture Manchester promotes, while the class and gender deviant, such as working-class women – the 'hens' – are discouraged.

More generally the issue is one of access to the public sphere and who qualifies as a 'representative' of the 'gay and lesbian community', cf. Clarke 2000.

INTERSECTIONS

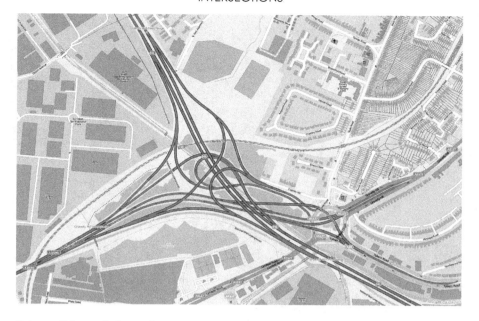

5.1 Map of Gravelly Hill Interchange in Birmingham
Source: OpenStreetMap from Wikimedia, reproduced on a Creative Commons Licence.

A38 (M) Aston Expressway in Birmingham, United Kingdom. The junction covers 30 acres (12 hectares), serves 18 routes and includes 4 km (2.5 miles) of slip roads, but only 1 km (0.6 miles) of the M6 itself. Across five different levels, it has 559 concrete columns, reaching up to a height of 24.4 metres (80 ft). Construction started in 1968 and the junction opened in November 1972. It immediately became known as Spaghetti Junction on account of its seemingly endless tangle of roads and flyovers in which drivers got lost – they still do.

The first question to ask is: From whose perspective do we see the intersection? I write 'see' because intersection strongly suggests a visual phenomenon, a position on high from which the entire intersection can be observed. What do we see when we survey an intersection?

Seen from on high in the form of a two-dimensional map (Figure 5.1) the intersection is simply a network of criss-crossing lines with little detail visible. If we descend to a lower altitude, structure emerges as in Figure 5.2. The lines transform into roads, many of which do not even touch, but pass over and under each other with no physical contact between them. Strictly speaking there is no intersection. There also seems to be some kind of hierarchy present, some roads are broader with several lanes of traffic, while others are comparatively narrow.

The roads also mutate as some smaller slip roads become part of larger routes, which in their turn merge with and become part of even larger motorways. If

5.2 Aerial view of Gravelly Hill Interchange, Birmingham a.k.a. Spaghetti Junction, September 2008

Source: Wikimedia, reproduced on a Creative Commons Licence.

you were to get really close and enter the intersection as a motorist, you might find yourself on a road passing under a flyover without any clear idea of the intersection as a whole.

There are some surprises in wait too. It turns out that not all the lines on the map are roads. There are in fact three canals running through the Gravelly Hill Interchange, the Grand Union Canal, the Birmingham and Fazeley Canal, and the Tame Canal. Horse-drawn barges still traffic their waters. There are also two rivers, the Tame and the Rea, and even railway lines (Figure 5.3).

The different modalities of power discussed by Brown are analogous to the different routes that make up an intersection in my metaphorical model – motorways, b-roads, slip roads, canals, rivers and railway tracks. These are not compatible with each other, although some are more compatible than others. Canals can combine with rivers, and slip roads can combine with motorways, but

5.3 Motorway, railway and waterway at Gravelly Hill Interchange, Birmingham, © Optimist on the run, 2009 / CC-BY-SA-3.0 & GFDL-1.2

Source: Wikimedia, reproduced on a Creative Commons Licence.

railway tracks remain, and must remain, in a category of their own. Obviously, all sections of the intersection must *not* intersect. If roads, canals, and railway lines were to meet, there would be catastrophe.

Rephrased in more theoretical terms, to navigate an 'intersection' it may be necessary to shift perspective and theoretical position radically within the intersection. In which case it is difficult to see an intersection as a node of ontologically separate categories although some treat it as such (Yuval-Davis 2006). We are after all looking at material practices, and materiality is always implicate, it folds within it the totality of relations that it partly expresses at any given moment (Ingold 2011: 237). Different formations will be more or less relevant depending on the theoretical trajectory and goals chosen. The result is always partial, never total. But not only do they have different physical natures, the parts of the intersection also have different temporalities, the leisurely barge on the canal, the car that proceeds in fits and starts in the traffic jam, and the high speed train. All proceed at their own pace, their own tempo. Again, in more theoretical terms, different dimensions of inequality exploit and subjectify at different rates and take hold of subjects most fully at different times in their lives. Gender and race usually begin at birth, if not earlier, whereas the 'wrong' sexuality will only be fully grasped by formations of sexuality at a later date, often but not always in the teens.

One question that follows from this is where is the intersection? What is to be counted as a part of the intersection when some of its component parts are mutually exclusive? Where do we 'draw the line', both in the sense of circumscribing our object of study and in the disciplinary sense of setting a limit? And finally, and of great interest to our drivers sitting in their cars somewhere in Spaghetti Junction, how does one escape the intersection? Where are the exits? It is now time to look more closely at lines.

Lines

To think of things is to think in terms of lines for, as Tim Ingold writes: 'Every thing is a parliament of lines' (Ingold 2007: 5). In Chapter 1, we saw that things are the result of deliberation and disputes at places, places that have been occluded by the static, Cartesian idea of a thing as an object occupying a particular point in time and space, and the only possible occupant of that specific coordinate. To reach these places we must follow lines, or paths, that converge on a point and think in terms of coordinates, the places where lines intersect.

An intersection is a place. According to Ingold, 'Once a moment of rest along a path of movement, place has been reconfigured in modernity as a nexus within which all life, growth and activity are *contained*' (2007: 96, emphasis in original). It is *inside* the containers – the places – that things happen. Between the containers are connections – lines – in the form of transport networks such as roads, tracks and air traffic routes that link towns, cities, and countries to each other. The lines themselves are static, things move *along* them, but do not create them. But what if the lines were not static and what if they did not stop at the place, in the manner of connectors between nodes? We would then have lines of movement that cross, circle and double back on themselves. The lines create a knot, but as Ingold puts it, these 'lines are bound together *in* the knot, but they are not bound *by* it' (2007: 100, emphasis in original). The point Ingold wishes to make is that if we see the lines as life courses, which is how Ingold encourages us to view life processes in general (2007: 103), or the movement of people and other living things, then the knots do not *contain* their lives, rather the lines *are* their lives unfolding. Life is not the line, which is only the trace it leaves, but the very endpoint of the line at its point of emergence. If life takes place along the lines it traces as it goes, then somehow our methods need to capture this movement as an unfolding or explicating line.

The important point to derive from Ingold's argument is that the lives of people are not confined to a particular place, a container. We may have constructed a Cartesian world of fixed coordinates, bound places, and connecting lines along which the commuter sitting in a car and stuck in a traffic jam (or Spaghetti Junction) moves from one place (home) to another place (work) along a motorway that passes through an anonymous landscape, but is this how we mostly live? The intersection metaphor, I would argue as others have done, leads to attempts to define people by their position at a particular point in space. There is an inevitable risk of fixity in this metaphor.

An intersection suggests a confluence or meeting point at which the subject stands. The sections are external to the subject, they are structures that precede the subject they produce. The very metaphor of intersection made up of converging lines suggests movement towards a *point* from elsewhere. But what is it that moves? There is a suggestion of external forces creating the subject. As we saw earlier, this external model of power as 'impact' fails to grasp how power, in a Foucauldian sense, inhabits subjects and the very processes of subjectification themselves. Such a model of power raises the question of how does the subject move? Does she have a line of her own? And if she does is it separate from the intersection that converges in/at her? In short, how does she move on from the coordinate created by the intersection? Remember that the word 'section' also means to sequester and incarcerate someone, often when they are deemed to be mentally ill. We might also want to recall here the significance of crossroads as sites for the burial of suicides and executed criminals. Considered to be social outcasts and ritually unclean they were buried at crossroads because, like a knot, a crossroads could incarcerate their troubled souls and prevent them from wandering around amongst the living. Employing the knotty metaphor of the intersection may well run its own risks of incarceration.

This ought, perhaps, to come as no surprise. Lines can ensnare us (a snare is after all a string or thread). Alfred Gell (1998) argues this point in his claim that complex patterns, such as Celtic loops inscribed onto the surface of a door, serve to protect what is behind them from evil spirits and demons. The spirits see the pattern and are so intrigued by it that they attempt to unravel it, but without success. The patterns eventually lead back to the point of origin and the spirits get stuck in them and never pass through the door. The pattern, writes Gell, acts like 'demon fly-paper' (1998: 84). As Ingold notes, Gell's striking simile presupposes a demon's eye view, an aerial perspective not unlike the intersectional viewpoint. Seen from on high an intersection does appear as lines on a map or surface, but once on the ground something happens. The lines take on solidity and become material, like the passageways of a maze or the network of roads. The intersection as an object disappears for the driver negotiating a particular stretch of Gravelly Hill. To get out we must follow these passageways or perhaps a lifeline, like the one given to Theseus by Ariadne, his very own line of flight out of the labyrinth of Knossos.

An intersection is then a good term for a coordinate or meeting place, but less useful for providing instructions about the nearest exit.

Textures

The ability of lines, qua threads, to cross, converge and loop allows them to create knots, and from these knots more complex things can result. If woven or knitted together, lines create materials or texts – the Latin for weave is *texere*.[6] Once woven together, lines change their character on becoming parts of the material, the matter, they create. Weaving lines together at the intersection may then produce something that is no longer recognisable as the lines that led us to it and formed it. If we regard the sections in intersectionality as converging threads, then what happens to them once they are woven together? Once intersected what is there to guarantee that something new is not created and if this is the case, do we still have gender, class, or race?

Weaving does not only create surfaces, it can also create depth and 3-dimensionality in the tissues of a body (the word tissue too is derived from *texere* via the French *tistre*). One of the original intersectional texts by Kimberlé Crenshaw (1991) employs a 2-dimensional metaphor. The intersection of race and gender produces one position to be occupied: gendered race or racialised gender. Other ways of conceptualising the interplay of modalities of power provide a more dynamic and layered model, such as Stuart Hall's (1996) concept of 'articulation'. Articulations are three-dimensional and reverberate *throughout* a social formation rather than creating a particular point within it. They are, we might say, holographic. The social is not a surface on which lines are drawn but a structure with depth, and also interconnections rather than intersections.

The metaphor of being woven as a subject, rather than inscribed as one (although inscriptions too involve lines), points toward the need for a disentanglement if we are to analyse what goes into a subject's formation. This is clearly conveyed in the following quotation which relies heavily on lines without

---

6 Even the word for line has a textual dimension. The seventeenth-century English word 'line' also meant lint, or flax, a type of cloth. Lint is derived from *linea*, originally meaning a thread made from flax, *linum*. Once woven together the threads produce the cloth now known as linen with which garments are lined (Ingold 2007: 61).

picking up the thread, so to speak, of some of the theoretical implications I explore here:

> One of the great strengths of social and cultural analysis is that it can tease apart the *ties* that connect gender and sexuality and reveal the multiplicity of *strands* from which they are *woven* and which, in turn, *weave* gendered and sexual relations into the wider social *fabric*. Queer theory has, of course, contributed to this project; some of its canonical *texts* sought to *disentangle* sexuality from gender and reveal the contingency of their relationship. (Jackson 2006: 39, emphases added)

The process of 'disentangling' of which Stevi Jackson writes demands a degree of reflexivity, whether on the part of the theorist attempting to understand others or on the part of a person attempting to isolate and understand 'components' of practice. Much of life proceeds at an unconscious, pre-reflexive level of practices, where there is no differentiation present, and where 'sections', whether for the person concerned or an outside observer, are neither relevant nor apparent. Some degree of reflexivity is needed to make them materialise, and this requires the creation of 'distance' between observer and observed. When practice becomes the object of reflection, it is divided within itself. But it is not only practices that can be divided, matter itself is cut up, sectioned, by the desire to create objects. To illustrate this, take the example of people classed by medical science as intersexed.

Vivi-sections

'[I]f culture demands gender, physicians will produce it, and of course, when physicians produce it, the fact that gender is "demanded" will be hidden from everyone' (Kessler 2000: 75). The case of people diagnosed as intersexed makes Evelyn Kessler's point abundantly clear. They are literally subject to a vivisection, a surgical cut that divides their living flesh in the interests of creating gender normativity. The cut sexes them. (See Chapter 1 on the sexing of matter and things.)

The term *inter*-sexed suggests a relation *between* sexes, but intersexed people are not between anything. The spatial language is misleading. There is no 'inter' in the bodies of the intersexed. There is no juncture, no crossroads, no convergence, no mixture and no intersection. There is a whole person already present. 'If my genital anatomy is other than male or female, this is not a defect or deformity; I am as I am meant to be. I affirm my capacity to be *whole* as an asexual person' (Kessler 2000: 78, emphasis added). So said Toby, who was born with non-standard genitals, was raised as a girl, lived as a boy from age twelve for five years, and now self-identifies as 'neuter'.

To sex the intersexed person requires a cut – categorical and surgical. The medical response to genital anomalies is to separate, to section, not to create a whole but to divide and remove. Some intersexed people talk of having been murdered, or at least that part of them that was subjected to surgical invasion. 'I have managed to calm down my murderous rage at [the] professionals, but I'll probably never get over what my parents did to me by trying to *kill me off*' (Kessler 2000: 85, emphasis added). People diagnosed as intersexed experience *intra*-sections which divide their flesh into parts or morphologies that are recognisable to medical science and in conformity with dominant models of sexed bodies, but not necessarily in accordance with how the people experience themselves. To sex is after all to assign to categories, which are mutually exclusive. Or, following Barad, the process is one of 'intra-action' in pursuit of the creation of a determinate object. Generally speaking, western medical science has found it hard to tolerate indeterminate sexes and has created determinate ones by cutting flesh.

Kessler provides examples of doctors talking of intersexed babies and children as if the penis or the vagina, as doctors believe they ought to appear, are simply waiting for the surgeon to reveal them, rather than cut them into shape in accordance with cultural expectations. Physicians 'reveal' a penis or a vagina which was hidden in a mixture that made it difficult, at first, to *determine* the individual elements. Katrina Karkazis' (2008) study of American medical practices reveals the extent of the heteronormative presuppositions surrounding gender assignment and sexuality. One doctor stated: 'If you're a woman with a big clitoris, you're likely to turn into a dyke. People never say it in that kind of cruel, inappropriate way, but that's the association people make' (Karkazis 2008: 149). Another expressed feelings of disgust: 'These girls don't look right. It's unsettling. It's repulsive. You just cannot leave them looking like that!' (Karkasis 2008: 147).

The surgical decisions do not only provide a determinate gender, they also produce parents of a gendered child. Just as to be a subject is to be a gendered subject, to be a parent is to be the parent of a gendered child. Kessler writes of one family in which the parents of an intersexed child told everyone that they had had twins, a boy and a girl. Once the sex of the child was determined by surgery, they told everyone that the other twin had died (Kessler 2000: 21). Parents, Kessler reports, were encouraged by doctors not to think of the intersexed child as a boy or a girl, but simply as a child, but apparently the parents were unable to do so (Kessler 2000: 21). To be a parent is to parent a child, and for a child to qualify as a child it must have a gender. Until that gender is determined parenthood is, at least for some people, itself on hold, indeterminate, as parents wrestle with the fact that they do not know how to parent an ungendered child.

The *productivity* of the surgical intervention does not stop with the child or the parents. To some extent the surgical cut also produces the physician. It certainly creates a type of physician, one who 'corrects' (both in the sense of to rectify but also perhaps to discipline) the body of the intersexed by bringing it into line (that word again) with heteronormative expectations surrounding sex, gender and sexuality.

Intra-actions Revisited

The making of divisions within practice, matter, and human flesh, returns us to agential realism and intra-actions discussed in Chapter 1.

'Race', 'class', 'gender', 'sexuality', 'ethnicity' and so on are often treated as the property of individuals, like objects. A point made by performative theories of gender is that gender is a doing, a practice, rather than the essence for which it is mistaken. This does not make it any less real because 'realness does not imply thingness'. It does not presuppose a world of pre-existing objects. Discourses make possible what can be said and are part of what they produce, they enact cuts and create objects from within phenomena in the form of a local determination that produces the observer of the objects and the objects observed. These objects can be described as a mixture, but the original entanglement (an appropriately knotty metaphor suggestive of lines) remains.

An intersectional analysis effects an agential cut and produces a mixture of separate objects. Different cuts resolve the ontological inseparability within the phenomenon along different lines depending on which category interests us. But if we take seriously the idea of material-discursive practices on which Barad draws, these objects are only local and temporary determinations that crystallise out of the original entanglement.

Phrased differently, the representational strategy needed to make sections appear effects a division internal to lived practice that results in the production of discrete 'objects' that are understood to be the products of wider material-discursive formations. Different theoretical (measuring) apparatuses will cut up the entanglement that is lived practice along different lines producing different combinations (mixtures) of sections. But once practice resumes, the division will subside back into the subject. The kind of reflexive stance needed to effect an agential cut can only make a difference in a local, specific and temporary way. However, the agential cuts that produce the observer and observed need not and almost certainly do not correspond to the implicate character of practices. Moreover, this cut can be accomplished not only by the analyst but also through the reflexive work of the people who are the entanglement that is disentangled by the agential cut. Intersectionality works with *mixtures*, a combination of individual or separate states or elements each with its own determinate value (in relation to the others). The mixture emerges as such once we measure certain properties. But because a measurement can only make certain things determinate, the properties that are not part of the experimental arrangement – and this includes our analytical categories – remain indeterminate and as such not part of the mixture. In other words, the cut always produces exclusions that prevent a total view, not all parts of the intersection can manifest themselves. To repeat Barad's words: '*only part of the world can be made intelligible to itself at a time, because the other part of the world has to be the part that it makes a difference to*' (Barad 2007: 351, emphasis in original).

Holistic Ambitions

Sections suggest a whole to which the sections contribute. What is this whole? Is there some kind of prior unity? Where is it located, in society, the subject, or only in the sociological imagination? Is the holism a product of the analysis itself, or is it already present in the unity of practice, the seamlessness of living which is of necessity broken apart to allow the analysis to commence?

Although holism has been a leitmotif of anthropology as part of its ambition to contextualise and render other cultures in as much detail as possible, there has never been, nor could there ever be, a fully holistic depiction of other cultures and societies.[7] Recognition of this fact has paved the way for mereological studies that deal with the relationship of parts to wholes, or sections to subjects in the parlance of intersectionality. Phrased simply, all knowledge is partial, about parts, even though we may aspire to provide holistic accounts. Such accounts are illusory, there can be no final, all-knowing perspective on the world because knowledge is always focused upon an object and objects, as I have repeatedly argued, emerge from exclusions and cuts. They involve extraction from a manifold or the partial disentangling of an entanglement or the actualisation of the virtual. Recognising that our knowledge is only ever part of what there is to know leaves room for other, sometimes complementary rather than simply competing, versions of the world. It also leaves room for new knowledge. Completeness must be abandoned although this does not and ought not to exclude attempts to be as comprehensive as possible.

Arguably, in the intersectional approach there is a longing for a holism able to account for all that contributes to the subject. Certainly, if an intersectional model is intended to fill in the blanks previously left by one-dimensional models of 'gender' or 'class' or 'race', and their simple addition in an ampersand model

---

7 For recent discussions of holism in anthropology, see Otto and Bubandt 2010.

– gender & race & class – then it appears to be an improvement. The subject can be de-*line*ated with the help of the converging lines of the intersection. But is a description of a fully present subject a realistic goal?

Intersectionality is interesting from a queer point of view precisely because it appears to have totalising ambitions: the mapping by a coordinated means of formations of oppression. This seems to promise a 'completion' of the subject and perhaps an overly socialised picture of it. As such, it is at least partly at odds with queer theory's interrogations of subject positions. Seen from this perspective it appears that intersectionality and queer theory are moving in opposite directions.[8]

The term 'position' itself suggests a place whose whereabouts is fully understood, like a map coordinate. Queer relationships to space point to the difficulty of equating where with here (see Graham 1998). The location and position of social agents – as constructed in analysis – does not automatically tell 'us' about 'their' authentic interests, and thereby enable us to attribute a correct or false consciousness to them.[9] Nor does it tell us how people themselves will interpret their own location, or what theories and models they will use to make sense of their positions. Subject positions do not exactly correspond to the experiences and practices of individuals as the earlier examples of transgender and transsexual people make clear. Conflating the two runs the risk of reducing people to oppressed subjects whose subjectivity is prefigured in the oppression that forms them at an intersection. This would make intersectionality pre-formative. In theory, we could play the intersectional process in reverse to find the real or the present in the possible of the past. An intersection can never therefore be exhaustive no matter at what level we pitch it. This point is perhaps obvious but nonetheless important when applied to the tendency to equate gay and lesbian identity with a queer subjectivity. The latter implies a denaturalising critique of identities that the former may not share: to be a lesbian or to embrace another local version of same-sex sexuality is not necessarily to be queer in any disruptive or challenging sense. Witness the writings of conservative gay men like Andrew Sullivan (1995) and Bruce Bawer (1993).

---

8 Some scholars argue that intersectionality and queer theory complement each other, see Dietze et al. 2007.

9 Anthropology has its own tradition of 'localising strategies' (Fardon 1990) that equate certain places with specific cultures. In, for example, studies of same-sex sexualities this includes the 'Sotadic zone' of the Middle East, the identification of semen exchanges with parts of Melanesia, hierarchies of sexual penetration in Latin America and ancient Greece, and third genders on the plains of North America. The problem with these strategies is that they simplify by adopting a dominant optic through which to view an entire culture or even geographical region, one calibrated to some details but unable to distinguish others.

I have made use of spatial themes on numerous occasions in this book and fully recognise the importance of spatiality to sexuality and gender (Graham 1998). That said, for the above reasons I also feel that caution is needed. To put someone or something 'in its place' is, as the saying implies, to place them — spatially and conceptually — where they ought to be. It is a form of discipline. As a spatial metaphor, intersection runs risks similar to any other localising strategy. Fixing is often a strategy of the privileged employed to control the weak. As I noted at the start of this chapter, intersectionality is not usually assumed to refer to the powerful and the wealthy. Furnishing the intersected with exit options ought, then, to be as much a part of any analysis (regardless of whether or not we call it intersectional) as the cartographic aim to find our coordinates.

Chapter 6
Failures

Queer oracle, the late Eve Kosofsky Sedgwick famously argued that in western cultures the heterosexual–homosexual divide maps onto a host of other cultural categories such as innocence v. initiation, domestic v. foreign, natural v. artificial, and so on, which are not immediately seen to be related to the heterosexual-homosexual binary, but nonetheless inform it. The first term in each couplet coincides with heterosexuality and is positively valued while the second pertains to homosexuality and has a negative valency (Sedgwick 1990: 11). At the same time, Sedgwick concedes, in a footnote, that: 'My casting of all these definitional nodes in the form of binarisms, I should make explicit, has to do with a felt need to schematise in some consistent way the treatment of social vectors so exceedingly various. The kind of falsification necessarily performed on each by this reduction cannot, unfortunately, itself be consistent' (Sedgwick 1990: 11, n.19). In short, binaries are by no means the entire story; indeed, they are an inevitable 'falsification' of a messy reality.

One of my main concerns in this chapter is to explore the implications of these arbitrary binaries for failure. Heteronormative regimes can do little else than cast queer sexualities in the role of failures – biological, moral, social, economic and cultural. According to Judith Halberstam 'success in a heteronormative, capitalist society equates too easily to specific forms of reproductive maturity combined with wealth accumulation' (2011: 2). She does not wish to redefine the criteria of success but to dismantle its logic, and argues that 'under certain circumstances failing, losing, forgetting, unmaking, undoing, unbecoming, not knowing may in fact offer more creative, more cooperative, more surprising ways of being in the world' (pp. 2–3). Rephrased: We learn from our mistakes. Avoiding the logic of success and failure can involve standing outside of, for example, patriarchal norms to reformulate what it means to be a woman (e.g. Wittig 1992). But doesn't this locate the alternatives in an outside, a margin? Halberstam's failure is reactive, a form of resistance. Although she concentrates on textual matters – film, biography and photography – she largely ignores the smorgasbord of failures amongst the 'successful' on offer in the genre examined herein and on the streets outside.

In this chapter, I want to examine the supposed dividing line between heterosexual and homosexual within the cultural imaginary and the assumption even demand that it map onto success v. failure by examining gossip magazines and 'real life' television programmes. Both the magazines and the programmes are almost unavoidable as they appear on billboards, television, the tabloid press and magazines at the supermarket checkouts. They are part of the repertoire of sexual stories that permeate western cultures (see Plummer 1995). Focusing on the sexual stories allows us to turn the tables and place heterosexuality under scrutiny. When doing so, we ought perhaps to recall that for Freud heterosexuality was the end result of a ghastly drama of envy, patricide, guilt, castration fears and trauma. Remember that Sophocles' play, *Oedipus Rex*, which Freud repeatedly refers to, is a tragedy. Freud himself regarded heterosexuality as a puzzle in need of an explanation, not a self-evident fact of nature. He certainly did not see it as the key to paradise, unlike many of his more sexually conservative followers and successors. Certainly, the mass media representations examined here lend little support to the notion that heterosexuality is a bed of roses.

Magazines

The material on which this chapter is based includes the Swedish magazines *Se & Hör*, *Hänt Extra*, *Veckans Nu!*, *Hänt bild* and *Svensk Damtidning* which I consulted during the period September 2003 to January 2004. Alongside the magazines, I have watched hours of television programmes devoted to heterosexual pairing. By this I mean the programmes in which heterosexual couples are either created through rather elaborate and contrived dating games, or tested to the point of breaking in equally contrived circumstances. These included *The Batchelor*, *For Love or Money*, *Meet My Folks*, and *Joe Millionaire*. However, in this chapter I shall confine my comments to the Scandinavian version of *Temptation Island*.

One of the most striking things to note about the magazines is their stylistic peculiarities. I refer to the exclamation mark! Most gossip magazines suffer from a severe rash of exclamation marks! Nothing is low key in this strange world of exaggerated enthusiasm. Every new relationship, personal revelation, 'confession', sordid detail, or snippet of gossip deserves an exclamation mark! The tempo in this world is nothing short of frantic.

Couples

What are the first impressions of heterosexuality we get from the magazines? What picture of heterosexuality do they paint? One of their most obvious features is their emphasis on couples. Page after page is covered with pictures of heterosexual pairs at various occasions, whether it be at a wedding, a celebrity party, or the premier of a film.

Whatever the event, it is an excuse to display heterosexuals arm in arm. Even celebrities not accompanied by a spouse or partner usually appear with a 'friend', rarely is anyone alone. Of course, bussing in dozens of celebrities to a party guarantees publicity and bestows the occasion, however banal, with a certain glamour that provides a backdrop for the heterosexual cavalcade, and the occasional gay or lesbian.

Royals

The obsession with royal families runs like a thread throughout the genre of gossip magazines. In only one issue of *Svensk Dam tidning* (8–14 January, 2004) we can read the following: A five-page article (2–5, 64) on Prince Charles and Camilla Parker Bowles: 'She has had to put up with a lot for love, but how many scandals can she take?' In fact, the piece is not about scandals at all. On the contrary, it paints a rosy picture of Charles and Camilla's relationship. 'Life is sweet for Charles and Camilla, who finally dare to have fun together and openly show the love they had to keep secret year after year.' For any other couple this would have been a story of a betrayed wife – Diana – false marriage vows witnessed by billions from the future King of England and Head of the Anglican Church in St Paul's Cathedral, and living a lie. But, it seems, in this case, it being a (half-) royal couple, it is the love that dared not speak its name. Five pages (6-10) telling readers about Queen Silvia of Sweden's sixtieth birthday, complete with family photos, the birthday cake, the party and guests – lots of couples featured – a night at the opera, and more guests. On two pages (36–7) in the same issue we can also read about Denmark's Princess Alexandra and Prince Joachim, her 'humble' beginnings in Hong Kong (she was the director of a marketing company), how she met her prince, their children, and her difficulties with the cold climate of Denmark. A two-page 'Royal Confection' about who is having a baby, who is buying a puppy, who is having a house extension, and so on.

Weddings

Weddings are an opportunity not to be missed. They are usually 'fairytale', there are plenty of photo opportunities as the famous and not so famous Swedish, and sometimes foreign, guests line up to be photographed. Everyone is radiant, the bride is overjoyed, her family is proud, and happiness is complete.

Divorces

Happy heterosexual couples are profiled, but it is an even better story when the happiness is shattered, preferably only a few weeks later. In September 2003 we read about Sven-Göran Eriksson, former manager of England's football team, and then partner Nancy Dell'Olio: 'Sven and Nancy's wedding happiness' and that 'the joy is complete. All the storm clouds have blown away'. In actual fact it's all about an ordinary holiday in the Mediterranean. Three months later we read: 'Has Svennis tired of his Italian full blood? Nancy has turned his life upside down and created a career of her own. It irritates him. Will she ever be Mrs. Nancy Eriksson? Loving kisses have been replaced by quarrels'. 'She wants to get married and have children. He does everything to avoid it' (*Se & Hör* 7 January 2004).

In a similar vein: 'Leonardo and Gisele together again, but for how long?' A double page spread shows actor Leonardo di Caprio on a bike 'walking' Gisele's dog: 'A man who walks a woman's dog is for life they say, but does Gisele notice? The neighbours have complained about their noisy fights. Gisele's once so impressive dinner service has shrunk a lot the last six months' (*Se och Hör* 17 September 2003).

Gossip

Then there is gossip. The meaningless chit chat that fills much of the magazines, often with a little sex to liven up what is otherwise a very uninteresting story, such as the following example: 'Robinson' Vincent reveals his past as a gigolo'. But readers can relax, all this happened far away in Los Angeles, not in Sweden. 'Vincent tried to make his way as an actor and fashion model'. 'The occasions when Vincent was an "escort" were full of celebrities and glamorous. The women were often millionaires and twice as old as the Robinson challenger.'

Lesbian Titillation

The treatment of homosexuality in these Swedish magazines is generally speaking politically correct. Homophobia is rarely present. Yet at the same time there is a small sub-genre of 'lesbian' stories in which foreigners feature in saucy lesbian escapades clearly intended to titillate the reader. This is a little puzzling as the magazines are aimed at a largely heterosexual female readership. Are they the ones to be thrilled, or is it their male companions? Here are a couple of examples involving rap star Eminem and Mel B, former member of the UK group Spice Girls:

> The relationship between Eminem and wife Kim has been very stormy to say the least. But Eminem is having difficulty breaking up because Kim is bisexual. The star's uncle told American television that the rapper doesn't just come home to his wife but to everyone else in bed. Why wouldn't you want to have a wife who waits for you with other women? Surely it's every man's dream! (*Se och Hör* 17 September 2003).

Mel B comes out of the closet, "Made love with a stripper in the Toilet!" It was last winter when Mel turned up at The Honeypot. Dawn Macintosh, one of the strippers, who performs under the name of Summer, recognized her immediately...I was lost from the first moment...and Dawn got her chance. Mel paid for a private show and Dawn took her by the hand and led her to a booth, sat her in the black velvet armchair and closed the curtain. Then she placed her hands on Mel's knee, leaned forward and whispered seductively in her ear: "I'll show you mine if you show me yours." But if Dawn and Mel B had been caught in the booth Dawn might have lost her job. The solution? "When Mel went to the toilet a moment later I simply followed her", says Dawn. "We squeezed into a cubicle and locked the door. She was really experienced, you could clearly tell", Dawn discloses for the readers.

Another example includes Madonna kissing Britney Spears and Christina Aguilera at the MTV gala. This was reported with four pages of supporting photographs in several magazines: 'Madonna makes an entry by kissing Britney Spears and Christina Aguilera with an open mouth, tongue, and everything.'

While it may not be acceptable to write homophobic articles, the fact that the antics, or alleged antics, of Eminem's bisexual wife, Mel B and Madonna are so eagerly exploited points to a continued ambivalence surrounding homosexuality. It is not condemned, not even when in a toilet, but it is still portrayed as out of the ordinary and just a little perverse, 'with an open mouth, tongue, and everything'. Notice that there are no gay men here. Lesbian sex, if indeed it is lesbian, is not a threat especially if it involves someone like Madonna who is already sexually ambiguous. What would the reaction be if two well known, contemporary young male entertainers, let us say the members of one of the current crop of boy bands, were to ram their tongues down each other's throats in full view of millions?

Television

The television programmes I have watched included the Scandinavian version of *Temptation Island*[1] which is devoted to encouraging partners to cheat on each other. Heterosexual couples, mostly in their twenties, are flown to a tropical paradise where they will be separated and then spend several days in the company of complete strangers. The first programme introduces the couples at home in Sweden, Norway and Denmark. They have all volunteered to put themselves in the way of temptation and all are entirely convinced that they will

---

1 The original series was produced by FOX Reality TV and aired in the USA between 2001 and 2003. The programme format was franchised to numerous countries.

be able to resist it. At least, that is what they say when interviewed prior to their incarceration on the island. Once there, the couples are gathered on the beach awaiting the arrival of their unknown companions. The women will be sent off with the unknown men and the men with the unknown women.

The first boat arrives at the beach with its cargo of women. They are all stunning with perfect bodies in skimpy bikinis, perfect tans, perfect hair and perfect smiles. They parade past the couples doing their best to look seductive for the men. The men look at them a little furtively while their partners look slightly anxious at the sight of the competition. The second boat arrives, this time carrying the male companions. The men are equally stunning, clad in swimming shorts, tall, tanned and with bulges in all the right places. Most of the women stare at them, although a few try to play disinterested. Their male partners do not look at all happy as the competition troops past.

The couples are treated to a beauty pageant of men and women. This is an interesting, if brief, moment in which the men look at the male strangers and assess their sex appeal and the women look at the female strangers to assess how attractive they are. This is a fairly routine activity carried out on a daily basis by heterosexuals whenever the threat from sexual competition must be assessed. On Temptation Island the situation makes it very obvious. But the queer moment does not last long before we quickly return to a world of compulsory heterosexuality.

Once in their separate villages, life revolves around partying, and spending time with the beautiful strangers whose sole task is to seduce the participants. Needless to say some of them succeed. The catch is that everything that goes on is captured by cameras which are placed around the village. There is nowhere to hide except inside the huts where the participants and guests sleep. If a man and a woman disappear into a hut together and don't emerge until the light of dawn, the viewers are left to draw their own conclusion. Back in the other village the male or female partner of the one who has transgressed will find out about it sooner or later. Result: trouble in paradise.

Myths of the Heteronormative

It is obvious that the media examined here do not explore a new theme. Failed and difficult other-sex relationships are one of the central obsessions of literature, film and theatre. Think of Aristophanes' *Lysistrate*, Sophocles' *Oedipus Rex*, Shakespeare's *The Taming of the Shrew* Strindberg's *Miss Julia*, or Edward Albee's *Who's Afraid of Virginia Woolf?*[2] However, the articles and the recent

---

2 There is also a rich vein of ethnography on the subject if one knows where to look. Ritual symbolism, for example, paints an anything but harmonious picture of

spate of documentary soaps, the 'real life' dramas unfolding every evening on television, are not sold as fiction, but neither, perhaps, are they seen as truth. They are after all referred to as *gossip* magazines, and gossip, however fascinating it may be, contains only dubious truths. I would like to suggest that these dramas are 'mythic'.

The main characteristics of myths are a narrative of events, the narrative has a sacred character, at least some of the events or things occur in a sacred or fantasy world, and the narrative refers to origins or transformations (Cohen 1969). To these we must also add the entertainment value of myths. These, then, are some of the basic characteristics of myth and they are all present in the material under scrutiny.

The narrative form is easily discernible in the stories about royalty, stars, minor celebrities, and public figures.

The sacred quality is not always obvious in a highly secularised society like Sweden unless we view the celebrity and the star as not-quite-ordinary beings. Royal Families are definitely not mere mortals and not surprisingly receive enormous attention. They represent a fantasy world of wealth, privilege and a heteronormative idyll. It is not unusual to find traditional royalty together with the new economic or celebrity 'royalty' in the same magazine, for example, the Beckhams and their glamorous lifestyle. 'David and Victoria Beckham – icons for a new lifestyle' (*Svensk Dam tidning* nr 39 18–24 September 2003). In their house in England, 'Beckingham Palace', everything is super luxurious with five bedrooms, three guestrooms, two dressing rooms as big as an average apartment, an ultramodern kitchen, wine cellar, sauna, and so on. We read that Victoria has had cosmetic surgery done on her breasts, that she likes Bombay pearls, that the engagement ring David bought her cost 225,000 (SEK) and that Victoria found the wedding ring in Paris for 750,000 (SEK). The queen of the jewelry collection is a bracelet with antique diamonds for 3,750, 000 SEK. The garage is crammed with Ferraris, Porsches, Bentleys, Aston Martins, Cadillacs, BMWs, and Harley-Davidson motorbikes. We learn that David's style is called 'metrosexual' and describes the modern guy, who plucks his eyebrows, shaves his chest and uses makeup. He waxes his legs, walks around in a sarong – or in David's case Victoria's panties – loves to be seen and cultivates his 'feminine side.'

The people in these stories may be real enough but the settings for some of the 'real life' soaps are definitely not of the real world. They are at parties, galas, and fairytale weddings. We don't normally meet people in ordinary city suburbs or housing estates. The real life television docu-soaps don't take place in everyday contexts either. The dramas are played out in specially constructed apartments, mansion houses, luxurious villas, tropical islands, and French

---

gender relations and sexuality (Moore 2007).

chateaux. People are locked into houses and deprived of all contact with the outside world. Cameras follow them even when they shower, and millions of viewers watch them on television or round the clock on the Internet. How, exactly, are we to understand these bizarre tales?

The Work of Myth

According to Lévi-Strauss (1976), the obvious content of myth, its narrative, is an important part of its entertainment value. But it is not the entire truth. He argues that the message of the myth lies 'deeper'. What the myths discuss are the insoluble contradictions of human life. If we read myths in the right way, we see that they encode these contradictions without mentioning them explicitly. By means of an endless repetition of details they convey the message that some of life's contradictions and conflicts must be endured.

The message in the magazines seems to be that all attempts to build heterosexual relationships, even within a heteronormative socio-cultural order, lead to frustration and disappointment: You will fail. At the same time there is nothing in the message that says that heterosexual relationships, as they are presented here, are problematic. On the contrary, all the problems are played out against a background assumption that heterosexuality is natural and unavoidable. In this way the gossip media are like psychoanalysis: they make it possible to live with the problem but they do not solve it.

With this in mind we can view *Temptation Island* as a back to nature programme reminiscent of William Golding's novel *Lord of the Flies*, only instead of polite, middle-class school boys turning into vicious savages, adult heterosexuals regress to the state of the promiscuous horde so beloved of nineteenth-century evolutionist theorists of human development. The heterosexual couple, it transpires, is a fragile thing in the face of libidos let loose on a tropical island. Given the chance, the programme seems to be saying, nature – the sex drive – will always win over heteronormative constraints – culturally prescribed monogamy.[3]

Another interpretation of myths emphasises their functionality. Myths are social charters that spell out and justify social relations and cultural truths. If we follow Bronislaw Malinowski's (1954) classic interpretation, in what sense is the material examined here a charter? What does it legitimate or prescribe?

---

3 As far as I know, none of the couples were married. Some were planning on marrying but none had yet done so. Breaking up a married couple would be too radical a move. It would amount to an assault on the institution that provides coupledom with its ultimate purpose and value in a heteronormative regime. It is significant that a show designed to split pairs does not go this far.

A pervasive theme in the magazines is the importance, even the necessity, of being part of a couple. You must have a mate. You must long for one if you don't already have one. You must long for a family. However, Malinowski also pointed out that the message of myths was open to discussion. We can thus interpret these sexual myths in several ways.

The transformations are the moral lessons to be drawn from the episodes that the celebrities have lived through. In *Temptation Island*, for example, the moral is rather ambiguous. Those who cheat on their other half appear suitably distraught and full of regret. Grown men cry over their stupidity as they confess their sins to the other guys and worry about how their female partner will react when presented with the evidence. Remember, everything that happens on *Temptation Island* is captured on camera. But if the cameras had not been there, would they have wept? Is their regret at having cheated or at having been caught in the act?

In the case of celebrities, we might want to see the coverage of their miseries as a kind of class revenge, or expression of resentment, in which the less privileged gloat at how the high and mighty, if not quite fallen, have nonetheless made asses of themselves.[4] Equally, we could see it as a way of preserving social distinctions based on wealth and privilege by trying to convince the majority that the rich and famous minority suffers and is really unhappy despite its privileges. Perhaps class resentment is wasted on it. Gossip can also reveal commonalities. No matter how rich or how famous 'they' are they are still basically the same as 'us'. Even royal bastions of the heteronormative are showing cracks. One only has to think of the exploits of the members of the British Royal Family over the years to realise that its most sacred manifestations have feet of clay.

Myths can also act as morality plays. The endless parade of minor 'tragedies', failed marriages, betrayals, cheating, and deceptions, are the human interest meant to capture the reader and perhaps evoke sympathy or contempt. After all, when all is said and done, their miseries are often self-inflicted. Why, for example, would any sane person travel to a tropical island to test their relationship in full view of millions of fellow Scandinavians? Unless, of course, they want a brief period of fame during which they will appear in the gossip magazines and avoid the queues into the trendiest nightclubs in Copenhagen, Oslo and Stockholm.

Another feature of mythological tales is their redundancy. Edmund Leach (1976) argues that a myth tends to have a repetitive structure in terms of plot and content in order to communicate effectively. Week after week the same faces appear in the magazines, the same dramas are enacted and re-enacted,

---

[4] Cross and Litter (2010) see in the *schadenfreude* surrounding celebrity failures a reaction that leaves intact the system which produces celebrities and the inequalities they represent. It is often expressed in a comic register and helps us to 'withstand the difficulties of living', a function attributed to myths.

the same mistakes made, the same lessons learned and then forgotten. But the endless repetition also suggests an attempt to convince us of something, but what? Perhaps the inevitability of heterosexuality and the gender order.

Finally, there is the entertainment value. These stories depict the seamy underbelly of heterosexuality. It is the *failed* performance of heterosexuality that is most interesting, not its perfect execution. Hence the dizzying succession of love affairs, engagements, marriages, and then separations and divorces, reunions, recriminations, deceptions, and so on. Too much heterosexual bliss becomes dull, and not very credible. Neither does it sell well. We are after all looking at commodities – magazines, newspapers and television programmes – that must make a profit. Humdrum heterosexuality needs to be spiced up with trouble and strife, but not to the point of rejecting the heteronormative as a whole.

A paradox of theories of myth is the following: Why are tales that provide normative justification for social relations (as in functionalism) or cognitive support for them (as in structuralism) told in otherworldly terms? One explanation is that myths are allegories that exaggerate or invert conventional premises and thereby draw attention to them and confirm them. Of course, the myths presented here are exaggerations of the contradictions, problems, and troubles inherent to heteronormative gender and sexuality. No one suggests that gossip presents an accurate account of the life of the average Smith or Svensson. The themes that are presented – relations, frustrations, betrayals, the search for Mr/Mrs Right – are all familiar to readers, even if they are portrayed by royalty, film stars, and sporting elites. The role of myths in maintaining social conventions is ambiguous and complex. On the one hand, they show how natural heterosexuality is by providing a model of how heterosexuality ought to be done. On the other hand, they paint a picture of heterosexuality likely to deter potential candidates. One could argue that the mythic repetition of these ambiguous messages – half farce, half celebration – conveys a kind of ambivalence rather than confirms the heteronormative order. They are hyperbolic in how they depict it, but they do not paint a picture that can simply be dismissed as false. It might be objected that the media under study are trivial and frivolous and they do not deserve any serious attention, not least because they do not say much about 'ordinary' people. Against this we can point out that this is the very character of myth. In them, thoughts and fantasies are not constrained by the everyday laws of nature, social convention or good taste. They can 'say' things, however obliquely, which would be out of place in any other context, precisely because myths themselves are, so to speak, out of place.

We are then confronted by a very ambiguous representation of heterosexuality in a very prominent part of the cultural system, a part that, even in this exaggerated form, reflects cultural tensions which derive from how people live their lives in accordance with heteronormative demands.

Much of what happens in places like *Temptation Island* is so exaggerated as to qualify as parody. Parody can be defined as 'a form of repetition within an ironic critical distance, marking difference rather than similarity' (Hutcheon 1985 xii). Repetition is potentially conservative as it implies mimicry, while difference is potentially revolutionary. Parody, then, is potentially authority and transgression at once, an 'authorized transgression' (Hutcheon 1985 26). If it is to succeed, parody demands recognition of that which is parodied otherwise it gets lost. The target of parody is another work of art or coded discourse. Because it is a representation of a modelled reality which is a representation of an original reality, the parodic exposes the model's conventions. By contrast, satire is critical, comic representation of real objects – people, morality, opinion and so on. The question here is whether the reality in real life television is indeed real or a form of fiction. If reality television is mythic, it does not mirror reality at all, but provides a distorted and at times unrecognisable version of it. This would position *Temptation Island* closer to parody than satire. Satire, like mockery, contains a critical component that parody need not contain. Parody on *Temptation Island* is more like confirmation than critique.

When understood in these terms, performativity, too, as the citation of *codified* gender norms, appears as a form of parody. Like parody it can shade into mockery and satire but need not do so. Indeed, for most of the time it does not involve the authorised transgression of parody. For performative theories, the creation of gender is associated with the risk that it will be created wrongly and thereby reveal its constructed nature and along with it the cultural arbitrary that creates the illusion of a natural heterosexuality. This seems partly to miss the mark when viewed against the backdrop of myths of heterosexuality examined here. If we are to believe the gossip media, the heteronormative appears to be falling flat everywhere. These failures and misdemeanours, which are eagerly consumed on a regular basis by hundreds of thousands, perhaps millions, of people in Sweden alone reflect the dissatisfaction that exists within the heteronormative order and the social and cultural practice of heterosexuals. If we are to believe the myths, these include gold digging, jealousy, a widespread tendency to cheat on one's partner, the difficulties of balancing careers with families, drug and alcohol abuse, oversized egos, and more besides. Yet because performative theories have often ignored contradictions and complexities within actually-existing-heterosexuality, their critique of it is referred to a rather abstract world of gender-related citations and indeterminate symbolic structures. To ignore the banquet of heterosexual failures served on a daily basis and instead choose to emphasise occasional moments of dubious gender citation or the inherent instability of signification provides rather meagre fare.

It is worth remembering a point made by Baudrillard here, namely that the Law – here gender norms – are always underwritten by the unwritten, or what Baudrillard terms the Rule. The Rule is the informal, the leeway within apparently Law-abiding behaviour. Those who conform to the letter of the Law do not support the Law, they risk making it appear foolish. Baudrillard asks:

> Does not [the] secret disobedience of a group to its own principles, this profound immorality and duplicity, reflect a universal order? We need to reawaken the principle of Evil active in Manichaeism and all the great mythologies in order to affirm, against the principle of Good, not exactly the supremacy of Evil, but the fundamental duplicity that demands that any order exists only to be disobeyed, attacked, exceeded and dismantled. (Baudrillard 1990b: 77)

The Evil keeps on generating what the Law is meant to prevent, its opposite. Baudrillard identifies this as a form of secret but one recognised by all.[5] It is for this reason that the perfect accomplishment of gender is not to be congratulated but, on the contrary, seems like a threat, or even zealousness. Perhaps this also explains why the perfect heteronormative couple in one issue of a magazine is replaced by its own abject failure in the next: Perfection must not go unpunished.

Impossible Ideals

This prompts an interesting question: When is a performance a failure? Performative failure and incorrect citation suggests a correct form somewhere, a form of the sign that is true. But exactly where is this to be found? Some people, as we all know, can enjoy and even admire the most awful and amateurish performances, while others are only satisfied with the most perfect execution. It is not enough to claim that the performance of gender and sexuality can fail; we also need to know how much 'failure' amounts to failure. When does the audience start asking for its money back? A striking feature of gender is the considerable variability found *within* gender categories (in part because gender is always informed by other social divisions, including class, race, ethnicity, sexuality, and so on), while the categories themselves are remarkably few and enduring (Delphy 1993). We ought to bear in mind that what seems like repeated failure or self-parody of the heteronormative may instead signal

---

5 There are some interesting parallels to be drawn here with the work of Michael Taussig who argues that faith (in religion) 'seems to require that one be taken in by what one professes while at the same time suspecting it as a lot of hooey' (Taussig 2006: 123). In other words, faith seems to demand a degree of scepticism and doubt. At the same time as one has one's own doubts, practitioners of religion wonder if others are true believers, or really possessed of supernatural gifts. Belief and doubt are not mutually exclusive, they go hand-in-hand (Taussig 2006: 135).

a deep commitment to it, even in the face of considerable dissatisfaction and anxieties. The obsessive repetition of the mass media, highly reminiscent of mythic structure, could therefore just as easily point to the immense social investment in impossible heterosexual ideals as constitute a critique of those ideals.

What type of heterosexuality is depicted in these mythic stories? Gender representations are generally traditional, even conservative. The women are glamorous and long for heterosexual romance. The men are ideally handsome and a real catch. Gender tends to be materialised correctly. The final result, however, as we have seen is a heterosexual horror story. It seems that it is not enough to follow the law of gender demands to achieve heteronormative heterosexuality in this mythical world.

Lauren Berlant and Michael Warner (2000: 320), writing about American chat shows that often feature heterosexual failures, note that on these shows no one ever blames the ideology and institutions of the heteronormative as such. Why? The reason they proffer is what they call 'an optimism for optimism', or 'cruel optimism' (Berlant 2011), an attachment to the heteronormative without the means to see its promises come true. 'A relation of cruel optimism exists when something you desire is actually an obstacle to your flourishing...These kinds of optimistic relations are not inherently cruel. They become cruel only when the object that draws your attachment actively impedes the aim that brought you to it initially' (Berlant 2011: ix). The failures of normative heterosexuality are interpreted as failings of the individual, not the system or institution itself. After all, there is so much therapeutic advice available that everyone *ought* to succeed in their relationships. What these guides promote is the attainment of perfect heterosexuality, they prescribe a performance principle, the sexual side of which, when necessary can now be chemically augmented. Think of Viagra. The result is that heterosexuality becomes increasingly compulsive and increasingly prone to failure (Jackson and Scott 2010: 98).

Popular culture that at first glance seems to confirm the heteronormative is also replete with examples of its failure. The message of these representations, as I read it, amounts to a question mark at the centre of a popular cultural genre. What they reveal is the paradox of performativity, not in the usual sense of conformity and more or less successful reproduction, but rather the inevitability, even 'desirability' of failure within conformity. This is a doubt that emanates from within rather than being imposed from without. They promote, or at least excuse, imperfection (regardless of the kind of gender or sexuality), because imperfection or failure is all we will ever have. They are, we might say, an act of revenge on all those who dare to aspire to perfection. Perfection leads inevitably to stasis, by its nature it cannot change without becoming other than perfect, im-perfect. If taken too far, conformity to gender norms – the Law – creates horrors, like Goya's sleep of reason. The perfect exponent of the Law appears deranged, even monstrous. The lesson of gossip magazines is perhaps an unexpected one: At the centre of even the apparently most normative cultural genre and its most successful expressions resides the worm of doubt and repeated failures.

Failed Repetition

Repetition is one of the central tenets of performativity, variously phrased as citation or reiteration, that repeats gender norms understood as exemplary reoccurrences. Yet exemplary recurrences are out of tune with capitalist modernity, which, as Marx pointed out, melts all that is solid in the interests of economic expansion. To counter this, new rituals are created or re-invented with rules and procedures that often give them a formal and inflexible structure. Their very stability is a nostalgic response to innovation and flux. As Paul Connerton puts it: 'it is not, therefore, the experience of recapitulative imitation, of *mythic* identification, but the display of formal structure that is the most evident mark of social rites' (Connerton 1989: 64, emphasis added). Recurrence in modernity is, he suggests, only ever a stopgap because the thrust of modernity is to deny the 'reliving of the prototypical'. Arguably, the plethora of manuals, television programmes, newspaper and magazine articles on how to do relationships and sexuality correctly is but another instance of the need for structure and rules in the face of uncertainty. Even the formalistic and repetitive failures that fill the popular media examined herein are a form of structure and predictability. Practical knowledge often becomes explicit and expressed as a 'rule' when a habit can no longer be relied upon to do the job. Where then does this leave performativity? Its stress on repetition in the form of exemplary recurrence appears to be out of step with modernity's denial of it. Instead of unidirectional external gender norms and intra-psychic processes, the compensatory strategy of a proliferation of 'rules' that are not always easy to formulate, apply and perhaps not always mutually compatible demands that social actors be selective, it requires not only repetition but reflexive, social actions, the absent middle of much performative theory.[6]

The desperate attempts to repeat, even the repetition of failure common to all (a burden shared is a burden halved), may therefore be a symptom of

---

6 We ought also to be wary of rules. To infer a rule from observed behaviour and then put it forward as the cause of said behaviour is to commit what Bourdieu (1977) (under Wittgenstein's influence) calls 'legalism' or the 'fallacy of the rule'. A reliance on the repetition of gender norms, the 'rules' for correct gender, confronts performativity with some of the problems of logical reversal that face gender essentialisms.

modernity and the gender unease it generates rather than intrinsic to the performative realisation of gender everywhere

Understanding gender as endless repetitions is reminiscent of Freud's description of acting out in 'Remembering, Repeating and Working Through'. For Freud, repetition is a pathological form of remembering (1973 [1915–17]: lecture 27). However, although Freud on memory is often associated with the memories of trauma, this was not his major interest. 'The central issue is not so much a matter of having "forgotten" an original event than of never really seeing what we commemorate in the patterns we repeat' (Antze and Lambek 1996: xxvii). In this chapter, it is about the repetition of failure and an 'optimism for optimism'.

This is perhaps the point and the message of the myths: You will fail and repeatedly so. It is not a matter of performative repetition of unachievable norms, but more a question of repetition of *failures* as much as, if not more than, success. The heteronormative unites people in their failed repetition, as part of a community of suffering, and an optimistic/fatalistic stance toward the promise of success, however unlikely, rather than being driven by traumas from the past hidden in the psyche.[7] *Failure*, akin to Baudrillard's Rule rather than execution of the Law, is the norm of performative heteronormativity, rather than the relatively (un)successful repetition of gender ideals. There is no way out, no exit option, which returns us to the point made by Lévi-Strauss about myths that console us in the face of inevitable and unavoidable contradictions. But there may be more to repetition than this.

At the very end of *Mythologiques* Lévi-Strauss writes: '*conter* (to tell a story) is always *conte redire* (to retell a story) which can also be written *contredire* (to contradict)' (1981: 644). In short, repeatedly telling stories can contradict the message itself. This is a theory of performativity over a decade *avant la lettre*, but with a twist. Repetition in performativity cements gender, albeit always provisionally because the repetition/citation might turn out to be a bad one. In the version of repetition Lévi-Strauss has in mind the repetition produces an *unheimlich* effect. Gender becomes 'going through the motions' and reveals itself as such. So rather than simply representing the world, albeit obliquely, and leaving it much as it is, as in the functionalist approach, myths can perform a 'dislocation' (Wagner 1978: 255) within convention.[8]

---

7 Judith Butler traces repetitive gender performance to traumatic denial of one's own gender demanded by Oedipal development. The patient repeats but is unaware what she is repeating.

8 Deleuze, sounding very much like David Hume, makes a similar point. He lays the work of continuity at the door of habit. But habits are not habitus, they do not simply reproduce for they 'draw something new from repetition – namely difference' (Deleuze 1994: 93).

If we broaden the canvas for a moment to include reality television, another dimension of obsessive gender repetition and the attempts to do it correctly emerges. Beverley Skeggs and Helen Wood (2012: 67) argue that much (UK) reality television, in which the working class making performative failures of themselves, in fact illustrates the limitations of class and gender norms and the ineffectiveness of performative governmentality that demands 'correct' (i.e. middle-class) forms of class, gender and sexual behaviour. They further suggest that the detailed attention to these behaviours amounts to a virtual do-it-yourself guide in which habit is atomised into its component parts and shown to be a contrivance. Reality television 'enables us to enter different temporal and spatial coordinates revealing the class relations that underpin the normative "standards" of gender, class and race as they are spectacularly performed'. In a similar vein, Bruce Kapferer, in his application of Deleuze to ritual, writes that ritual virtuality is 'an opening up within ongoing existential realities' (Kapferer 2006: 674). By this he does not mean that the virtual re-presents some version of reality so that it can become an object of reflexive contemplation. Rather, he argues that it is about 'slowing the flow that is and enabling an entry into the compositional dynamics of process within which a temporality is integral' by putting certain aspects of the process on hold (Kapferer 2006: 683). Likewise, Graeber, whom I quoted in Chapter 4, wants us to assess what we are actually doing in the doing of it. In all three cases, the temporality of practices and habits is put on hold allowing them to be prised apart and assessed. Myths too rarely occupy the same temporal coordinates of the quotidian. They also interrupt the flow of the taken-for-granted and self-evident. This also makes them ethical phenomena.

Ethical Failures

Recent anthropological writings on morality and ethics have identified two broad approaches: either attention to a moral code or system that determines actions, or to the details of ethical conduct and the work individuals put into attaining their version of the good life (Fassin 2012). According to Joel Robbins (2007) the difference between them is that between the reproduction of a moral and social order in a Durkheimian fashion, or ethical freedom, choosing whom one wishes to be (cf. Laidlaw 2002). Anthropologists, suspicious of the abstractions of philosophers, have a penchant for the latter approach which obliges us to pay close attention to ethics as mundane activity woven into the fabric of everyday life. The ethical preference also seems to clear a space for 'agency' rather than the mechanical norm-governed moral reproduction of the social order. Jarrett Zigon (2007) favours attention to the ethical work occasioned by what he terms 'moral breakdown'. It is when moral systems can no longer be taken for granted that the ethical work of reflection and reflexivity begins as people refashion their moral universe and attempt to re-establish a moral order. In some respects this lies closest to queer theoretical concerns. Queer theory isn't so much a response to moral breakdown as an instigator of it by means of its deconstructive critique. This assault on the given is by definition an ethical enterprise.

There are, however, differences between Zigon's approach and queer theory. The latter, at least in my rendering of it, implies the sheer ordinariness of ethics. If change, differentiation and multiplication and the emergence of the new are routine matters of fact, or even facts of matter,[9] then ethics too in the sense of reworking the given, is an ontological fact rather than an exception occasioned by breakdown. Or perhaps I can rephrase what I mean in terms of the topic of this chapter. Breakdown is woven into the fabric of the everyday in the form of failures, not necessarily in any spectacular sense but in a routine manner.

Beyond the Monolithic

The upshot of all of this is that the cultural system and symbolic structures are by no means monolithically in favour of the heteronormative, the practice of which is rife with contradictions, hopeless failures, farcical desperation, plain stupidity, masochism, sadism, indifference, resignation, and going through the motions in the absence of a viable alternative. The social tends to be recursive once set in motion, not because of obscure psychic mechanisms, but because, practically speaking, there is often little alternative for most people even if they might wish for things to change (and an awful lot of people do) because they lack the resources to make it happen.

How we depict and theorise the heteronormative (indeed any normative) ought to reflect this. Yet many queer writings depict a rather uniform, not to say monolithic, heterosexuality. Part of the problem lies in queer theory's repeated failure to engage with the social. No person is only intra-psychic processes inferred from Lacanian psychoanalysis plus regularised and repressive gender norms impinging from an outside. Regardless of whether or not the intra-psychic processes are of the kind Lacan argues, it is social actors who are reflexive, and constantly in interaction with other people, cultural imaginaries, the material world, and not least their own embodiment. The performative version of the

---

9 If we adopt Deleuze's ideas on becoming, whatever happens each instant is only ever a fraction of what might have been, of matter's potential. Each becoming of matter, each actualisation is a success story of sorts, but it is also a failure and the failures far outnumber the successes. All that could have happened but never did. In this respect matter succeeds even as it fails.

reflexive social agent emphasises the instability of the significatory structures that produce gender identity, but this is much denuded version of social action.

Much of the blame for this rather uniform theoretical depiction of heterosexuality is attributable to heteronormative discourse that exaggerates its own integrity and its differences from homosexuality, especially when claiming to be superior to the latter. The same applies, albeit to a lesser extent, to homonormative discourses that exaggerate the internal consistency of homosexuality. As I pointed out in the Introduction, queer theory itself may be overly reactive against the heteronormative, which is portrayed in too stark a contrast to homosexuality. Homosexual and heterosexual in practice and in fantasy are not opposites. The opposition is effected when they are formalised into categories for comparison. Discursive contrasts, policy and legal distinctions and bifurcations come into play. Standard replies, clichés, and the like all simplify a complex situation. While an opposition can be seen in legislation, when, for example, certain rights are reserved for heterosexuals but not for the rest, then, perhaps, we can talk about opposites: You either enjoy the right or you do not. But the binary model, as Sedgwick's quote at the start of the chapter recognises but does not explore in any detail, only poorly captures the more chaotic representations of heterosexuality circulating in the cultural sphere, not to mention actual practices.

If, for just one moment, we were to accept that homosexuality is a failed copy of heterosexuality, then there is no shortage of alternatives to heteronormative heterosexuality to mimic, and no shortage of ghastly examples of why not to mimic it. But can we turn this argument around and argue on the basis of the material presented here that it is heterosexuality that is mimicking homosexuality? Are we witnessing the queering of heterosexuality in which at least some of the constraints of heteronormative gender relations and sexuality are losing their grip? Nowadays we can watch television programmes where gay men style heterosexual men and make then 'gayish'. Metrosexual Beckham is gay in all but sexual preference. Mel B has been married, has children, and has sex with whomsoever she pleases regardless of their gender.

An Anthropology of Failure

This brings me back to the subject of failure. By failure I am not thinking first and foremost of those who turn failure into a project. There are important examples of this. Feminism is all about a certain kind of failure: the 'failure' of women to be men, and the very real failures of patriarchy. Nor am I necessarily thinking of the most obvious forms of failure measured by economic misery, lack of power and social standing. Anthropology has a long tradition of studying the underdog who suffers these kinds of defeats, if nothing else because the weak and the unfortunate have often been the people most willing to speak when spoken to. Yet despite this attention the discipline has tended to write the success stories however modest they might appear to an outsider. The stories of the people who call the shots, the big men, the chiefs, the representatives of the group, the elders, the ritual experts, the talkative ones, the exemplars of their culture, the personalities that thrive in its ethos. It is important at the very least to consider the possibility that some people simply don't care about success and don't define themselves in accordance with the local criteria for a successful life. Not least because these criteria may well have been drawn up by others elsewhere whose perspective the 'unsuccessful' do not share. Failure is, among other things, a perspective and before we label anything a failure we need to know whose perspective we have adopted.

As a form of critical theory, queer theory runs the risk of becoming resistance studies if it pays too much attention to the victim perspective and forgets that people are not always 'negative', are not defined totally by their resistance, if indeed they engage in any.[10] This brings us close to what I mean here by failure. Would any of the people who fail to live up to heteronormative ideals see themselves as failures? Perhaps not, yet failure is ever present in their and our lives regardless of the ideals we try or don't try to live up to. We need to look closely at not only what success entails but also at what coexists alongside it, constant, routine failure. Of course, this includes more conventional senses of failure, but it also encompasses disappointments, meaninglessness, obsessive repetition, resigned going through the motions, as well as getting by and making do. It extends to chronic if suppressed doubts – 'Is that all there is?' – and to those moments or phenomena – things, people, ideas and situations – that cause pauses, hesitations or delays, instances of reflection, our encounters with the *unheimlich*, the strange, the hitches, snags and tears in the fabric of everyday life when we get occasional and tantalising glimpses of something else.

---

10 There are, of course, people who do resist, and there is no shortage of anthropological accounts of resistance. But resistance has become a rather tarnished word since its heyday in the 1990s (Abu-Lughod 1990). It is simply too common; it can be found everywhere. Labelling something 'resistance' risks turning those who resist into reflexes of their oppressors or recasts them as heroic, pulling through against all the odds, and exemplars of an anti-culture.

Chapter 7
Explications

As Adam Early in the Morning,
Walking forth from the bower refresh'd with sleep,
Behold me where I pass, hear my voice, approach,
Touch me, touch the palm of your hand to my body as I pass,
Be not afraid of my body.
                Walt Whitman[1]

Welcome is every organ and attribute of me…
not an inch nor a particle of an inch is vile,
and none shall be less familiar than the rest.
                Walt Whitman[2]

At numerous places in this book we have stopped to question the self-evident status of objects. This final chapter is no exception but instead of looking out into the world it turns inwards to scrutinise the status of an object that has so far been taken for granted, the anthropologist.

The two poems by Walt Whitman serve as the chapter's bookends. In the first, 'Adam Early in the Morning', we meet a body that is visible, tangible and audible, fully formed and no doubt pristine. In the second, 'Song of Myself', the body of Adam has given way to 'particles' and 'inches'. There is no longer any apparent unity or hierarchy to it. Whitman's body has become egalitarian, perhaps also democratic: Every inch is equal to every other inch and all deserving of equal respect. It's interesting that in the second poem Whitman councils us to dispel our fears and revulsion lest they keep us at a distance. He seems to realise that something about the body decomposed is disturbing, even vile. Whitman's bodies are ontological not representational, we can and should get to know them. The transition from the complete molar body of Adam, fresh from the imprint of God's will, to the particles and inches of Whitman's body charts a trajectory similar to that followed in this chapter. It begins its exploration at the molar level and the *de fault* dominance in Euro-American cultures of particular masculine models of the body that emphasise containment and stability. Unavoidably, this leads to questions about sexuality because these gender-specific masculine models strongly reflect and support

---

1 'As Adam Early in the Morning', in Murphy 1975: 145.
2 Walt Whitman 'Song of Myself', in Murphy 1975: 67.

a particular kind of sexual body one that has acted as a conceptual template for theoretical statements which have exercised considerable influence in anthropology. It then adopts an increasingly molecular focus as it explores affects, things, and intuition. This final chapter is not a conclusion. It does not attempt to tie together all the threads and loose ends to deliver a neat package or final pronouncements. As its title suggests, it ex-plicates what is implicated in the anthropologist by unfolding some of the themes found in previous chapters. It is, like Whitman's poems, an invitation not an adjudication.

To start with we look at one kind of body – a normative, theoretical and metaphorical body – whose presence haunts the social sciences: The body of Émile Durkheim.

Bodies in Denial

According to Durkheim, men differentiate themselves from the natural world by becoming social beings, while women remain bemired in their biological nature (Lehmann 1994). '[Durkheim's] masculine ontology of the social…relies on the counterpositioning of *female corporeality* and *male sociality*…The very concept of the social, as it comes to be articulated in the sociological imaginary, relies on the simultaneous exclusion of the corporeal and of women' (Witz and Marshall 2003: 351, emphasis in original). It is this male body 'that grounds most of the disciplinary corpus, but is rarely explicitly named as such' (Witz and Marshall 2003: 351). But not all men's bodies are of a piece; there are significant differences between them, not least in connection to their sexuality. Durkheim's male body ought ultimately to acquiesce to control; more specifically, it should be disciplined in and by the institution of heterosexual marriage. Durkheim is very explicit on this point: Men who are not subjected to the matrimonial regime are sad creatures whose bodies – more specifically their sexuality – gain the upper hand, and who are plagued by sexual anomy and suicidal tendencies (Witz and Marshall 2003: 348). The social is therefore not only male; it is predicated on a specific form of male body framed, or rather restrained, by heterosexual marriage. (What we have here is an early statement of Habermas's claim, taken up in Chapter 4, about the emergence of the self within the conjugal couple and alongside it a gloomy diagnosis of the dangers facing the autological self that exists outside conjugal bonds.) The homosexual male body, emerging as a sexual species around this time, is, like a woman's body, saturated by its sexuality. It is not in control of itself, and certainly not disciplined in marriage, which Durkheim calls the 'communion of the most intimate kind between two conscious beings'.[3] Durkheim therefore

---

3 For a discussion of Durkheim that identifies the conservative implications of his views on women and marriage, see Gane (1993: 21–58).

locates the social not in all male bodies, and not even all heterosexual male bodies, but in a specific kind of heteronormatiove male body. The male body Durkheim prescribes – and his sociology here is normative – maps easily onto a body that is sealed, disciplined, stable and predictable, not a body given to anomy and suicidal tendencies one suspects, but one organised in accordance with a specific western bourgeois schema.

Moving to anthropology, A. R. Radcliffe-Brown is not usually regarded as a theorist of bodies and embodiment (and he was certainly no theorist of gender or sexuality), but in key texts he does employ biological analogies that suggest certain forms of bodies. Taking his cues from Durkheim he compares the relationship between the social function of an institution and how it contributes to the continued existence of society or social structure with the physiological function of an organ and how it contributes to the 'organic structure', the continued life of the organism (Radcliffe-Brown 1952 (1940): 200). Radcliffe-Brown's well known functionalist organic analogy resonates with much older metaphors, such as the body politic of Hobbes. It is also part of a positivist sociological tradition that privileges stability and continuity over change. His 'organic structure' is but another expression for a stable molar body, very like a specific kind of male body that was refined and made hegemonic in modernity in the form of a middle-class, white, European, heterosexual, and able-bodied male. In short, it is the body of Durkheim and Radcliffe-Brown.

My point, if it is not already obvious, is that there is a sexual subtext to somatic metaphors like Durkheim's and Radcliffe-Brown's that is entangled in ideas about the nature of the body, the extent to which it can change, academic approaches to male sexual embodiment, and popular understandings of the body, including the metaphors used to describe it. It is also, of course, deeply implicated in gender hierarchies. Recall that Edwin Ardener (1975) made an explicit link between structural-functional models (the kind influenced heavily by Radcliffe-Brown) and the exclusion of women and other 'muted' groups from structural-functional ethnographies. Any theories that make use of Durkheim and bodily analogies, ought then to be keenly aware of the foundation on which they rest and their sexual and gender implications.

The Anthropological Body

Although you need a body to do fieldwork and every body brings its own skills and limitations to the field, relatively little has been written on the body of the ethnographer (Coffey 1999: 59–75, Okely 2007). Judith Okely argues that 'the anthropologist needs to unlearn or at least be able to recognise the bodily knowledge from his/her lived past that informs interpretations in the field' (2007: 65). Okely asks us to scrutinise our experience, but she is surely aware that feminism has interrogated the assumptions behind a naive empiricism's faith in the self-evident truth of experience and what it can teach us (Scott 1992). What we recognise as part of our lived past is only ever a fraction of what we have lived and are still living. Whatever our 'somatic modes of attention' (Csordas 1993) might reveal cannot simply be taken at face value, nor is it exhaustive.

Phenomenological accounts of embodiment provide some insights into how we live as gendered and sexual bodies, but do not always make explicit the subterranean processes that are active in the constitution of those bodies. In effect, Okely is asking us to unearth the genealogy of our bodies. On the subject of genealogy, Moira Gatens argues that we must 'understand and remember how we became what we are, not in order to live what we have become as our "truth" but rather as our condition of possibility for that which we may become' (1996: 77). It is the 'became' in what Gatens writes above that is important. Both she and Okely call on us to explore how the 'body' is constituted, how it is put there, 'objected'. But we need to be careful when we employ the term 'possibility'. If what becomes simply emerges directly out of the possible, then it is already preformed, inevitable. Under the influence of Bergson, I prefer to grant the body more leeway than a possible lain down in the past.

One highly influential approach to embodiment within anthropology that makes a great deal of the past in the present is Bourdieu's (1977) work on the habitus, which he defines as a system of dispositions – mental and physical – that creates a common-sense and moral world which it tends to reproduce. The durability of the habitus lies in the fact that it is an embodied history – a past – that has become 'second nature'. Bourdieu concedes that a habitus can change when new circumstances make novel demands on practices (Bourdieu 1992: 133), however he tends to emphasise the objective *determination* of the body. For him, once habituated, the matter of the body is smooth, synchronised and homogenous. It contains few if any surprises. For all his insights, Bourdieu treats the body more as an object than a thing.

Yet studies of embodied knowledge and practices reveal that they do not necessarily add up to a coherent whole. The body is *heterogeneous*, not *homogeneous* (Hunter and Saunders 1995). It is not always perfectly internally synchronised. Embodied dispositions, which Bourdieu argues are 'transposable' and therefore have the effect of imposing a homogeneity throughout the body, are not as easily transposable as he assumes. Learning (and unlearning) is patchy and discontinuous (Downey 2007: 237).[4] If we recall Lacan's Imaginary stage, the coherent body imago it precipitates is never more than an illusion – and a very

---

4 Nor need the process be largely unconscious. A habitus can be the result of diligent and repeated practices aimed at the cultivation of an ethical self (see Mahmood 2012). Both practice theory and performative theories of gender tend to neglect this active, conscious, ethical and creative labour.

masculine one at that – of a body that is centred, whole and fully under conscious control. Bourdieu's habitus reflects this (narcissistic) masculine fantasy. It installs a form of molarity that generates a specific form of heterosexual male body, what Brian Massumi (1992: 89) calls 'The standard Man-form...the personification of anti-becoming'.

How might we conceive of the body differently? What other templates are available that are not wedded to Radcliffe-Brown's organic structure, Bourdieu's homogenous body, or Oedipal molarity? I shall consider but two of many possibilities: the body's libidinal organisation and its heterogeneity or multiplicity. First, I turn to a modern classic, *Homosexual Desire*, by Guy Hocquenghem ([1972]1993: 96–7).

Anal Speculations

Hocquenghem argues that in the West the anus is the centre of the private male person. 'Every man', he writes, 'has an anus which is truly his own, in the most secret depths of his own person. The anus does not exist in a social [or sexual] relation, since it forms precisely the individual and therefore enables the division between society and individual to be made' (1993: 97). He contrasts the private anus with the penis, a fleshy appendage that might not always amount to much, but which enjoys nonetheless the privilege of being associated with 'The Great Social Phallus' (1993: 97). Possession of a penis is the passport that guarantees access to legitimate phallic power in society.

The social status of the penis is evident in the humorous books written about the relationship men have to it, and in the metaphors used to describe it, including words like 'tool' and 'weapon' that suggest an extension of the person in the service of domination. The penis may even receive a personal name – 'Willy', 'Dick', 'Mr Percy', or whatever – that marks its status as a unique *individual* among others.[5] The anus, unlike the penis, does not usually receive a personal name and is neither meant to extend personhood nor to be the site of social or sexual exchange with others. When it is, it tends to be tabooed (this includes same and other-sex sexuality).[6] Normative male heterosexuality privileges the penis and denies or downplays the sexual potential of other parts

---

5 For some interesting observations on the relationships of Western men to their penises, see Bordo 1999: 15–104, and Murphy 2001.

6 There are exceptions. The 1993 Canadian film musical *Zero Patience*, directed by John Greyson, tells the story of flight attendant Gaetan Dugas, allegedly the man who introduced HIV into North America. It includes a scene from a gay bathhouse where two arseholes are engaged in conversation with each other.

of the male body, especially the anus which threatens to confuse male and female gender because both possess one.

Hocquenghem's observations on the sexual zoning and demarcations of the body echo the insights of Freud, who, in 1915, wrote: 'I have been led to ascribe the quality of erotogenicity to all parts of the body and to all internal organs' (1953: V11. 184). In all social orders sexual embodiment is zoned to specific sites and organised into a hierarchy of licit and illicit pleasures that are sedimented into a sexual habitus supportive of a (hetero)normative regime and hence specific forms of gender and sexuality. In order to disrupt the sexual habitus, Hocquenghem advocates a polymorphous perversity based on 'annular' sexuality, and 'anal grouping', a plugging in of organs, or what he terms a horizontal sociality rather than a hierarchical Oedipal order, a system of 'polyvocal desire plugged in on a non-exclusive basis' (1993: 131). The language is taken from Deleuze and Guattari. Hocquenghem emphasises the disruptive consequences of changes to the body's libidinal organisation for the social body, and especially the public status and power of men.[7] The point is not to advocate a gay bathhouse, although Hocquenghem does sing the praises of gay male cruising, but to challenge the privatisation of desires within the Oedipal family whose eros is framed by homophobia and channelled into the service of capitalist production. In short, he posits a different embodied ontology as a model for sociality.[8] It is one very much in keeping with the assemblage world

---

7 Without denying the insights of Hocquenghem's argument it risks essentialising gay male embodiment as some sort of ontological ground for a reformed masculinity and through that the entire social order. Hocquenghem displays a common tendency of the late 1960s to romance the margins. Yet there is nothing *inherently* subversive about male-male anal intercourse. It was firmly integrated into sections of classical Greek society (Dover 1978), and its widespread if often cloaked existence in many other cultures is well documented, see Schmitt and Sofer (1992), Murray (1995). Nor does being a gay male automatically translate into becoming a freedom fighter. Moreover, essentialising a positive gay sexual embodiment also has the effect of reintroducing, and even strengthening, the heterosexual-homosexual binary that supports the masculine notion of the body as a closed system. Last but by no means least, he very conspicuously fails to consider women's embodiment in general and lesbian embodiment and sexuality in particular.

8 The vitalist politics of Michael Hardt and Antonio Negri (2005) provide a similar appeal to ontology as Hocquenghem. They call for a new physiology, one that takes account of the dissolution of *de corpore*, the traditional political-social bodies. They write: 'From the perspective of political order and control, then, the elemental flesh of the multitude is maddeningly elusive, since it cannot be entirely corralled into the hierarchical organs of a political body' (2005: 192). Unlike the traditionalists, new movements like Queer Nation and ACT UP (their examples), which do not cohere into the stable, predictable actors of yore point the way and for this reason they claim

of connections we now see emerging but which was much less in evidence when he wrote in the late 1960s and early 1970s. In effect, Hocquenghem is reminding us of the body's heterogeneity, its multiplicity, rather than the homogeneity that results from the imposition of an Oedipal grid.

Yet arguably we need to dig even deeper than Hocquenghem if we are to grasp bodies. Genealogy is usually understood to be a matter of knowledge, discourses and epistemologies that are enfolded into or inscribed onto bodies. The Oedipal grid is one example but there are other molecular and larval processes at work in the body's emergence that are not straightforwardly genealogical in nature.

Singular Bodies

Following Deleuze, one way to conceive of the heterogeneous body is as a combination of the ordinary and the singular. The ordinary is the stability of the object, the routine and the repetitive. Singularities, by contrast, are points when and where something happens in the original sense of happenstance and haphazard – unpredictable, unforeseen random and chaotic – and even happiness, a chance confluence of pleasant circumstances. Bodies, just like things, are a combination of the ordinary and the singular, a multiplicity in flux capable of acting in several and sometimes unpredictable and contradictory ways. In every encounter in the world between minds and minds, bodies and bodies, people and the material, we cannot know in advance what will happen argues Deleuze (1988: 17–18) under the influence of Spinoza. Bodies are susceptible to events and events are unique conjunctures, no matter how routinised or predictable, they never repeat themselves perfectly, difference is inherent to them.

As the body becomes more organ-ised, its range of potential narrows and fades but it does not completely disappear; bodies are full of echoes.[9] A multiplicity endures that can still be actualised. All anthropologists enter the field with a body that is organised in a culturally sensible and ordinary way *and*

---

are considered monstrous by the institutional Left (2005: 191). Drawing explicitly and enthusiastically on queer theory and ideas of performativity, Hardt and Negri argue that queer and feminist ideas of the body are in fact against 'the body', in the sense of a gendered and sexed object, and for the 'performativity of queer social flesh' (2005: 199). A weakness of their argument is that this flesh remains ungendered. While this is in keeping with some strands of queer theory, it ignores the fact that not to mention gender is often to gender something male by de fault.

9 This would correspond to the content of the Real in Lacan's tripartite schema forever bubbling up to disturb the Imaginary and Symbolic registers.

an implicit body full of echoes and potential singularities capable of springing surprises under the impact of events, of causing a dis-ease that can shock challenge, stymie, or inspire.

Foucault, I believe, was on a similar track when he wrote that: 'It is the agency of sex we must break away from, if we aim – through a tactical reversal of the various mechanisms of sexuality – to counter the grips of power with the claims of bodies, pleasures, and knowledges, in their multiplicity and their possibility of resistance. The rallying point for the counterattack against the deployment of sexuality ought not to be sex-desire, but bodies and pleasures' (Foucault 1978: 157). Critics argue that his call for 'bodies and pleasures' places them beyond the reach of power (e.g. Fraser 1989, Butler 1990: 97). Although there is some ambiguity in his position, such as his notorious reference to a rural past of 'inconsequential bucolic pleasures' in which he completely ignores gender and age asymmetries (Foucault 1990: 31), I do not understand Foucault to be making this claim. Rather, I read him as saying that we need a non-subjective way of looking at sex (which includes sexuality and gender). Bodies and pleasures may gravitate around the vortex of sexuality without being sucked in and pressed into the service of creating the sexual subject. Some bodily pleasures may not even be regarded as sexual, but can become so, such as the sado-masochistic practices that Foucault embraced (see Halperin 1995: 85–112). Or, it may be the case that pleasures not previously experienced by a person are not easily reconciled with their sex, gender and sexuality. These pleasures can be assimilated to the regime of sexuality, for example, as either heterosexual or homosexual (or some 'perversion') and force a choice to be made, but such an assimilation is not guaranteed.

Pleasures, in Foucault's usage, are like events that open the body to the intrusion of the unexpected, singularities that dislocate previous understandings. Under propitious circumstances they can cause a mismatch between the conceptual grid through which we comprehend our bodies and the feelings and affects of embodiment that move us to forge new concepts and make sense anew.[10]

---

10 I am not suggesting that ethnographers deliberately put themselves into each and every situation that will challenge their sexual habitus in order to sharpen their conceptual prowess any more than authors who have written on sexuality in the field – a topic close to that of the present chapter – prescribe sexual relations as a necessary part of fieldwork, see Kulick and Willson 1995, Lewin and Leap 1996, Markowitz and Ashkenazi 1999. For one thing, writing of sexuality can easily shade into pornography, a genre with which few scholars want to be associated, even assuming they could write it well and that anyone would want to read it. The social sciences have never been strong on intensely subjective experiences, like embodiment and not least sexuality. They are not good at confession. Witness some of the reactions to the so-called reflexive turn in anthropology in the mid- and late-1980s which was dismissed as self-indulgent navel gazing. It is perhaps no coincidence that male scholars in the humanities have

It is true to say that anthropology has displayed a strong tendency to look at the ordinary, the everyday, the repetitive and habitual rather than the singular, the 'tipping points', or catastrophic moments: The differences that make a difference. These happenings need not be on the scale of hurricanes and earthquakes. What I have in mind, as I wrote at the end of Chapter 6, are the mundane, low-key 'catastrophes' (the sudden turns), unquiet moments when we glimpse not necessarily alternatives fully formed but the possibility of alternatives. The moments, or failures if you like, when we sense the virtual beneath our feet.

Below the Radar

Bodies respond to the impact of events, but events in the sense used here belong to the Real, they are ontological rather than representational, and they introduce something beyond representations, a remainder. We must not forget that the becoming of the materiality of the body goes well beyond the form onto which identities are attached and with which human subjects are moulded. It encompasses processes of mattering that are independent of subjectivity and conscious thought. Regardless of how diligently we perform our gender and sexuality, or any other social expectations, our bodies are not docile, they are not fully compliant subjects and they are not totally inhabited by the external demands of discourse, no matter how insistent and violent those demands.

Vicki Kirby (2008) criticises those who claim as self-evident fact that matter, whatever it happens to be up to, is of interest only once it is made an explicit object of human interpretation. So long as it is not admitted into cultured society we need not concern ourselves with it. Performative positions on the body and the material in general posit an unknowable matter that can only be approached as a sign, an element of culture. Matter only matters when codified. By contrast, other approaches, such as process philosophy presented in Chapter 1, consider matter to be active and inventive in itself independently of human intentions. For Kirby, nature does not simply provide the ontological raw material for culture. Bodies and biology are never outside culture because neither the biological nor the cultural are closed systems, they both partake of characteristics of the other, nature is cultural and vice-versa.[11] Witness the

---

often taken the lead in writing about male sexual embodiment, as they are arguably better versed in putting into words the personal and subjective that is so closely tied to sexuality than their male (and female) sociological and anthropological colleagues, e.g. Bersani 1994, Reid-Pharr 2001, Thomas 2002.

11 A note of caution. This should not be read to suggest that there is always symmetry between the human and the non-human. There may be colossal asymmetries

communicative abilities of cells, genetic materials, signal substances, and the de-cisions of matter. These are all characteristics more often associated with culture than the stuff of biology. As a consequence, much of the body's business evades verbalisation and remains opaque to us. To consider these aspects of the body is to shift attention from the phenomenology of bodies and perhaps also their genealogy, to other dimensions less amenable to language.

One candidate for our attention is affect.

Affectations

Recent work on affect understands it as autonomic, in excess of or below consciousness and therefore not coterminous with subjects and subjectivities, as an a-subjective force that can impel or inhibit action (Gibbs 2010: 188), something that augments or diminishes a body's capacity to act (Clough 2010: 207), or as an impersonal intensity that establishes connections and expands or contracts our horizons. (In many respects it is a resurgence of Lacan's Real.) Affect is also ambiguous. Celebrants of affect emphasise its liberatory potential as something excessive and beyond control, a corrective to oversocialised constructivist approaches.[12] However, affect in an abstract sense doesn't really interest me very much. Whatever affect's dynamism and corrosive properties at some point the brake is applied and it is made available for social and cultural translation and codification. Affect as endless novelty and flux is an appealing but ultimately exhausting notion. Rather like Weber's charisma – an early sociological version of affect – it eventually becomes routinised. When this happens, affect can be marshaled and manipulated to effect control and impose consensus and conformity, not only undo them. For example, the Global Culture Industry (see Chapter 2) can and does exploit affect by investing it in media-things that lend it specific emotions and values and thereby forge links between affect and capitalism. What of affects that dissolve, realign, undermine and refigure, the affects that expand horizons? Take the example of disgust.

Disgusting

Disgust is a visceral reaction to the world a feeling of revulsion anchored in the guts. Disgust positions us on a boundary between mind and matter,

---

working in either direction. The relationship between the animate and inanimate is not one of straightforward reciprocity, even less a Hegel-style recognition.

12 There is a libertarian emphasis in writings on affect reminiscent of earlier writings on the promise of Eros found in works by Norman Brown, Herbert Marcuse, Wilhelm Reich and the polymorphous perversity of Hocquenghem encountered earlier (Dollimore 1991: 205–6)

epistemology and ontology, rational and irrational, the tangible and intangible. Gut feelings are felt but need not be reasoned through or spelled out (Durham 2010: 137). A visceral reaction can contradict better judgement in someone who doesn't consider herself, to be prone to homophobia or racism, but reacts nonetheless with disgust or distaste: 'I ought to know better than to feel like this, but I can't help it.' What our bodies are partial to need not agree with our expressed preferences, likes or dislikes. Sometimes affects follow their own agendas.

Disgust also acts as a bridge between self and other. It requires some kind of proximity. Disgust can span huge distances, but it will not arise from indifference and disinterest. As Deborah Durham (2011: 151) states: 'Active disgust is simultaneously both transgressive, rooted in boundaries maintained with moral force, and also transcendent, successful insofar as the person feeling disgust is caught up in the experience of another. A moment of transcendence is required to create the moment of "transgression" that is often observed in disgust – an erasure of the distinction is part and parcel of the intimate, and imaginative, act of disgust.' Smells, the topic of Chapter 3, act as just such a bridge. They are molecular connections between people and people, people and other beings and people and things. They are tangible, to smell something is literally to touch it. Perhaps for that reason smells are often the focus of disgusted reactions and moral outrage. To make a stink about something is to turn it into a moral stench.

It is obvious to any anthropologist that visceral reactions like disgust are a potential resource for an ethnographer. By exposing somatic biases, including fears, embarrassment, squeamishness, prudishness, and disgust (but also pleasures) we use the knowledge gained to direct our attention to those aspects of the people we study that have evoked or provoked such reactions. More than an ethnographic tool, affective fieldwork also draws attention to non-subjective, visceral, sometimes molecular processes. The lowly, often disavowed and frequently organic aspects of ethnography: bowels, digestion, fatigue, ennui, listlessnss, bad moods, temper tantrums, elation, euphoria, fear and loathing. This is the stuff often consigned to diaries. Their frequent neglect is yet another symptom of the absent body. Here is a little food for thought.

The Alimentary Anthropologist

There is a growing awareness of how foodstuffs are caught up in vast and complicated networks of agribusiness, transport, environmental impacts, and the global relations of poverty and inequality. Anthropologists have long written about the social and cultural significance of food, including the massive symbolism surrounding food and eating. All this is obvious. So too are the class, ethnic, racial and national dimensions of food. We use food to mark ourselves off from others. Our food is delicious, theirs is disgusting. But food *does* things in a much more tangible sense than symbolisation. We become what we eat. Food makes bodies, fat or thin, healthy or unfit. The rich eat better than the poor and they tend to live longer. There is now a large and growing literature on the effects of foodstuffs on everything from personality, intelligence, concentration span, violent behaviour, allergies, and psychological disorders. Food also orders time, most obviously by meal times. When we eat the national dish on the appointed holidays, we synchronise the guts of the nation through alimentary processes of ingestion, digestion and defecation. The latter connects us all to yet another complex organisation with which we are in frequent and unavoidable contact, shit and how it is taken care of. (Now there is a topic seriously underresearched by anthropologists.)[13] From the simplest hole in the ground (and perhaps not even that) to the industrial-scale treatment of human faeces in the sewage systems of the world's cities, we cannot escape our shit, the end result of our food. Once tourist attractions we now prefer to ignore these huge subterranean worlds flowing just below our feet. Food's impact is also molecular. For example, we are usually unaware of the digestion of food, unless our food 'disagrees' with us. Then battle commences and the offending tenant is expelled often in ways largely beyond our conscious control, such as projectile vomit or sudden and violent diarrhea. Even normal defecation can only be postponed for so long. What makes food enjoyable is also often under the radar. We like the taste of the cheese but are unaware of the microbes that lend it its numerous flavours, or the yeast that creates wine and beers. We are unable to feel the growing of our muscles as they bind protein to themselves. All these processes take place within the molar realties of the agricultural and food industries and the cultural and social ordering of food, but they are not always answerable to them and we fail to notice many of them. If we were to attend to every particle and inch of the anthropologist, we would soon start to look at our food and our shit. This would be a molecular study of the ethnographer. It is a gigantic undertaking but it is also a profoundly ethical one, because all of these processes, regardless of whether they impinge on our thoughts or our body's somatic attention, connect us to actors, organisations and processes with social and political implications. This would also be a queer

---

13 Recent research by anthropologists into infrastructures does bring us close to the topic. Infrastructures are, sometimes, the obscene but indispensable supplements necessary for successful society. Other examples than sewers include bridges, motorways and hydroelectric dams that are very visible manifestations of infrastructure and intended to be so. These frequently political and often emotive projects cultivate civic and national pride and make possible citizens, travellers, and sometimes anthropologists. For a recent review, see Larkin 2013.

and perhaps even post-human endeavour. The anthropologist eating, and all anthropologists eat, would be a surface effect on a sea of food and all that makes food possible.

Thus far I have decomposed the body – its metaphors, organisation and affectual states – but as we have just seen in the case of food, bodies are not alone. They are connected in diverse ways to things. I want now to consider in a little more detail than hitherto another quality of things addressed in the work of Adorno, their non-identity.

Things (Still) Matter

Adorno (1973) wrote against the predominance (at least in the Euro-America tradition) of the subject over the object. In the identitarian thought he critiques subjects deploy concepts that both represent and purport to describe the object exhaustively. The result is a direct identity between thought and the world with no remainder. The apparent unity of the subject, its sense of being in control, is made possible by the demotion of the material world to a mere reflection of its own thought. Like the ego of Lacan's Imaginary, and Baudrillard's mirror of production, subjects falsely assume a wholeness that objects reflect back to them. But objects have elements of the Real about them, a surplus that escapes concepts and militates against closure. According to Adorno, this material recalcitrance is experienced by the subject as a threat to its sense of unity and dominance. Minting new concepts in a vain attempt to exhaust the object is not a fruitful response in Adorno's opinion. We must relinquish any such ambition and make room for non-identity, a concept that refers to the out of reach, the feeling that there is more going on than awareness reveals, that regardless of how much we grasp there is always more to comprehend because 'objects do not go into their concepts without leaving a remainder'. It is important to be able to identify those things that harbour non-identity and for subjects to be open to their otherness and not regard it as a threat to their own integrity.[14] These are the things that leave us perplexed – the fetishes of fieldwork that do not simply mirror concepts and representations. Things we cannot make *sense* of, that we find difficult to assimilate to our sensible world, in both senses. Things that are sensational, excessive and extravagant, things that wander off the beaten track, and are out of bounds.[15]

---

14 Adorno traces part of the difficulty in grasping this otherness to the axiology of capitalism, which attaches exchange values to things in order to render them equivalent, thus suppressing the thing's particularity and its incomparability, its use value.

15 David Sneath et al. (2009: 6) write about what they call 'technologies of the imagination' that include things and practices which produce phenomena whose

Adorno's 'negative dialectics' is actually a method for the detection and acceptance of non-identity. Jane Bennett (2010: 159) summarises it succinctly: 'The self-criticism of conceptualisation, a sensory attentiveness to the qualitative singularities of the object, the exercise of an unrealistic imagination, and the courage of a clown. By means of such practices one might replace the "rage" against non-identity with respect for it, a respect that chastens our will to mastery'.

Reflexive critique, skirting around the real, aesthetic appreciation and fooling around are all methods in tune with queer theory. I particularly like the reference to the clown. If you want to make sense of things, you have to be a bit of a buffoon and what ethnographer hasn't landed in that position at some point in time? The word clown appears to be derived from the English clod or clot, something lumpy, thrown together, a coagulated substance or frozen motion. The clown is a being not entirely finished and loosely connected. Clowns are also internally heterogeneous, ambiguous and even contradictory, at one moment comic and clumsy, the other serious and controlled. Like mediaeval fools, they dissolve the world around them just as they themselves are always on the edge of falling apart. As Don Handelman puts it, the clown is a 'consistent solvent of states or reality, and its essence seems to be that of process' (1990: 243). It is 'an embodiment of uncertainty, and so a device for the dissolution of boundaries' (1990: 264). Not surprisingly, clowns appear at rituals and public events where status alters and change is in the air. Clowns project their own internal flux and inconsistencies, their very own non-identity, into their surroundings and lead them towards becoming other than they are. Clowning would seem to be a good method when out to interrogate the object's self-evident character imposed by the subject's concept, and crack open its carapace to set free its non-identity.

We can also clown around in a more conventional sense. According to Freud (1938: 795) when we encounter the new we can react in one of two ways. We can compare it with something we already know, which requires standards, objects of comparison and epistemological distance. Or, we can choose to mimic the thing by doing or being it. The latter is an ontological stance towards

---

conditions of emergence are not fully conditioned. What they call the imagination is 'the space of indeterminacy in social and cultural life'. And, like the arguments proffered here, they consider ethnography with its attention to specifics of time and place as indispensable for the study of the imagination (2009: 25). They thus provide a definition of imagination and creativity compatible with Bergson's ideas surrounding the future that emanates from but is not determined by the past. Another reaction to unfamiliar things is to think 'through' them, to use them as tools with which to generate new concepts (e.g. Henare et al. 2007). This would make things events, in the sense mentioned earlier.

the thing which Freud associated with children. It is also an intensive and sensible relationship. Children lose themselves in things through playfulness, sheer nonsense and immediacy that involve finding out, experimentation and improvisation. We sense things and try to make sense of them by bringing them into the sensible orbit even as they shift its coordinates. Ethnographers too can be distanced observers intent on comparison with what they already know or playful neophytes trying to grasp the new from the inside.

The Material Anthropologist

As the example of food illustrates, no thing is an island. To employ a terminology currently in vogue, and also Deleuzean, things, including bodies, belong to assemblages. An assemblage is not comprised of self-identical objects whose combination is simply additive, so that the result is a mere summation of the components. In such an arrangement novelty is prefigured in the parts themselves. In an assemblage of multiplicities differentiation is central to it. Elizabeth Grosz describes an assemblage as 'the provisional linkages of elements, fragments, flows of disparate status and substance: ideas, things – human, animate, and inanimate – all have the same ontological status' (1994: 167). The assemblage stands in contrast to the integrated and unified body of the Imaginary, the dominant masculine imago, in which the parts are subordinated to a whole as organs are subordinated to a body. An assemblage does not stand alone; it too is caught up in other assemblages. Out of this entanglement bodies and structures stabilise. Connections to other assemblages help them to do this: collective practices, rituals, and routines laid down by institutions, all of which are themselves assemblages.

Assemblage is a very appropriate leitmotif for ethnographic fieldwork as it brings into focus the encounter between the ethnographer's body and persons and things, perhaps unfamiliar and novel, that contribute through linkages and exchange to this process of assembling. (In fact, what I have described corresponds to a non-sexual version of Hocquenghem's anal grouping and polymorphous perversity based on couplings and decouplings. Other non-sexual versions of similar ideas go under the name of actor network theory.)

Ethnography is material not only because it involves the study of things but also because of its conditions of possibility, the material framework that supports it. What material assemblage makes and has made anthropology possible? Here is a short list: Universities and all their institutional paraphernalia, letters of introduction, grant applications, grant committees, funding agencies, pens, pencils, notepads, paper, erasers, cameras, sound recorders increasingly of a digital kind, video recorders, virtual tools like Skype and iCloud, iPods, websites, blogs, satellites, telephones, mobiles, email, postal services, letters, telegrams, parcels, packages tied up with string, stamps, tape, glue, USB memory sticks, flashcards for cameras, extra computer memory, CDROM, DVDS, clothing, pith helmets, shorts, mosquito nets, t-shirts, good boots, good sandals, as little clothing as possible, as much clothing as possible, machetes, axes, knives, medical kits, laxatives, toilets, vaccinations, malaria pills, healthcare facilities, water purification tablets, maps, charts, diagrams, guidebooks, dictionaries, language courses, bearers, porters, interpreters, adopted kin, friends and acquaintances, local currency, passports, visas, immigration authorities, travel tickets, trains, planes, cars, busses, bicycles, lorries, jeeps, vans, canoes, boats (steam, turbine, motor, sailing, rowing) helicopters, hotels, apartments, rooms in houses, own house, tent, hut, hammock, blankets, food, alcohol, drugs, colonial and post colonial relationships, the following very material positions and statuses (class, gender, sexuality, age, ethnicity, race, nationality, and religion), publishing companies, libraries, journals, the editors of journals, the peer reviewers for journals, books, articles, conference papers, conferences and all their paraphernalia, reports, televisions, radios, newspapers, the organisations and institutions we study, material culture, the natural environment (an immensely complicated phenomenon). The people we study.

I doubt any of the above, in what is a very incomplete inventory, will surprise readers. It took only a few minutes of reflection to jot it down and it is far from exhaustive. Any number of different anthropologists and ethnographers can be extruded out of this assemblage depending on when, where and how they did their fieldwork. Pith helmets are not so common nowadays but we still use pens and notepads. This is how material we are. This is also very easily overlooked.[16] The sheer scale of anthropology's material support is astonishing and difficult to assimilate to an object of thought. Its full extent will always, I suspect, be beyond our ken.

This immediately raises ethical questions. Just how much of this complexity can we attend to in fieldwork? How much food for thought can we stomach to return to the alimentary anthropologist? Where do we draw the line? Although anthropology often presents itself as holistic, it cannot include everything, and never does whether it be the ethnographic product or its attention to its own material base. There is always a cut, a de-cision, deliberate or not, to include and

---

16 The material scaffolding that supports the production and dissemination of knowledge is strikingly and famously apparent in the case of physicist Stephen Hawking. His motorised chair, his electronic voice, the computer hardware and software that helps him work and communicate, students who aid him, nurses who tend him, as well as the paraphernalia of fame, including television appearance and even a statue in his honour, have all contributed to what Hélène Mailet (2012) in her ethnography calls *Hawking Incorporated*. Yet we are all of us corporations.

exclude that implicates us in the inequalities of fieldwork, its material conditions of possibility.

In Excess

To summarise the point, ethnographic and anthropological practice in general is always beyond itself. It can never be fully self-aware, and never fully in possession of itself. There is always a remainder to anthropology as a discipline and the actual person and body of the anthropologist, an excess if you like.

All of the chapters that feature herein explore aspects of excessive or extravagant phenomena: the indeterminate nature of matter, the litigious character of things, the unrepresentable fetish, the secretive commodity, the ambiguous and superfluous gift, nomadic smells, implicate value, repeat failures, the unheimlich in the everyday, and now the anthropologist's body. Excessive phenomena are not recognisable by their scale – size *doesn't* matter – but by their capacity to depart, to go beyond, to roam and wander off the beaten track.

Excess has long been a problem for the sociological and anthropological imaginations (Pawlett 1997). Yet it is present in modern thought though rarely at the theoretical and empirical centre. Pawlett traces an excessive genealogy from Nietzsche through Bataille to Baudrillard. Where these thinkers overlap is their, at times imperious, hostility towards the utilitarian principles of classical economics and conventional sociology. Marx's elevation of productivity and use-value to the status of defining characteristics of our species being is but one example. Within anthropology, functionalism defined swathes of social practices in terms of their usefulness (functionality) for society conceived of as a functioning whole. Whatever threatened stability was dealt with either as pathological or functional in its own right (Durkheim on the role of deviance and crime). An argument that reappeared much later in the theoretical guise of post-structuralism under the rubric of supplementarity and constitutive outsides that stabilise the boundaries of dominant categories, and as such are functional for them, even if in a troubling and uncanny way.

Yet Durkheim himself wrote that it is the superfluous and excessive acts that we find the most appealing, even as they contradict the demands of sound economy (Pawlett 1997). (The classic example is the potlatch – again.) Yet, despite what Durkheim wrote, he did not launch a sociology or anthropology of excess. Quite the opposite, his positive sociology is preoccupied with order and stability. If anything, excess has been corralled in anthropology, made part of classificatory regimes,[17] and domesticated as a hybrid, which nowadays does

---

17 More recently, attempts to make sense of excessive phenomena, such as alterity and violence, catch it in 'grammars', e.g. Baumann and Gingrich 2004.

not appear particularly threatening. In part, this reflects a neglect of subjectivity. Two of the most influential theoretical currents of the last few decades, despite their considerable insights, Bourdieu's practice theory and Foucault's discursive-power approach, both fail to take individual subjectivity and variation seriously and turn the largely faceless people in their texts into exemplars of what is rather than harbingers of what might be or could have been.

Without labouring the point, then, excess and anthropology tend not to go hand-in-hand.[18] Yet ironically, and as I mentioned in the Introduction, anthropology is often equated with the purveyance not only of the exotic but also the extravagant and the excessive – the uncivilised, the grotesque, the untamed, the alarming, the bizarre, the immoral and repugnant, the irrational, the utterly other. It might be just those moments of otherness and strangeness for anthropologists that are most illuminating.

Intuition

Jason Throop (2010) argues that it is in moments of maximum opacity 'where failure in our attempts at understanding reveal the limits of interpretability, that there is a true acknowledgment of the integrity of that other, the alter, the full being that stands before us'. Adopting a cultural phenomenology of moral experience Throop has studied illness and intense pain and suffering on the Micronesian island of Yap. The intensive pain of other people is not something we can take upon ourselves, we cannot experience it, because it resists meaning and verbalisation. It is excessive. Drawing on Levinas, Throop argues that it is in extra-ordinary 'limit experiences' like pain that we glimpse the 'integrity and mystery of the other'.

I believe that Throop's point can be generalised beyond the example of pain and suffering to include less extreme situations. He argues that the 'anthropological attitude' emerges out of the frustrations of ethnography and recurrent failures to understand other lifeworlds. The stuff we label 'culture', he reasons, is whatever destabilises us, throws us off kilter, and produces vulnerability and an openness as preconceived ideas and assumptions crumble. Rendered thus 'their' culture appears decidedly queer in its effects. The non-

---

18 Even in its attention to the anthropological writing excess got short shrift. The reflexive anthropology of the 1980s focused on the tropes and conventions (often unrecognised) that underlie the dominant realist textual tradition (Marcus and Fischer 1986). Seen from a different angle, what this reflexive turn addressed was how the chaotic, strange, and incomprehensible parts of fieldwork, not least embodiment, are excluded once ethnography is broken down and reassembled in the form of a written product, a text that conforms to conventions.

identity of excessive things, like fetishes, can elicit the same kind of reaction. The difficulty of pinning down the meaning of gifts and especially their extreme manifestations such as sacrifice, challenge our capacities to represent them. Another example could be glossolalia, which transcends language but holds meaning within its meaninglessness and intensely embodied performance and expression. All things make sense but in excess of themselves because sense is always to some extent excessive there is a superabundance of signifiers over signifieds.

How then do we make sense of whatever seems to escape sense? One candidate is intuition. Intuition is something anthropologists employ all the time but a capacity which is itself very difficult to put into words and perhaps even more difficult to teach and communicate to students. Grosz calls intuition a 'luxurious and excessive operation [tuned to the] myriad connections, entwinements, and transformations that make up even the most stable objects of analysis' (2004: 240). Intuition in Bergson's hands is very much an ontological stance to being in the world.[19] It is a way of approaching duration. Unlike intelligence, which is practical in its orientation and divides being into units and objects, intuition is about grasping the unity or the multiplicity of duration. While intellect apprehends from the outside and is extensive, intuition is intensive, it demands an insider approach, an immersion in the materiality of the world. This is why Bergson calls it 'true empiricism'. He writes: 'We call intuition here the sympathy by which one is transported into the interior of an object in order to coincide with what there is unique and consequently inexpressible in it' (quoted in Grosz 2004: 237). It even suggests playfulness. In this respect, intuition is searching for something akin to Adorno's non-identity of the object, the thingness that evades the concept. Intuition attends to what the intellect must perforce neglect.

This is not an easy task. Intuition cannot withstand for long the demands of the intellect for objects, concepts, representations, and measurements. Whatever intuition intuits must be transformed into the recognisable garb of the intellect. We need both intellect and intuition. The development of intuition demands taking part, being there, immersion in the world. It is very much an empirical exercise despite its associations with guesswork based on flimsy or minimal evidence.

Intuition, whose origins are always difficult to pinpoint, is what emerges when the visceral and molecular processes this chapter has sketched impinge on consciousness. It crystallises out of the emergent and inchoate. It is the actualisation of thought's virtual, its implications. It is when the umbra of inscrutable things gives way to a penumbra of insight. It is when we grasp, if

---

19 My understanding of Bergson is here indebted to Elizabeth Grosz' *The Nick of Time* (2004).

only fleetingly and at the risk of causing a commotion, the 'truth' of a gift. It is when smells actualise often poignantly the past that dwells in the present. It is when the *unheimlich* causes a shudder and a snag in the flow of life and forces us to take a closer look at just what it is we are up to. These, in brief, are moments of intuition and these are the content of a querying, sometimes querulous, and queer anthropology.

References

Abelson, E. 2000. 'Shoplifting Ladies', in Scanlon, J. (ed.), *The Gender and Consumer Culture Reader*. New York: New York University Press, pp. 309–29.

Abu-Lughod, L. 1990. 'The Romance of Resistance: Tracing and Transformations of Power through Bedouin Women', *American Ethnologist* 17(1): 41–55.

Adams, V. and Pigg, S.L. (eds), 2005. *Sex in Development: Science, Sexuality, and Morality in Global Perspective*. Durham, NC: Duke University Press.

Adorno, T. 1973. *Negative Dialectics*, trans. E.B. Ashton. New York: Continuum.

Alaimo, S. and Hekman, S. 2008. 'Introduction: Emerging Models of Materiality in Feminist Theory', in Alaimo, S. and Hekman, S. (eds), *Material Feminisms*. Bloomington, IN: Indiana University Press, pp. 1–19.

Althusser, L. 1971. 'Ideology and Ideological State Apparatuses', in *Lenin and Philosophy and Other Essays*. New York: Monthly Review.

Altman, D. 1993[1971]. *Homosexual Oppression and Liberation*. New York: New York University Press.

Anthias, F. and Yuval-Davis, N. 1992. *Racialized Boundaries: Race, Nation, Gender, Colour and Class and the Anti-racist Struggle*. London: Routledge.

Antze, P. and Lambek, M. 1996. 'Introduction', in Antze, P. and Lambek, M. (eds), *Tense Past: Cultural Essays in Trauma and Memory*. London: Routledge, pp. xi–xxxviii.

Appadurai, A. 1986. 'Introduction', in Appadurai, A. (ed.), *The Social Life of Things: Commodities in Cultural Perspective*. Cambridge: Cambridge University Press, pp. 3–63.

Ardener, E. (1975). 'Belief and the problem of women', in Ardener, S. (ed.), *Perceiving Women*. London: Malaby Press, pp. 1–17.

Aristotle. 1998. *Politics*, trans. Ernest Barker, revised by R.F. Stalley. New York: Oxford University Press.

Austin J.L. 1975. *How to Do Things with Words*. Oxford: Oxford University Press.

Badgett, M.V.L. 2001. *Money, Myths and Change: The Economic Lives of Lesbians and Gay Men*. Chicago: University of Chicago Press.

Bailey, F. 1971. *Gifts and Poison: The Politics of Reputation*. Oxford: Blackwell.

Bar-On Cohen, E. 2011. 'Events of Organicity: The state abducts the war machine', *Anthropological Theory* 11(3): 259–82.

Barad, K. 2007. *Meeting the Universe Halfway: Quantum Physics and the Entanglements of Matter and Meaning*. Durham, NC: Duke University Press.

Barad, K. 2008. 'Posthumanist Performativity: Toward an Understanding of How Matter Comes to Matter', in Alaimo, S. and Hekman, S. (eds), *Material Feminisms*. Bloomington, IN: Indiana University Press, pp. 120–54.

Barker-Benfield, G.J. 1976. *Horrors of the Half-known Life: Male Attitudes toward Women and Sexuality in Nineteenth-Century America*. New York: Harper & Row.

Bataille, G. 1988. *The Accursed Share: An Essay on General Economy*, trans. R. Hurley. New York: Zone.

Bataille, G. 1985. 'The Notion of Expenditure', in Stoekl, A. (ed.), *Visions of Excess: Selected Writings: 1927–1939*, trans. A. Stoekl, C. Lovitt and D. Leslie. Minneapolis: University of Minnesota Press, pp. 116–29.

Bateson, M.C. 1984. *With a Daughter's Eye: A Memoir of Margaret Mead and Gregory Bateson*. New York: William Morrow.

Baudrillard, J. 1975. *The Mirror of Production*, trans. M. Poster. St. Louis: Telos Press.

Baudrillard, J. 1981[1972]. *For a Critique of the Political Economy of the Sign*, trans. C. Levin. St. Louis: Telos Press.

Baudrillard, J. 1988. *Consumer Society: Myths and Structures*. London: Sage.

Baudrillard, J. 1990a, *The Transparency of Evil*, trans. J. Benedict. London: Verso.

Baudrillard, J. 1990b. *Fatal Strategies*. London: Pluto Press.

Baudrillard. J. 1993. *Symbolic Exchange and Death*, trans. I.H. Grant. London: Sage.

Baudrillard, J. 2005. *The System of Objects*, trans. J. Benedict. London : Verso.

Baumann G. and Gingrich, G. (eds), 2004. *Grammars of Identity/Alterity*. New York: Berghahn.

Bawer, B. 1993. *A Place at the Table: The Gay Individual in American Society*. New York: Touchstone.

Beck, U., Giddens, A. and Lash S. 1994. *Reflexive Modernization*. Cambridge: Polity.

Benhabib, S. 1992. *Situating the Self: Gender, Community and Postmodernism in Contemporary Ethics*. Cambridge: Polity.

Bennett, J. 2010. *Vibrant Matter. A Political Ecology of Things*. London: Duke University Press.

Bentley G. 1987 'Ethnicity and Practice', *Comparative Studies in Society and History*, 29: 24–55.

Berlant, L. 2011. *Cruel Optimism*. Durham, NC: Duke University Press.

Berlant, L. and Warner, M. 2000. 'Sex in Public', in Berlant, L. (ed.), *Intimacy*. Chicago: Chicago University Press, pp. 311–30.

Bersani, L. 1994[1987]. 'Is the Rectum a Grave?', in Goldberg, J. (ed.), *Reclaiming Sodom*. London: Routledge, pp. 249–64.

Biehl, J. and Locke, P. 2010. 'Deleuze and the Anthropology of Becoming', *Current Anthropology* 51(3): 317–51.

Binnie, J. 2004. *The Globalization of Sexuality*. London: Sage.

REFERENCES

Blackwood, E. 2010. *Falling into the Lesbi World: Desire and Difference in Indonesia*. Honolulu: University of Hawai'i Press.

Blaser, M. 2009. 'The Threat of the Yrmo: The Political Ontology of a Sustainable Hunting Program', *American Anthropologist* 111(1): 10–20.

Bloch, M. and Parry, J. (eds), 1989. *Money and the Morality of Exchange*. Cambridge: Cambridge University Press.

Boellstorff, T. 2007. 'Queer Studies in the House of Anthropology', *Annual Review of Anthropology* 35: 17–35.

Bohm, D. 1980. *Wholeness and the Implicate Order*. London: Routledge.

Bordo, S. 1993. *Unbearable Weight*. Berkeley: University of California Press.

Bordo, S. 1999. *The Male Body: A New Look at Men in Public and in Private*. New York: Farrar, Straus and Giroux.

Borch-Jacobsen, M. 1991. *Lacan: The Absolute Master*, trans. D. Brick, Stanford: Stanford University Press.

Bourdieu, P. 1977. *Outline of a Theory of Practice*, trans. R. Nice. Cambridge: Cambridge University Press.

Bourdieu, P. 1984. *Distinction: A Social Critique of the Judgement of Taste*, trans. by R. Nice. London: Routledge & Kegan Paul.

Bourdieu, P. 1990. *The Logic of Practice*, trans. R. Nice. Stanford CA: Stanford University Press.

Brown, W. 2005. *Edgework: Critical Essays on Knowledge and Politics*. Princeton, NJ: Princeton University Press.

Butler, J. 1990. *Gender Trouble: Feminism and the Subversion of Identity*. London: Routledge.

Butler, J. 1991. 'Imitation and Gender Insubordination', in Fuss, D. (ed.), *Inside/Outside: Lesbian Theories, Gay Theories*. New York: Routledge, pp. 13–31.

Callari, A. 2002. 'The ghost of the gift: The unlikelihood of economics', in Osteen, M. (ed.), *The Question of the Gift: Essays across Disciplines*. London: Routledge, pp. 248–65.

Campbell, J. 2000. *Arguing with the Phallus*. London: Zed Books.

Candea, M. 2011. 'Our Division of the Universe: A Space for the Non-Political in the Anthropology of Politics', *Current Anthropology* 52: 3: 309–34.

Cantle, T. 2001. *Community Cohesion: A report of the independent review team*. London: Home Office.

Cantle, T. 2005. *Community Cohesion: A New Framework for Race and Diversity*. Basingstoke: Palgrave Macmillan.

Carrier, J. 1995. *Gifts and Commodities: Exchange and Western Capitalism since 1700*. London: Routledge.

Carrier, J. and Miller, D. 1999. 'From Private Virtue to Public Vice', in Moore, H. (ed.) *Anthropological Theory Today*. Cambridge: Polity, pp. 24–47.

Chasin, A. 2000. *Selling Out: The Gay and Lesbian Movement Goes to Market*. New York: Palgrave.

Clarke, E.O. 2000. *Virtuous Vice: Homoeroticism and the Public Sphere*. Durham, NC: Duke University Press.
Classen, C., Howes, D. and Synnott, A. 1994. *Aroma*. London: Routledge.
Clifford, J. 1988. *The Predicament of Culture: Twentieth-Century Ethnography, Literature and Art*. Cambridge, MA: Harvard University Press.
Clough, P.T. 2010. 'The Affective Turn: Political Economy, Biomedia, and Bodies', in Gregg, M. and Seigworth, G.J. (eds), *The Affect Theory Reader*. London: Duke University Press, pp. 206–26.
Coffey, A. 1999. *The Ethnographic Self: Fieldwork and the Representation of Identity*. London: Sage.
Cohen, A. 1974. 'Introduction', in Cohen, A. (ed.), *Urban Ethnicity*. ASA Monographs, 12. London: Tavistock, pp. ix–xxiv.
Cohen, P. 1969. 'Theories of Myth', *Man* NS 3(3): 337–53.
Collins, J. 2003. *Threads: Gender, Labor and Power in the Global Apparel Industry*. Chicago: University of Chicago Press.
Collins, P. 1998. 'It's all in the family: intersections of gender, race, and nation', *Hypatia* 13(3): 62–82.
Commission for Racial Equality (CRE) 2004. *Strength in Diversity: Towards a community cohesion and race equality strategy. A response*. London: CRE.
Connerton, P. 1989. *How Societies Remember*. Cambridge: Cambridge University Press.
Cooper, D. 2004. *Challenging Diversity: Rethinking Equality and the Value of Difference*. Cambridge: Cambridge University Press.
Crenshaw, K. 1991. 'Mapping the Margins: Intersectionality, Identity Politics, and Violence against Women of Color'. *Stanford Law Review* 43(6): 1241–99.
Crenshaw, K. 1989. 'Demarginalizing the Intersection of Race and Sex: A Black Feminist Critique of Antidiscrimination Doctrine, Feminist Theory and Antiracist Politics', *University of Chicago Legal Forum*: 139–67.
Cross, S. and Litter, J. 2010. 'Celebrity and Schadenfreude: The cultural economy of fame freefall', *Cultural Studies* 24(3): 395–417.
Csordas T.J. 1993. 'Somatic modes of attention', *Cultural Anthropology* 8(2): 135–56.
Davis, K. 2011. 'Intersectionality as Buzzword: A Sociology of Science Perspective on What Makes a Feminist Theory Useful', in Lutz, H., Vivar, M.T.H. and Supik, L. (eds), *Framing Intersectionality: Debates on a Multi-Faceted Concept in Gender Studies*. Farnham: Ashgate Publishing, pp. 43–54.
Davis, S.G. 2010. *Gender Diversity in Indonesia: Sexuality, Islam and Queer Selves*. London: Routledge.
Dean, T. 2000. *Beyond Sexuality*. Chicago: University of Chicago Press.
Deleuze, G. and Guattari, F. 1984. *Anti-Oedipus*. London: Athlone Press.
Deleuze, G. and Parnet, C. 1987. *Dialogues*, trans. H. Tomlinson and B. Habberjam. London: Athlone Press.

REFERENCES

Deleuze, G. 1988 /1966. *Bergsonism*, trans. H. Tomlinson and B. Habberjam. New York: Zone Books.
Deleuze, G. 1988. *Spinoza: Practical Philosophy*, trans. R. Hurley. San Francisco: City Light Books.
Deleuze, G. 1994. *Difference and Repetition*. London: Athlone Press.
Delphy, C. 1993. 'Rethinking Sex and Gender', *Women's Studies International Forum* 16(1): 1–19.
Derrida, J. 1992. *Given Time: I. Counterfeit Money*, trans. P. Kamuf. Chicago: University of Chicago Press.
Devereux, G. 1937. 'Institutionalized Homosexuality of the Mohave Indians', *Human Biology* 9: 498–513.
Devereux, G. 1978[1965]. 'Ethnopsychoanalytical Reflections on the Notion of Kinship', in *Ethnopsychoanalysis: Psychoanalysis and Anthropology as Complementary Frames of Reference*. Berkeley: University of California Press, pp. 177–215.
Dietz, G., Haschemi Yekani, E. and Michaelis, B. 2007. '"Checks and balances"Zum Verhältnis von Intersektionalität und Queer Theory', in K. Walgenbach, G. Dietze, A. Hornscheidt and K. Palm (eds), *Gender als interdependente Kategori. Neue Perspektiven auf Intersektionalität, Diversität und Heterogenität*. Opladen: Barbara Budrich.
Dollimore, J. 1991. *Sexual Dissidence*. Oxford: Clarendon Press.
Douglas, M. and Isherwood, B. 1979. *The World of Goods: Towards an Anthropology of Consumption*. Harmondsworth: Penguin.
Dover, K. 1978. *Greek Homosexuality*. London: Duckworth.
Downey, G. 2007. 'Seeing with a "Sideways" Glance: Visuomotor "Knowing" and the Plasticity of Perception', in Harris, M. (ed.), *Ways of Knowing*. New York: Berghahn Books, pp. 222–41.
Durham, D. 2011. 'Disgust and the Anthropological Imagination', *Ethnos* 76(2): 131–56.
Ebert, T. 1993. 'Ludic Feminism, the Body, Performance and Labor. Bringing Materialism back into Feminist Cultural Studies', *Cultural Critique* 23: 5–50.
Ereshefsky, M. 2010. 'Species', in *Stanford Encyclopedia of Philosophy*. http://plato.stanford.edu/entries/species.
Ethnos. 2009. Theme Issue 'Transnationalizing Desire', 74(3).
Ethnos. 2010. Theme Issue, 'Performing Nature at World's End', 75(3),
European Journal of Women's Studies 2006. 'Intersectionality', No. 13.
Fardon, R. 1990. *Localizing Strategies: Regional Traditions of Ethnographic Writing*. Edinburgh: Scottish Academic Press.
Fassin, D. (ed.) 2012. *A Companion to Moral Anthropology*. Chichester: Wiley-Blackwell.
Fassin, E. 2001. 'Same Sex, Different Politics. "Gay Marriage" debates in France and the United States', *Public Culture* 13(2): 215–32.

Fausto-Sterling, A. 1985. *Myths of Gender: Biological Theories about Men and Women*. New York: Basic Books.

Firth, R. 1936. *We the Tikopia: A Sociological Study of Kinship in Primitive Polynesia*. London: George Allen and Unwin.

Florida, R.L. 2002. *The Rise of the Creative Class: and How it's Transforming Work*. New York: Basic Books.

Florida, R. 2005. *Cities and the Creative Class*. New York: Routledge.

Ford, C. and Beach, F. 1952. *Patterns of Sexual Behavior*. New York: Harper and Brothers.

Foucault, M. 1977. *Discipline and Punish: The Birth of the Prison*, trans. A. Sheridan. Harmondsworth: Penguin.

Foucault, M. 1978. *The History of Sexuality: Vol. 1, An Introduction*. New York: Pantheon.

Foucault, M. 1990. *The History of Sexuality: An Introduction*, trans. R. Hurley. New York: Vintage Books.

Freud, S. 1938. *The Basic Writings of Sigmund Freud*, trans. and with an Introduction, A. Brill. New York: Random House.

Freud, S. 1953–65. *The Standard Edition of the Complete Psychological Works of Sigmund Freud*, trans. J. Strachey, et al. London: Hogarth Press.

Freud, S. 1973. *Introductory Lectures in Psychoanalysis*, trans. J. Strachey. Harmondsworth: Pelican.

Friedan, B. 1963. *The Feminine Mystique*. New York: Norton.

Gane, M. 1993. *Harmless Lovers? Gender, Theory and Personal Relationships*. London: Routledge.

Gatens, M. 1996. *Imaginary Bodies: Ethics, Power and Corporeality*. London: Routledge.

Geertz, C. 1973. *The Interpretation of Cultures*. New York: Basic Books.

Gell, A. 1977. 'Magic, Perfume, Dream ... ,' in Lewis, I. (ed.), *Symbols and Sentiment*. London: Academic Press.

Gell, A. 1998. *Art and Agency: An Anthropological Theory*. Oxford: Clarendon Press.

Gibbs, A. 2010. 'After Affect: Sympathy, Synchrony and Mimetic Communication', in Gregg, M. and Seigworth, G.J. (eds), *The Affect Theory Reader*. London: Duke University Press, pp. 186–205.

Giddens, A. 1991. *Modernity and Self-Identity: Self and Society in the late Modern Age*. Cambridge: Polity.

Giddens, A. 2001. 'Introduction', in Giddens, A. (ed.), *The Global Third Way Debate*. Cambridge: Polity, pp. 1–22.

GLQ: A Journal of Lesbian and Gay Studies 2002 'Queer Tourism: Geographies of Globalization', No. 8.

Gluckman, M. 1954. *Rituals of Rebellion in South-East Africa*. Cambridge: Cambridge University Press.

REFERENCES

Goldman, M. 2009. 'An Afro-Brazilian Theory of the Creative Process: An Essay in Anthropological Symmetrization', *Social Analysis* 53(2): 108–29.

Gouldner, A. 1973. 'The Norm of Reciprocity. A Preliminary Statement', in *For Sociology*. London: Penguin Books, pp. 226–59.

Grace, V. 2000. *Baudrillard's Challenge: A Feminist Reading*. London: Routledge.

Graeber, D. 2001. *Toward an Anthropological Theory of Value: The False Coin of our Own Dreams*. Basingstoke: Palgrave.

Graham, M. 1992. *British Discourses on Race and Ethnicity. The construction of Britain's Black population as a problem in a post-imperial society*. Unpublished ms.

Graham, M. 1997. 'Welcome to the Land of Anthropology: Need Queers Apply? *Antropologiska studier*, 58: 7–25.

Graham, M. 1998. 'Follow the Yellow Brick Road. An Anthropological Outing in Queer Space', *Ethnos* 63(1): 102–32.

Graham, M. 2004. 'Sexual Things', *GLQ* 10(2): 299–303.

Graham, M. 2006. 'Queer Smells: Fragrances of Late-Capitalism or Scents of Subversion?' in Drobnick, J. (ed.), *The Smell Culture Reader*. Oxford: Berg.

Graham, M. 2010. 'Method Matters: Ethnography and Materiality', in Browne, K. and Nash, C. (eds), *Queer Methods and Methodologies: Intersecting Queer Theories and Social Science Research*. Farnham: Ashgate Publishing, pp. 183–94.

Gray, J. 1982. *Modern Process Thought*. Lanham, MD: University of America.

Greenberg, D. 1988. *The Construction of Homosexuality*. Chicago: University of Chicago Press.

Gregor, T. and Tuzin, D. (eds), 2001. *Gender in Amazonia and Melanesia*. Berkeley: University of California Press.

Gregory, C.A. 1982. *Gifts and Commodities*. London: Academic Press.

Grosz, E. 1994. *Volatile Bodies: Toward a Corporeal Feminism*. Bloomington and Indianapolis: Indiana University Press.

Grosz, E. 2004. *The Nick of Time: Politics, Evolution and the Untimely*. London: Duke University Press.

Grosz, E. 2009. 'The Thing', in Candlin, F. and Guins, R. (eds), *The Object Reader*. London: Routledge.

Gudeman, S. 2001. 'Postmodern Gifts', in Cullenberg, S., Amariglio, J. and Ruccio, D. (eds), *Postmodernism, Economics and Knowledge*. New York: Routledge, pp. 459–74.

Halberstam, J. 2011. *The Queer Art of Failure*. London: Duke University Press.

Hall, D. 2003. *Queer Theories*. Basingstoke: Palgrave Macmillan.

Hall, S. 1996. 'On postmodernism and articulation: an interview with Stuart Hall', in Morley, D. and Chen, K-H. (eds), *Stuart Hall, Critical Dialogues in Cultural Studies*. London: Routledge, pp 133–50.

Hallward, P. 2006. *Out of This World: Deleuze and the Philosophy of Creation*. London: Verso.

Halperin, D. 1995. *Saint Foucault: Towards a Gay Hagiography.* Oxford: Oxford University Press.

Hamer, D. and Copeland, P. 1994. *The Science of Desire: The Search for the Gay Gene and the Biology of Behavior.* New York: Simon and Schuster.

Handelman, D. 1990. *Models and Mirrors: Towards an Anthropology of Public Events.* Cambridge: Cambridge University Press.

Hardt, M. and Negri, A. 2005. *Multitude: War and Democracy in the Age of Empire.* London: Penguin.

Harmon, D. 2001. 'On the Meaning and Moral Imperative of Diversity', in Maffi, L. (ed.), *On Biocultural Diversity: Linking Language, Knowledge and the Environment.* Washington and London: Smithsonian Institution Press, pp. 53–70.

Harvey, D. 1996. *Justice, Nature and the Geography of Difference.* Oxford: Blackwell.

Haug, W. 1986[1971]. *Critique of Commodity Aesthetics: Appearance, Sexuality & Advertising.* Cambridge: Polity.

Haugerud, A., Stone, M.P. and Little, P. (eds), 2000. *Commodities and Globalization: Anthropological Perspectives.* Boulder: Rowman & Littlefield.

Hechter, M. 1978. 'Group Formation and the Cultural Division of Labor', *American Journal of Sociology* 84(2): 293–318.

Hekman, S. 2008. 'Constructing the Ballast: An Ontology for Feminism', in Alaimo, S. and Hekman, S. (eds), *Material Feminisms.* Bloomington, IN: Indiana University Press, pp. 85–119.

Henare, A., Holbraad, M., and Wastell, S. 2007. 'Thinking Through Things', in Henare, A., Holbraad, M. and Wastell, S. (eds), *Thinking Through Things: Theorizing Artefacts Ethnographically.* London: Routledge, pp. 1–31.

Hennessy, R. 2000. *Profit and Pleasure: Sexual Identities in Late Capitalism.* New York: Routledge.

Herzfeld, M. 1997. 'Anthropology: A Practice of Theory,' *International Social Sciences Journal* 153: 301–18.

Hey, J. 2001. *Genes, Categories, and Species: The Evolutionary and Cognitive Causes of the Species Problem.* Oxford and New York: Oxford University Press.

Hocquenghem, G. 1993[1972]. *Homosexual Desire*, trans. D. Dangoor. Durham, NC: Duke University Press.

Hodges, M. 2008. 'Rethinking Time's Arrow, Bergson, Deleuze and the Anthropology of Time', *Anthropological Theory* 8(4): 399–429.

Hogbin I. 1970. *The Island of Menstruating Men: Religion in Wogeo, New Guinea.* Prospect Heights: Waveland Press.

Holbraad, M. 2012. *Truth in Motion: The Recursive Anthropology of Cuban Divination.* Chicago: University of Chicago Press.

Home Office 2004. *Strength in Diversity: Towards a Community Cohesion Strategy.* London: Home Office.

REFERENCES

Hopkins, T. and Wallerstein, I. 1986. 'Commodity Chains in the World Economy prior to 1800', *Review* 10(1): 157–70.

Horkheimer, M. and Adorno, T. 1997. *Dialectic of Enlightenment*, trans. John Cumming. London: Verso.

Howes, D. 1987. 'Olfaction and Transition,' *Canadian Review of Sociology and Anthropology*, 24(3): 398–416.

Howes, D. 2003. *Sensual Relations. Engaging the Senses in Culture and Social Theory.* Ann Arbor: University of Michigan Press.

Howson, A. 2005. *Embodying Gender.* London: Sage.

Huffer, L. 2009. *Mad for Foucault: Rethinking the Foundations of Queer Theory.* New York: Columbia University Press.

Humphrey, C. 2008. 'Reassembling Individual Subjects: Events and Decisions in Troubled Times', *Anthropological Theory*, December: 357–80.

Hunter, I. and Saunders, D. 1995. 'Walks of Life: Mauss on the Human Gymnasium', *Body and Society* 1(2): 65–81.

Hutcheon, L. 1985. *A Theory of Parody: The Teachings of Twentieth-Century Art Forms.* New York and London: Methuen.

Iansiti, M. and Levin, R. 2004. 'Strategy as Ecology', *Harvard Business Review* 82, March: 68–78.

Ingold, T. 2000. *The Perception of the Environment: Essays in Livelihood, Dwelling and Skill.* London: Routledge.

Ingold, T. 2006. 'Rethinking the animate, reanimating thought', *Ethnos: Journal of Anthropology* 71(1): 9–20.

Ingold, T. 2007. *Lines: A Brief History.* London: Routledge.

Ingold, T. 2011. *Being Alive: Essays on Movement, Knowledge and Description.* Abingdon: Routledge.

Jackson, S. 2006. 'Heterosexuality, Sexuality and Gender: Re-thinking the Intersections', in Richardson, D., McLaughlin, J. and Casey, M. (eds), *Intersections between Feminism and Queer Theory.* Basingstoke: Palgrave, pp. 38–58.

Jackson S. and Scott, S. 2010. *Theorizing Sexuality.* Maidenhead: Open University Press.

Jagose, A. 1996. *Queer Theory.* Carlton: Melbourne University Press.

Jameson, F. 1984. 'Postmodernism, or the Cultural Logic of Late Capitalism', *New Left Review* 146: 53–93.

Jeffries, M.J. 2006. *Biodiversity and Conservation*, 2nd edition. London: Routledge.

Jensen, CB. 2010. *Ontologies for Developing Things: Making Health Care Futures Through Technology.* Rotterdam: Sense.

Kapferer B. 2006. 'Virtuality', in Kreinath, J., Snoek, M. and Stausberg, J. (eds), *Theorizing Rituals.* Brill Academic Publishers, pp. 671–84.

Karkazis, K. 2008. *Fixing Sex: Intersex, Medical Authority, and Lived Experience.* Durham. NC: Duke University Press.

Katz, J. 1995. *The Invention of Heterosexuality.* New York: Dutton.

Kelty, C. and Landecker, H. 2004. 'A Theory of Animation: Cells, L-systems, and Film', *Grey Room*, September: 30–63.

Kessler, S.J. 1998. *Lessons from the Intersexed*. New Brunswick, NJ: Rutgers University Press.

Kessler, S.J. and McKenna, W. 1978. *Gender: An Ethnomethodological Approach*. New York: Wiley.

Kirby, V. 2006. *Judith Butler: Live Theory*. London: Continuum.

Kirby, V. 2008. 'Natural Convers(at)ions: Or, What if Culture Was Really Nature All Along?', in *Material Feminisms*, Alaimo, S. and Hekman, S. (eds), Bloomington: Indiana University Press, pp. 214–36.

Kirsch, M. 2000. *Queer Theory and Social Change*. London: Routledge.

Kirton, G. and Greene, A. 2005. *The Dynamics of Managing Diversity: A Critical Approach*. Oxford: Elsevier.

Knapp, G-A. 2005. 'Race, Class, Gender: Reclaiming Baggage in Fast Travelling Theories', *European Journal of Women's Studies* 12(3): 249–65.

Kopytoff, I. 1986. 'The Cultural Biography of Things: Commoditization as Process', in Appadurai, A. (ed.), *The Social Life of Things. Commodities in Cultural Perspective*. Cambridge: Cambridge University Press, pp. 64–91.

Kostenbaum, W. 1993. *The Queen's Throat*. New York: Vintage Books.

Kulick, D. and Willson, M. (eds), 1995. *Taboo: Sex, Identity and Erotic Subjectivity in Fieldwork*. London: Routledge.

Lacan, J. 1977. *Ecrits*, trans. A. Sheridan. New York: Norton.

Laidlaw, J. 2002. 'For an Anthropology of Ethics and Freedom', *Journal of the Royal Anthropological Institute* 8(2): 311–32.

Lamphere, L., Rapp, R. and Rubin, G. 2007. 'Anthropologists Are Talking' About Feminist Anthropology', *Ethnos: Journal of Anthropology*, 72(3): 408–26.

Lancaster, R. 2003. *The Trouble with Nature: Sex in Science and Popular Culture*. Berkeley: University of California Press.

Laplanche, L. and Pontalis, J-B. 1973. *The Language of Psychoanalysis*, trans. D. Nicholson-Smith. New York: Norton.

Laqueur, T. 1990. *Making Sex: Body and Gender from the Greeks to Freud*. Cambridge, MA: Harvard University Press.

Larkin, B. 2013. 'Politics and Poetics of Infrastructure', *Annual Review of Anthropology*, 42: 327–43.

Lash S. and Lury C. 2007. *Global Culture Industry: The Mediation of Things*. Cambridge: Polity.

Lash, S. 2010. *Intensive Culture: Social Theory, Religion and Contemporary Capitalism*. London: Sage.

Lash, S. and Urry, J. 1994. *Economies of Signs & Space*. London: Sage.

Latour, B. 1993. *We Have Never Been Modern*. Cambridge, MA: Harvard University Press.

REFERENCES

Layton, R. 1997. *An Introduction to Theory in Anthropology*. Cambridge: Cambridge University Press.

Leach, E. 1976. *Culture and Communication*. Cambridge: Cambridge University Press.

Leach, J. 2004. 'Modes of Creativity', in Hirsch, E. and Strathern, M. (eds), *Transactions and Creations: Property Debates and the Stimulus of Melanesia*. New York: Berghahn Books, pp. 151–75.

Lehman, J.M. 1994. *Durkheim and Women*. Lincoln: University of Nebraska Press.

Lehrer, A. 1983. *Wine and Conversation*. Bloomington: Indiana University Press.

Leonardo, M. di. 1998. *Exotics at Home: Anthropologies, Others, American Modernity*. Chicago: University of Chicago Press.

LeVay, S. 1993 *The Sexual Brain*. Cambridge MA: MIT Press.

Lévi-Strauss, C. 1969[1949]. *The Elementary Structures of Kinship*, trans. J. Harle Bell, J. Richard von Sturmer and R. Needham. Boston: Beacon Press.

Lévi-Strauss, C. 1976. 'The Story of Asdiwal', in *Structural Anthropology Vol. 2*. New York: Basic Books.

Lévi-Strauss, C. 1981. *The Naked Man*. New York: Harper & Row.

Levin, D. (ed.) 1993. *Modernity and the Hegemony of Vision*. Berkeley: University of California Press.

Levy, R. 1973. *Tahitians: Mind and Experience in the Society Islands*. Chicago: University of Chicago Press.

Lewin, E. and Leap, W. (eds), 1996. *Out in the Field: Reflections of Lesbian and Gay Anthropologists*. Chicago: University of Illinois Press.

Local Government Association (LGA), Office of the Deputy Prime Minister, Home Office, Commission for Racial Equality, Inter-Faith Network 202 *Guidance on Community Cohesion*. London: LGA Publications.

Lock, M. and Scheper-Hughes, N. 1987. 'The Mindful Body', *Medical Anthropology Quarterly* 1(1): 6–41.

Ludwig, A. 2006. 'Differences between Women? Intersecting Voices in a Female Narrative', *European Journal of Women's Studies* 13(3): 245–58.

Lukács, G. 1971. 'Reification and the Consciousness of the Proletariat', in *History and Class Consciousness: Studies in Marxist Dialectics*, trans. Rodney Livingstone, London: Merlin.

Lutz, H., Vivar, M.T.H. and Supik, L. (eds), 2011. *Framing Intersectionality: Debates on a Multi-Faceted Concept in Gender Studies*. Farnham: Ashgate Publishing.

Lykke, N. 2010. *Feminist Studies: A Guide to Intersectional Theory, Methodology and Writing*. New York: Routledge.

Lyons, A. and Lyons, H. 2004. *Irregular Connections: A History of Anthropology and Sexuality*. Lincoln and London: University of Nebraska Press.

MacCormack, C. and Strathern, M. (eds), 1980. *Nature, Culture and Gender*. Cambridge: Cambridge University Press.

Mahmood, S. 2012. *Politics of Piety: The Islamic Revival and the Feminist Subject*, 2nd Edition. Princeton and Oxford: Princeton University Press.

Malinowski, B. 1922. *Argonauts of the Western Pacific*. London: Routledge.

Malinowski, B. 1926. *Crime and Custom in Savage Society*. London: Routledge.

Malinowski, B. 1954. *Magic, Science and Religion*. Garden City, NY: Doubleday Anchor Books.

Malinowski, B. 2001 [1927]. *Sex and Repression in Savage Society*. London: Routledge.

Mandel, E. 1975. *Late Capitalism*, London: New Left Books.

Marcus, G. 1995. 'Ethnography in/of the World System: The Emergence of Multi-sited Ethnography', *Annual Review of Anthropology* 24: 95–117.

Marcus, G. and Fischer, M. 1986. *Anthropology as Cultural Critique: An Experimental Moment in the Human Sciences*. Chicago: University of Chicago Press.

Markowitz, F. and Ashkenazi, M. (eds), 1999. *Sex, Sexuality, and the Anthropologist*. Chicago: University of Illinois Press.

Martin, E. 1994. *Flexible Bodies: Tracking Immunity in American Culture from the Days of Polio to AIDS*. Boston: Beacon Press.

Marx, K. 1975. *Early Writings*. Harmondsworth: Penguin/New Left Review.

Marx, K. 1995. *Capital, Vol. 1*. London: Lawrence and Wishart.

Massumi, B. 1992. *A User's Guide to Capitalism and Schizophrenia: Deviations from Deleuze and Guattari*. Cambridge MA: MIT Press.

Mauss, M. 1979. *Sociology and Philosophy*. London: Routledge & Kegan Paul.

Mauss, M. 1990. *The Gift: The Form and Reasons for Exchange in Archaic Societies*, trans. W.H. Hall. London: Routledge.

McCall, L. 2005. 'The Complexity of Intersectionality', *Signs: Journal of Women in Culture and Society*, 30(3): 1771–1800.

McClary, S. 1994. 'Constructions of Subjectivity in Schubert's Music,' in Brett, P., Wood, E. and Thomas, G. (eds), *Queering the Pitch*. New York: Routledge, pp. 205–33.

McGhee, Derek. 2008. *The End of Multiculturalism? Terrorism, Integration and Human Rights*. Maidenhead: Open University Press.

McKinnon, S. and Silverman, S. (eds), 2005. *Complexities: Beyond Nature and Nurture*. Chicago: University of Chicago Press.

Mead, M. 1928. *Coming of Age in Samoa. A Psychological Study of Primitive Youth for Western Civilization*. New York: William Morrow.

Mead, M. 1949. *Male and Female*. New York: William Morrow.

Meigs, A. 1984. *Food, Sex and Pollution*. Brunswick, NJ: Rutgers University Press.

Mesle, C.R. 2008. *Process-relational Philosophy: An Introduction to Alfred North Whitehead*. Conshohocken, PA: Templeton Press.

Mialet, H. 2012. *Hawking Incorporated: Stephen Hawking and the Anthropology of the Knowing Subject*. Chicago: University of Chicago Press.

Miller, D. 1988. *The Novel and the Police*. Berkeley: University of California Press.

REFERENCES

Miller, D. 2008. *The Comfort of Things*. Cambridge: Polity.

Mintz, S. 1974. *Caribbean Transformations*. Chicago: Aldine.

Mintz, S. 1985. *Sweetness and Power: The Place of Sugar in Modern History*. New York: Viking.

Moore, H. 1994. *A Passion for Difference*. Cambridge: Polity.

Moore, H. 2007. *The Subject of Anthropology: Gender, Symbolism and Psychoanalysis*. Cambridge: Polity.

Mor-Barak, M. 2005. *Managing Diversity: Toward a Globally Inclusive Workplace*. London: Sage.

Moran, L. and Skeggs, B, with Tyrer, P. and Corteen, K. 2004. *Sexuality and the Politics of Violence and Safety*. London: Routledge.

Munn, N. 1986. *The Fame of Gawa: A Symbolic Study of Value Transformation in a Massim (Papua New Guinea) Society*. Cambridge: Cambridge University Press.

Murphy, F. (ed.) 1975. *Walt Whitman: The Complete Poems*. Harmondsworth: Penguin.

Murphy, P.F. 2001. *Studs, Tools and the Family Jewels: Metaphors Men Live By*. Madison: University of Wisconsin Press.

Murphy, T. 1997 *Gay Science: The Ethics of Sexual Orientation Research*. New York: Columbia University Press.

Murray S. 1995. *Latin American Male Homosexualities*. Albuquerque: University of New Mexico Press.

Murray, D. (ed.) 2009. *Homophobias: Lust and Loathing across Time and Space*. Durham NC: Duke university Press.

Nanda, S. 1990. *Neither Man nor Woman: The Hijras of India*. Belmont, CA: Wadsworth.

Nestle, J., Howell, C. and Wichins, R. (eds), 2002. *Genderqueer: Voices from beyond the Sexual Binary*. Los Angeles: Alyson Books.

Nussbaum, M.C. 1999. 'The Professor of Parody', *The New Republic* 22 February: 37–45.

Oakley, A. 1972. *Sex, Gender and Society*. London: Maurice Temple Smith.

Okely, J. 2007. 'Fieldwork Embodied', in Shilling, C. (ed.), *Embodying Sociology: Retrospect, Progress and Prospects*. Malden, MA: Wiley-Blackwell, pp. 65–79.

Oliver, K. 2001. *Witnessing: Beyond Recognition*. Minneapolis: University of Minnesota Press.

Ong, A. and Collier, S.J. (eds), 2005. *Global Assemblages: Technology, Politics, And Ethics as Anthropological Problems*. Oxford: Blackwell.

Ortner, S. 1974. 'Is Female to Male as Nature is to Culture?', in Rosaldo, M. and Lamphere, L. (eds), *Woman, Culture, and Society*. Stanford, CA: Stanford University Press, pp. 68–87.

Osteen, M. 2002. 'Introduction: Questions of the Gift', in Osteen, M. (ed.) *The Question of the Gift: Essays across Disciplines*. London: Routledge, pp. 1–41.

Otto, T. and Bubandt, N. (eds), 2010. *Experiments in Holism: Theory and Practice in Contemporary Anthropology*. Oxford: Wiley-Blackwell.

Ouseley, H. 2001. *Community Pride not Prejudice*. Bradford: Bradford Vision.

Pálsson, G. 2007. *Anthropology and the New Genetics*. Cambridge: Cambridge University Press.

Parry J. 1986. '*The Gift*, the Indian gift, and the "Indian gift"' *Man* 21: 453–73.

Pawlett, W. 1997. 'Utility and Excess: The Radical Sociology of Bataille and Baudrillard', *Economy and Society* 26(1): 92–125.

Pedersen, M.A. 2012. 'Common Sense: A Review of Certain Recent Reviews of the "Ontological Turn"', *Anthropology of this Century*, 5.

Pels, P. 1998. 'The Spirit of Matter: On Fetish, Rarity, Fact, and Fancy', in Speyer, P. (ed.), *Border Fetishisms: Material Objects in Unstable Places*. New York: Routledge, pp. 91–121.

Peraino, J.A. 2006. *Listening to the Sirens: Musical Technologies of Queer Identity from Homer to Hedwig*. Berkeley: University of California Press.

Phillips, T. 2004. Interview in *The Times*, 3 April, 2004.

Pietz, W. 1985. 'The Problem of the Fetish I', *Res* 9: 5–17.

Pietz, W. 1987. 'The Problem of the Fetish II', *Res* 13: 23–45.

Pietz, W. 1988. 'The Problem of the Fetish III', *Res* 16: 105–23.

Pinney, C. 2005. 'Things Happen: Or, From Which Moment Does That Object Come?', in Miller, D. (ed.), *Materiality*. Durham NC: Duke University Press, pp. 256–72.

Plummer, K. 1995. *Telling Sexual Stories: Power, Change and Social Worlds*. London: Routledge.

Povinelli, E.A. 2006. *The Empire of Love: Toward a Theory of Intimacy, Genealogy and Carnality*. Durham, NC: Duke University Press.

Putnam, R.D. 1993. *Making Democracy Work: Civic Traditions in Modern Italy*. Princeton NJ: Princeton University Press.

Putnam, R. D. 2000. *Bowling Alone: The Collapse and Revival of American Community*. New York: Simon and Schuster.

Radcliffe-Brown, A.R. 1952. *Structure and Function in Primitive Society*. London: Routledge & Kegan Paul.

Reaka-Kudla, M.L., Wilson, D.E. and Wilson, E.O. (eds), 1997. *Biodiversity11*. Washington, DC: Joseph Henry Press.

Reid-Pharr, R. 2001. *Black Gay Man*. New York: New York University Press.

Rescher, N. 1996. *Process Metaphysics: An Introduction to Process Philosophy*. New York: SUNY Press.

Rich, A. 1983. 'Compulsory heterosexuality and lesbian existence', in Snitow, A., Stansell, C. and Thompson, S. (eds), *Powers of Desires: The Politics of Sexuality*. New York: Monthly Review Press.

Richardson, D., McLaughlin, J., and Casey, M. (eds), 2006. *Intersections between Feminism and Queer Theory*. Basingstoke: Palgrave.

REFERENCES

Robbins, J. 2007. 'Between Reproduction and Freedom. Morality, Value, and Radical Cultural Change', *Ethnos*, 72(3): 293–314.

Robertson, J. (ed.), 2005. *Same-sex Cultures and Sexualities: An Anthropological Reader*. Oxford: Blackwell.

Rofel, L. 2007. *Desiring China: Experiments in Neoliberalism, Sexuality and Public Culture*. Durham, NC: Duke University Press.

Rolston, H. III. 1985. 'Duties to Endangered Species', *BioScience* 35(11): 718–26.

Rosaldo, M. 1974. 'Woman, Culture, and Society: A Theoretical Overview', in Rosaldo, M. and Lamphere, L. (eds), *Woman, Culture, and Society*. Stanford, CA: Stanford University Press, pp. 17–42.

Roscoe, W. 1998. *Changing Ones: Third and Fourth Genders in Native North America*. New York: St. Martin's Press.

Roughgarden, J. 2004. *Evolution's Rainbow: Diversity, Gender, and Sexuality in Nature and People*. Berkeley: University of California Press.

Rubin, G. 1975. 'The Traffic in Women: Notes on the "Political Economy" of Sex', in Reiter, R.A. (ed.), *Toward an Anthropology of Women*. New York: Monthly Review Press, pp. 157–210.

Rubin, G. 1984. 'Thinking Sex: Notes for a Radical Theory of the Politics of Sexuality', in Vance, C. (ed.), *Pleasure and Danger: Exploring Female Sexuality*. New York: Routledge & Kegan Paul.

Ruffolo, D. 2009. *Post-Queer Politics*. Farnham: Ashgate Publishing.

Sahlins, M. 1972. *Stone Age Economics*. Chicago: Aldine.

Sahlins, M. 1976. *Culture and Practical Reason*. Chicago: University of Chicago Press.

Schapera, I. 1966[1940]. (2nd edition). *Married Life in an African Tribe*. London: Faber & Faber.

Schmitt, A. and Sofer, J. (eds), 1992. *Sexuality and Eroticism among Males in Moslem Societies*. New York: The Haworth Press.

Schneider, D. 1968. *American Kinship: A Cultural Account*. Englewood Cliffs, NJ: Prentice-Hall.

Scott, J. 1992. 'Experience', in Butler, J. and Scott, J. (eds), *Feminists Theorize the Political*. New York and London: Routledge, pp. 22–40.

Scott, M.W. 2013. 'The Anthropology of Ontology (Religious Science?)', *Journal of the Royal Anthropological Institute* 19(4): 859–72.

Sedgwick, E.K. 1985. *Between Men : English Literature and Male Homosocial Desire*. New York: Columbia University Press.

Sedgwick, E.K. 1990. *Epistemology of the Closet*. Berkeley: University of California Press.

Sedgwick, E.K. 2003. *Touching Feeling: Affect, Pedagogy, Performativity*. Durham NC: Duke University Press.

Seidman, S. 1997. *Difference Troubles*. Cambridge: Cambridge University Press.

Simpson, M. (ed.) 1996. *Antigay: Homosexuality and Its Discontents*. London: Cassell.
Simpson, M. 1999. *It's a Queer World: Deviant Adventures in Pop Culture*. Binghamton, NY: Haworth Press.
Skeggs, B. 2004. *Class, Self, Culture*. London: Routledge.
Skeggs, B. and Wood, H. 2012. *Reacting to Reality Television: Performance, Audience and Value*. London: Routledge.
Slater, D. 1997. *Consumer Culture and Modernity*. Cambridge: Polity Press.
Smart, A. 1993. 'Gifts, Bribes and *Guanxi*: A Reconsideration of Bourdieu's Social Capital', *Cultural Anthropology* 8: 388–408.
Smith, A.M. 1994. *New Right Discourse on Race and Sexuality: Britain 1968–1990*. Cambridge: Cambridge University Press.
Smith, P.J. (ed.), 1999. *The Queer Sixties*. New York: Routledge.
Sneath, D., Holbraad, M. and Pedersen, M.A. 2009. 'Technologies of the Imagination: An Introduction', *Ethnos* 74(1): 5–30.
Snediker, M. D. 2009. *Queer Optimism: Lyric Personhood and other Felicitous Persuasions*. Minneapolis: University of Minnesota Press.
Somerville, J. 1989. 'The Sexuality of Men and the Sociology of Gender', *Sociological Review* 37(2): 277–307.
Spelman, E. 1988. *Inessential Woman: Problems of Exclusion in Feminist Thought*. Boston: Beacon.
Speyer, P. (ed.), 1998. *Border Fetishisms: Material Objects in Unstable Places*. New York: Routledge.
Stacey, J. 1991. 'Promoting Normality: Section 28 and the Regulation of Sexuality', in Franklin, S., Lury, C. and Stacey, J. (eds), *Off-Centre: Feminism and Cultural Studies*. London: Harper Collins, pp. 284–304.
Stonewall 2003. *Diversity Champions: promoting diversity in the workplace*. London: Stonewall.
Stonewall 2005. *What is Diversity Champions?* London: Stonewall.
Stonewall n.d. *The Employment Equality (Sexual Orientation) Regulations. Guidelines for Employers, 2nd Edition*. London: Stonewall.
Strathern, M. 1987. 'An awkward relationship: the case of feminism and anthropology', *Signs: Journal of Women in Culture and Society* 12: 272–92.
Strathern, M. 1988. *The Gender of the Gift: Problems with Women and Problems with Society in Melanesia*. Berkeley: University of California Press.
Strong T. 2002. 'Kinship Between Judith Butler and Anthropology? A Review Essay', *Ethnos* 67(3): 401–18.
Sullivan, A. 1995. *Virtually Normal*. New York: Alfred A. Knopf.
Sullivan, N. 2003. *A Critical Introduction to Queer Theory*. Edinburgh: Edinburgh University Press.
Taussig, M. 1993. *Mimesis and Alterity: A Particular History of the Senses*. New York: Routledge.

REFERENCES

Taussig, M. 2006. 'Viscerality, Faith, and Skepticism: Another Theory of Magic' in *Walter Benjamin's Grave*. Chicago: University of Chicago Press, pp. 121–55.

Taylor, R. 1997. 'The Sixth Sense,' *New Scientist*, 616: 36–40.

Thomas, C. 2002. 'Reenfleshing the Bright Boys; or, how male bodies matter to feminist theory', in Gardiner, J.K. (ed.), *Masculinity Studies and Feminist Theory: New Directions*. New York: Columbia University Press, pp. 31–59.

Throop, J. 2010. *Suffering and Sentiment. Exploring the Vicissitudes of Experience and Pain in Yap*. Berkeley: University of California Press.

Trnka, S., Dureau, C. and Park, J. (eds), 2013. *Senses and Citizenships: Embodying Political Life*. London: Routledge.

Valentine, D. 2007. *Imagining Transgender: An Ethnography of a Category*. Durham, NC and London: Duke University Press.

Vance, C. 1991. 'Anthropology Rediscovers Sex', *Social Science and Medicine* 33(8): 865–907.

Viveiros de Castro, E. 1998. 'Cosmological Deixis and Amerindian Perspectivism', *Journal of the Royal Anthropological Institute* 4(3): 469–88.

Wade, P. 2002. *Race, Nature and Culture: An Anthropological Perspective*. London: Pluto Press.

Wagner, R. 1978. *Lethal Speech: Daribi Myth as Symbolic Obviation*. Ithaca, NY: Cornell University Press.

Waites, M. 2005. 'The fixity of sexual identities in the public sphere: biomedical knowledge, liberalism and the heterosexual/homosexual binary in late modernity', *Sexualities* 8(5): 539–69.

Walby, S. 2007. 'Complexity Theory, Systems Theory and multiple Intersecting Social Inequalities', *Philosophy of the Social Sciences*. 37(4): 449–70.

Waldby, C. 1995. 'Destruction: Boundary Erotics and Refigurations of the Heterosexual Male Body', in Grosz, E. and Probyn, E. (eds), *Sexy Bodies: The Strange Carnalities of Feminism*. London: Routledge, pp. 266–77.

Walton, J. 2001. *Fair Sex, Savage Dreams: Race, Psychoanalysis, Sexual Difference*. Durham NC: Duke University Press.

Warner, M. 1999. *The Trouble with Normal: Sex, Politics and the Ethics of Queer Life*. New York: The Free Press.

Weston, K. 1993. 'Lesbian/Gay Studies in the House of Anthropology', *Annual Review of Anthropology*, 22: 339–67.

Whatmore, S. 2002. *Hybrid Geographies: Natures, Cultures, Spaces*. London: SAGE.

Wheeler, Q.D. and Meier, R. (eds), 2000. *Species Concepts and Phylogenetic Theory: A Debate*. New York: Columbia University Press.

Whitehead, A.N. 1929. *Process and Reality: An Essay in Cosmology*. New York: Macmillan.

Whitehead, H. 1981. 'The Bow and the Burden Strap: A New Look at Institutionalized Homosexuality in Native North America', in Ortner, S. and

Whitehead, H. (eds), *Sexual Meanings: The Cultural Construction of Gender and Sexuality*. Cambridge: Cambridge University Press.

Wikan U. 1977. 'Man become Woman: Transsexualism in Oman as a Key to Gender Roles', *Man* n.s. 12(2): 304–19.

Willerslev, R. 2007. *Soul Hunters: Hunting, Animism, and Personhood among the Siberian Yukaghirs*. Berkeley: California University Press.

Wittig, M. 1992. *The Straight Mind*. Hemel Hempstead: Harvester Wheatsheaf.

Witz, A. and Marshall, B.L. 2003. 'The Quality of Manhood: Gender and Embodiment in the Classical Tradition', *Sociological Review* 51(3): 339–56.

Yanagisako, S. and Collier, J. 1987. 'Toward a unified analysis of gender and kinship', in Collier, J. and Yanagisako, S. (eds), *Gender and Kinship: Towards a Unified Analysis*. Stanford: Stanford University Press.

Young, A. 2000. *Women Who Become Men: Albanian Sworn Virgins*. Oxford: Berg.

Young, I.M. 1990. *Justice and the Politics of Difference*. Princeton, NJ: Princeton University Press.

Young, I.M. 1997. *Intersecting Voices*. Princeton, NJ: Princeton University Press.

Yuval-Davis, N. 2006. 'Intersectionality and Feminist Politics', *European Journal of Women's Studies*, 13(3): 193–210.

Zigon, J. 2007. 'Moral Breakdown and Ethical Demand. A Theoretical Framework for an Anthropology of Moralities', *Anthropological Theory* 7(2): 131–50.

Index

ACT UP (activist organisation) 132n8
Adorno, Theodor 139–40, 145
    Dialectic of Enlightenment 52
affect 136–7
Aguilera, Christina 111
Alaimo, Stacey 20, 36
Albee, Edward, *Who's Afraid of Virginia Woolf?* 112
American Congressional Research Service (2000) 73
Appadurai, Arjun 32, 34n17
Ardener, Edwin 129
Aristophanes, *Lysistrate* 112
Aristotle 37, 72
Austin, John Langshaw 12

Bachofen, Johann Jakob 1
Bahati, David x
Bailey, Frederick, *Gifts and Poison* 46
Barad, Karen 28–31, 102, 103–4
Barthes, Roland 40
Bataille, George 48–50
Bateson, Mary 2
Baudrillard, Jean 32, 38–44, 49–50, 85, 117–18
    The Transparency of Evil 65
Bawer, Bruce 106
Beach, Frank 1, 3n2
Beauvoir, Simone de 19
Beckham, David 113, 124
Benedict, Ruth 2, 3n1
Bennett, Jane 140
Bergson, Henri 23, 24–5, 31, 145

Berkeley, George 19
Berlant, Lauren 119
biodiversity 73–5
Bloch, Maurice 51
Bohm, David 6n8
Bohr, Niels 28–30
Bourdieu, Pierre 15, 47, 120n6, 130–1, 144
Brown, Melanie 110–11
Brown, Wendy 93
Burton, Richard 1
Butler, Judith 12–13, 20n1, 45, 67, 121n7

Callari, Antonio 46n6
Calvin Klein 62–3
candomblé religion 35
Cantle, Ted 78, 85, 86n12
clowns 140
Collier, Janet 19n1
commodities 38–40, 45, 51–3
Connerton, Paul 120
Crenshaw, Kimberlé 91, 100

Darwin, Charles 24, 31n14, 88–9
    The Origin of Species 72–3, 74
Deleuze, Gilles 24, 27–8, 121n8, 123n9, 133
Derrida, Jacques 8, 47
Devereux, George 3n1, 46
Di Leonardo, Micaela 2
diversity
    biological 71–2, 73–6
    cultural 77–81, 85

sexual 81–3
DNA (perfume) 57
Douglas, Mary, *The World of Goods* 32
Durham, Deborah 137
Durkheim, Émile 32, 48, 128–9, 143

Ellis, Havelock 2
Eminem 110–11
Engels, Friedrich 1

feminism
    and intersectionality 91–2
    and materiality 19–21
    and queer theory 14n16
fetishes 33–6
Firth, Raymond 1, 3n1
Florida, Richard 77
Ford, Clellan 1, 3n2
Foucault, Michel xi, 7–8, 11, 13–14, 71, 134, 144
    History of Sexuality 11
France
    gay marriage xi, 4
    Pacte Civil de Solidarité (PACS) 4
Frazer, James 1
Freud, Sigmund 2, 7, 8, 42, 66–7, 108, 121, 132, 140–1
Friedan, Betty 2
functionalism 116, 129, 143

Gatens, Moira 130
    A Critique of the Sex/Gender Distinction 19
Gates, Gary 77
'gay' perfume 58–61
Gell, Alfred 65, 99
Giddens, Anthony 79
gifts 46–54
Global Biodiversity Assessment (1995) 73
Golding, William, *Lord of the Flies* 114

Goldman, Marcio 35
Gouldner, Alvin 46
Grace, Victoria 41–2
Graeber, David 86–7, 122
Gravelly Hill Interchange, Birmingham 94–8
Grosz, Elizabeth 141, 145
Gudeman, Stephen 47

Habermas, Jürgen 84, 128
Halberstam, Judith 107
Hall, Stuart 100
Handelman, Don 140
Hardt, Michael 132n8
Haug, Wolfgang 37
Hawking, Stephen 142n16
Hegel, Georg W.F. 8
Heisenberg, Werner 30n12
Hekman, Susan 20, 36
Hennessy, Rosemary 64
Héritier, Françoise 4
heterosexual relatinships, portrayed in the media 108–14
Hey, Jody 72, 73
Hocquenghem, Guy, *Homosexual Desire* 131–3
Hogbin, Ian 3n1
Horkheimer, Max, *Dialectic of Enlightenment* 52
Hua people, Papua New Guinea 56–7
Hutcheon, Linda 117

Iansiti, Marco, *Strategy as Ecology* 76
Ingold, Tim 26n9, 33, 68n10, 98–9
INTENSE (pheronome product) 58–60
intersectionality 91–106
intersexed people 101–3
intuition 145–6
Isherwood, Baron, *The World of Goods* 32

INDEX

Jackson, Stevi 101
James, Henry 23

Kapferer, Bruce 122
Karkazis, Katrina 102
Kato, David x
Kessler, Evelyn 101–2
Kessler, Suzanne 20n1
Kinsey, Alfred 8n10
Kirby, Vicki 20, 135
Kirsch, Max 64
Kopytoff, Igor 34

Lacan, Jacques 9–11, 16, 31n13, 67, 123, 130
Laqueur, Thomas 20n1
Lash, Scott 52–4
Latour, Bruno 33n15
Leach, Edmund 115
Levien, Roy, *Strategy as Ecology* 76
Lévi-Strauss, Claude 4, 46, 51, 85, 114
  The Elementary Structures of Kinship 46
  Mythologiques 121
Linnaeus, Carl 72
Lukács, György 12
Lury, Celia 52–4
Lyons, Andrew 1
Lyons, Harriet 1

MacLennan, John Ferguson 2
Madonna 111
magazines, popular 108–11
Malinowski, Bronislaw 2, 3, 47, 114–15
Marshall, Donald Stanley, *Human Sexual Behavior* 3
Marx, Karl 1, 35, 37, 38–9, 41, 44, 45, 49–50, 143
Massumi, Brian 131
materiality 20–1, 24–8, 31–6
Mauss, Marcel 6, 15, 46, 47, 50

The Gift 48
Mayhew, Henry 1
McClary, Susan 67
McKenna, Wendy 20n1
Mead, Margaret 2
Melanesia 15, 56, 65, 105n9
Merleau-Ponty, Maurice 68n10
Mesle, C. Robert 26, 27
Miller, Daniel 32, 45
Morgan, Lewis H. 4
multiculturalism 78
Munn, Nancy 86–8
musicology, and queerness 67
myths, and representation of gender 112–22

Negri, Antonio 132n8
New Labour philosophy 77–9, 84–5
Nude (pheronome product) 60–1

Okely, Judith 129–30
ontology 29n11, 53–4, 74, 128, 132n8
orixás (deities) 35
Ortner, Sherry 19n1
Osteen, Mark 48

Parry, Jonathan 47, 51
Pels, Peter 34
performativity 12–14, 28, 33n15, 65–9, 74, 85, 103, 117–22, 130n4, 135
perfume advertisements 55–64
pheromone products 58–61, 66
Plato 72
Possess (pheronome product) 60
post-structuralism 28
potlatch 48–50, 143
Povinelli, Elizabeth 5, 83–4
process philosophy 24–8
psychoanalysis 9, 15–16, 66

quantum physics 28–31
Queer Nation (activist organisation) 132n8

Radcliffe-Brown, A.R. 4, 129
reification 12, 23, 55
Rescher, Nicholas 31
Rich, Adrienne 19
Rivers, W.H. 2
Robbins, Joel 122
Rolston, Holmes 74
Rosaldo, Michelle 19n1
Russell, Bertrand 2
Russia, anti-homosexuality legislation x–xi

Sahlins, Marshall 39, 46
Saussure, Ferdinand de 40, 45
scents 55–69
Schapera, Isaac 3n1
Schneider, David 4
Schubert, Franz, *Unfinished Symphony* 67
Sedgwick, Eve 45, 107
Seidman, Steven 5
Shakespeare, William, *The Taming of the Shrew* 112
Skeggs, Beverley 87, 94n5, 122
Sophocles, *Oedipus Rex* 108, 112
Spears, Britney 111
Spencer, Herbert 74
Spinoza, Baruch 24
Stonewall (lobby organisation) 81–2
Strathern, Marilyn 45
Strindberg, August, *Miss Julie* 112
structural-functionalism 3, 13, 15, 129
structuralism 40–1, 86, 116
Suggs, Robert Carl, *Human Sexual Behavior* 3
Sullivan, Andrew 106

Svensk Dam tidning (magazine) 109, 113

Taussig, Michael 16, 118n5
Temptation Island (television programme) 111–12, 114–15, 117
Throop, Jason 144
transgender 93–4

Uganda, Anti-Homosexuality Act x
Umeda people 65
UN Convention on Biodiversity (1992) 74
unisex perfume 62–4
United Kingdom
    Commission for Equality and Human Rights (2004) 79n4
    Commission for Racial Equality (2004) 78
    and gay marriage xi
    Gravelly Hill Interchange, Birmingham 94–8
    New Labour philosophy 72, 77–9, 84–5
    Section 28 (Local Government Act) 81
    Stonewall (lobby organisation) 81–2

Valentine, David 93–4
Vance, Carole 1, 2

Warner, Michael 119
Westermarck, Edvard 2
Whitehead, Alfred North 24, 25–7, 31, 75
Whitehead, Harriet, *The Bow and the Burden Strap* 32
Whitman, Walt 127
Wittig, Monique, *The Straight Mind* 12
Wood, Helen 122

INDEX

Yanagisako, Sylvia 19n1
Young, Iris Marion 47n9, 86n12

Zero Patience (film) 131n6
Zigon, Jarrett 122
Žižek, Slavoj 10n15

CPSIA information can be obtained
at www.ICGtesting.com
Printed in the USA
BVHW041429071219
565929BV00003B/20/P